Appreciating Don DeLillo

The Moral Force of a Writer's Work

PAUL GIAIMO

PRAEGER

AN IMPRINT OF ABC-CLIO, LLC
Santa Barbara, California • Denver, Colorado • Oxford, England

Library of Congress Cataloging-in-Publication Data

Giaimo, Paul.
   Appreciating Don DeLillo : the moral force of a writer's work / Paul Giaimo.
      p. cm.
   Includes bibliographical references and index.
   ISBN 978-0-313-38624-4 (hardcopy : alk. paper) — ISBN 978-0-313-38625-1 (ebk.)
   1. DeLillo, Don—Criticism and interpretation.   2. Good and evil in literature.
   3. Ethics in literature.   I. Title.
   PS3554.E4425Z655   2011
   813'.54—dc22   2011011400

ISBN: 978-0-313-38624-4
EISBN: 978-0-313-38625-1

15 14 13 12 11   1 2 3 4 5

This book is also available on the World Wide Web as an eBook.
Visit www.abc-clio.com for details.

Praeger
An Imprint of ABC-CLIO, LLC

ABC-CLIO, LLC
130 Cremona Drive, P.O. Box 1911
Santa Barbara, California 93116-1911

This book is printed on acid-free paper ∞

Manufactured in the United States of America

Contents

Preface

If a work of art is rich and vital and complete, those who have artistic instincts will see its beauty and those to whom ethics appeal more strongly will see its moral lesson. (Oscar Wilde as qtd. in Holland and Hart-Davis 441)

This volume is for all who would like to know more about the rich and vital work of Don DeLillo but who may be intimidated by the vast amount written about him by literary critics. Certainly one of the best-known, most admired, and enjoyable of American writers, DeLillo has taken the enduring power of literature and coupled it with the fresh vision afforded us by the explosion of new media technologies. My purpose in choosing to write this book relates to my belief about the underlying moral lessons of DeLillo's work—moral lessons that, in the quote above, Wilde attributes to all great art. As with the American writers of the past who cared very deeply about making their country and the world a better place, the numerous awards, outstanding critical reception, and sales one finds for these texts point to the accuracy of one of Wilde's drier observations.

Books like Samuel Clemens's *Adventures of Huckleberry Finn* or Harriet Beecher Stowe's *Uncle Tom's Cabin* brought up the issue of slavery and showed to readers many people and events that would lead them to believe that slavery was wrong. DeLillo, trained by the Jesuits (as I was) to unite a respect for knowledge with a drive to help and serve other people, seems to be to be concerned with performing a similar task. Though we don't have chattel slavery here in the United States, a host of other problems—including terrorism, the bursting of the housing bubble, tremendous national debt, weapons of mass destruction, and environmental catastrophes—still plague us. In his 16 novels written under his own name, Don DeLillo takes on all these issues as the earlier American writers did, not only to criticize these problems but to suggest the impact that these problems have had on individuals.

Above and beyond the personal background I share with DeLillo, there are other important aspects of the Jesuit influence on this writer that critics ought to note in their attempts to classify these novels into common categories. Turning here to the speech given by Father Peter-Hans Kolvenbach in 1989 at Georgetown University and Georgetown Prep, we can discern the vision of education in service that informs DeLillo's approach to his readership:

> Our purpose, then is to form men and women "for others."...We want graduates who desire to eliminate hunger and conflict in the world and who are sensitive to the need for more equitable distribution of the world's goods. We want graduates who seek to end sexual and social discrimination and who are eager to share their faith with others. (Boston College Website)

I reproduce this selection of the Jesuit ideal vision of education for the purposes of comparing and contrasting it to the way DeLillo's major novels function. By such detailed presentation of the contemporary individual's perspective under the sway of the attendant social ills of our time, DeLillo's formational impact on the reader parallels the Jesuit ambition for their graduates: a transformation or awakening of moral conscience through a deepening of social consciousness. Proof is offered in this book, through a close reading of each novel against the postmodern grain, with the Aristotelian unities of plot, character, and theme intact. Justification for doing so can be found simply in response to the fact that most critics indeed miss the humor and the pathos suggested by ignoring the cultural surfaces of the writing. DeLillo's work, with its reference to crucial cultural surfaces far beyond the socially approved borders of American literary criticism, demands the reader wake up to the urban, gritty, zealously religious, and frequently ethnic surfaces that are ignored by most academics—as downtown Blacksmith and its scruffy fish hatcheries are by the good upper-class residents of *White Noise*'s fictional College-on-the-Hill. The radical moral/political implications of works like *Point Omega* and *Underworld* can no longer be ignored.

When we hear the phrase "moral force," we might be thinking of some quasi-mystical or Hollywood-inspired mythological reading of fiction, but

I derived this from DeLillo's writing: "There's a moral force in a sentence when it comes out right. It speaks the writer's will to live" (*Mao II* 48). Writing has a moral force to propel readers and writers in their personal lives. But the moral lessons of much good art also suggest solutions for our greatest social evils and thus carry a moral force beyond the writer's individual life and toward the world.

Unlike other overviews published recently, this text takes a fresh look at the artist as an agent of moral change and examines DeLillo's work very closely in light of our responsibility to change the world. I hope that this first foray into the mystery of good and evil as it emerges in DeLillo's art is of some help to both new readers and people already well aware of this American author's work.

Acknowledgments

There are many people I thank for help in the preparation of this book. Being a community college instructor in English and philosophy can give one the opportunity to write, but I would not have been able to find the time to assemble the pieces without a very generous sabbatical grant from Highland Community College. The people who helped that happen were Thompson Brandt, members of the board, and Executive Officers Joe Kanosky and Jeff Davidson. Special thanks to the hardworking members of the faculty senate led during this time by Steve Mihina. To my colleague Kent Johnson: your encouragement and sense of humor led the way as you have for years been a trailblazer in the world of publication.

Every writer needs a sense of community and individuals who are fellow travelers, empathetic to the unique needs and specific concerns of his or her project, and I received that heartfelt support from all my dear friends in the American Italian Historical Association and its associated groups. You are passionate crusaders all for Italian American literature and culture and a very patient and nurturing audience for my work presented over the years in journals, conferences, and newsletters. To Fred Gardaphé: without your original scholarship and unprecedented initiatives tirelessly made for 20 years in the field this book would never have been conceived. With Fred, thanks to Anthony Tamburri and Dominic Candeloro who each have administrated and guided our group with tremendous expertise and efficacy, ensuring that literary scholarship will henceforth be more receptive to the work of Italian and Italian American writers, scholars, and artists of every media than in days past. To Mary Jo Bona, who along with Veronica

Makowski did perform kind and patient work with me editing my article in *M.E.L.U.S.*, which ultimately culminated in some of the viewpoints
expressed herein. To my many friends who attended panels and shared so
generously: Alessandra Cenzoni, Michelle Fazio, Joanne Ruvoli, George
Guida, Joe Sciorra, and Laura Ruberto. To my coconspirator in forging
academic connections between the study of Italian American culture and
the study of DeLillo's fiction, Alan Gravano: many thanks, and our best
adventures yet await us. And to Maria Giura, for ongoing prayerful support, inspiration, and enthusiasm much needed and appreciated. Above all
to Dr. John Paul Russo, professor emeritus in the best possible sense. I am
eternally grateful for consistent editing and guidance not only on chapter 5
and the content of the writing but in guiding me toward the band of scholars who would provide encouragement and spur me on to pursue completion of this book.

Of course I would be remiss not to acknowledge the fact that I found a
like spirit of scholarly compassion among the members of the Don DeLillo
Society. Jacqueline Nina-Zubeck provided excellent guidance for ideas presented at the 38th Annual Louisville Conference on Literature and Culture since 1900, along with my colleague Dr. Giséle Manganelli Fernandes.
Anne Longmuir provided excellent editing of my analysis of *Point Omega*
published in the society's online newsletter. Much gratitude is also offered
to our listserv moderator Matt King, who provides aid generously to the
ever-expanding global community of readers of Don DeLillo's work.

At Greenwood and Praeger I have been blessed to work with several
talented editors: Emmanuel S. Nelson, George Butler, and Kaitlin Ciarm-
iello. Special thanks goes to the editor of this book, Dan Harmon, who was
always available during my struggles and infinitely patient. I also acknowledge friends who gave me needed personal help in other areas of life taxed
during the writing process: Chris Hoffman, the Dave Ramsey Financial
Peace Community, Kim Castenada, Dr. Pat Petrie, Dr. Tim Fior, and Rev.
George Malkmus in his groundbreaking work on nutrition, recommended
herein to all readers and writers.

To Don DeLillo the primary debt is owed as his tireless efforts both behind
the typewriter and in the struggle for freedom of information and for writers everywhere are duly noted. Finally, to my spouse Sarah, daughter Clare,
and son Michael: thank you for all the loving support and the numerous
sacrifices you made to help me find the time and space to write.

_____ *Chapter 1* _____

Don DeLillo and the Novel— Neither Modern nor Postmodern

Because of Don DeLillo's phenomenal success, many writers and professors doing research on the author have responded to his topical and technical excellence. Important concepts that have emerged for people studying the author's work in relationship to the genre of the novel are the ideas of "modern" and "postmodern" as types of fiction. In this section, we will define some of these terms and see how they are used by other readers who have written important books about Don DeLillo's work. Despite the fact that many prior readers stress elements of DeLillo's work that are easily labeled "postmodern" or "modern," more important elements related to the moral force of DeLillo's work hearken back to older styles of the novel and are not quite so easily put into categories. More specifically, my case is that DeLillo's tendency is to show some elements of mimetic realism as well as those features of modernism and postmodernism. Furthermore, the aesthetic influence of Nelson Algren is ignored by the majority of critics. This influence of the American urban author of *The Man with the Golden Arm* (and another mimetic realist) shows up in DeLillo's clear and compassionate portrayals of the American underclass and of social injustice more generally, two of Algren's great thematic concerns.

To begin, a major trend in DeLillo criticism is to identify the author as a postmodernist. For novelists, postmodernism refers to a literary style beginning after World War II and coming to fruition in the late 1960s and early 1970s on the heels of the antiauthoritarian social revolution going on concurrently. Its principle views on literature include a radical resistance to pinning down particular texts to particular meanings. Postmodernists see the truth behind words as something socially constructed, relative to the power structures of race and gender that exist in a culture. Frequently, the postmodernist author will adopt an ironic stance, almost seeming to be aware of the reader's attempts to create sense of the narrative or story he or she is reading. This kind of stance is also called a metafictive point of view. Postmodernist readers distrust any sort of artificially created order and all categories of logical thinking. As you might be thinking, it is very difficult to conceive of a truly postmodernist reading or an interpretation of anything, since it would seem to defy the logical structures that govern the way we communicate. Furthermore, how can we talk about anyone's fiction if we can't attach meaning to language? Postmodernists tend toward a relativist view of language. As if we are in an infinite series of Chinese boxes or Russian nesting dolls, one contained within the other, we never arrive at the end of our quest for true meaning. So the absolute postmodernist would say that DeLillo's work ironically undercuts our attempts to read it for a deeper level of meaning.

The claim that DeLillo is a postmodernist author begins obviously enough with the idea that several of the tenets of postmodernism are easily demonstrated via DeLillo's novels. For example, in one of the most-discussed scenes in DeLillo's own interviews and published criticism, Jeremy Green and John Duvall claim in their essays in *The Cambridge Companion to Don DeLillo* (Duvall, *Cambridge Companion*) that DeLillo includes a metafictive point of view in the novel *Libra* in the form of the character of Nicholas Branch. Branch is a CIA historian who some time after the Kennedy assassination is attempting to come up with a logical narrative explaining the assassination completely. Green and Duvall narrow Branch's choices down to either the commonly accepted "lone gunman" approach of Lee Harvey Oswald as the sole shooter or a fully finalized version of the conspiracy theory in that the reader knows precisely the identity of each and every conspirator. Of course this is not DeLillo's purpose, so Duvall summarizes that DeLillo then leaves us to "wander in the multiple possibilities of conspiracy theory" (Duvall, "Introduction" 7). Exemplifying this argument easily enough, Green points to the passage from *Libra* in which CIA historical analyst Nicholas Branch is completely swamped by the massive evidence he must sift through to come up with a coherent and perfectly accurate explanation of the conspiracy. Branch does fail to come up with such a theory and falls apart with reading his files, falling asleep in his chair and having neurotic reactions to his Sisyphean responsibilities. He begins to fear that he does not deserve his paycheck (*Libra* 183). Because Branch begins to fail in his quest for logic and truth that is not socially constructed, the critics argue, the postmodern sensibility of not attempting to make sense of things is strongly favored as the dominant viewpoint in *Libra*.

However, a closer examination of *Libra* yields a contradictory point. Even if Branch's failure indicates that postmodern ways of reading DeLillo are necessarily the way to go, there is the historical context to consider. The debate about the relative virtues of the postmodernists' deconstruction of notions of the "real" or objective world existing beyond our words becomes more complex when we look at the case of Lee Harvey Oswald, Kennedy, and the narrative of *Libra* treated by Green, Duvall, and others. Simply enough, *Libra* is DeLillo's retelling of the story of the assassination of John F. Kennedy, told from multiple points of view including that of Lee Harvey Oswald, multiple coconspirators from the CIA and neo-Battista contras, Oswald's mother Marguerite, John Birch Society demagogue General Walker, Jack Ruby, and many others. No published scholar would seek to reduce DeLillo to the purely relativist worldview he so masterfully skewers. For if we take the question of history, it is absurd to suggest that, for example, the words "Kennedy assassination" do not refer to anything, because clearly this was a real-world event.

To say with the postmodernists something along the lines of Siskind's "Once you've seen the signs about the barn, it becomes impossible to see the barn" (*White Noise* 12–13) in regards to the actual killing of Kennedy, or the actual events of September 11 for that matter, is much more exciting and fruitful. It may be so that discovering the truth of such over-reported events is a conundrum at the very least if not impossible due to the ubiquitous plethora of repeated media about such events. But I would not agree that we are simply left to wander in them, as if the purpose of *Libra* was to solve the actual mystery of JFK's murder. The relationship between DeLillo's work and actuality is not as simple as that.

Libra exists neither to posit a solution to the JFK mystery nor as a testimony to the opposite extreme that any and all claims to historical fact regarding the assassination are merely social construction. Writers like John Duvall refer fairly accurately to work like DeLillo's as historiographic, meaning it is drawn from historical sources. The author himself is quick to add a disclaimer, stating, "I've made no attempt to furnish factual answers to any questions raised by the assassination" (*Libra* 457). Despite what some claim, the overall purpose of the treatment of historical materials is not an investigation of the facts at all. Nicholas Branch is certainly not the idealized reader, put forth as some sort of figure for actual readers to identify with or to make a statement about the act of finding meaning.

If anything, Branch's confusion builds suspense late in the novel as we move closer to the actual crime. Yet our last view of Branch is in juxtaposition to the grief of Beryl Parmenter, wife of one of the CIA coconspirators, the oddly disengaged Larry Parmenter. Branch's final impression of his convoluted task and labyrinth of the Warren Commission Report evidence is not simply the postmodernists' joking or regretful sense of futility in the finding or creating of ordered meaning but rather one of a palpable horror: "There are times when he thinks he can't go on. He feels disheartened, almost immobilized by his sense of the dead. The dead are in the room. And photographs of the dead work a mournful power on his mind.... But he persists, he works on, he jots his notes" (455). Beryl too feels an unfathomable grief that is not channeled into endless detective work at the loss of Kennedy, "crying and watching" the multiple shootings all weekend (446). A purely relativist theorist discussing DeLillo's work would have to envision both the characters and the readers as disengaged detectives or elites like *White Noise*'s Murray Siskind gleefully elaborating on the significance of Elvis beneath a toxic cloud. So it is not true that Branch's bewilderment at his task demonstrates that reading history or novels from a postmodern perspective is favored by the author.

Despite this fact, other passages from different works by DeLillo are typically brought in to prove this postmodernist claim extensively. Despite the fact that some critics complain that the character is analyzed too often, it is worthwhile to bring up *White Noise*'s Murray Siskind, who as I have noted elsewhere clings to an aimless, drifting lifestyle of sequential polygamy. Siskind also articulates the viewpoint of complete relativism that I here associate with a postmodern approach to DeLillo. Murray and Jack Gladney (our protagonist, as I have noted in a later chapter) frequently engage in what the postmodern Elvis scholar Siskind calls "theoretical talk." At one point, these two chic cultural studies professors examine "THE MOST PHOTOGRAPHED BARN IN AMERICA" (12). Murray comments that because the barn has so many signs erected in its honor "it becomes impossible to see the barn" due to the excessive number of images around and about it and that one can no longer really experience or capture the reality of the barn "before it was photographed" at this point (12–13). Like the photographs and like Murray's endless affairs, language cannot be tied to any one real truth or experience. Like the crowd surrounding the barn in DeLillo's brilliant satire, we who discuss books are simply "taking pictures of taking pictures" (13) in a socially constructed endless maze or labyrinth of words. So here again DeLillo's work can demonstrate the tenets of postmodernism, and even though the scene is often analyzed, some will take it as such a demonstration.

Yet when postmodern theorists appear in DeLillo's best-known and best-loved novels, their portrayals are anything but flattering to the relativist avant-garde school in question here. To prove this, we have one of the most loyal disciples of postmodernism among the unique characters who populate DeLillo's work: billionaire Wall Street capitalist Eric Packer of 2003's major novel *Cosmopolis*. Resembling the disgraced Wall Street figure Bernard Madoff in more ways than one, Packer buys into the tenets of postmodern theory fervently, even hiring a chief of theory to mentor him, one Vija Kinski, whose job it seems is to "think about the art of money-making" with the young capitalist Packer (*Cosmopolis* 77–107).

This figure articulates the tenets of postmodernism and also encourages Packer to embrace them and live along the lines they suggest. Kinski lives in an amoral world, because she believes that "in fact it's all random phenomena" (85); her view of life is identical to the fluctuation of capital and international monetary exchange rates. She is one of the many hangers-on who follow Packer around in his limousine, caught up in the wealth, glamour, and excitement. But here again it would in this case be a mistake to assume that the author is in agreement with the main character's point of view. Though he rejoices in her relativist view and even thinks he "loved Vija Kinski" (85), Eric Packer does not in any way benefit from her words. He knows in some sense that he does not operate to the same "nihilistic degree... where all judgments are baseless" (85), yet he lives as though her view is the right one. After she leaves the limousine, the amoral capitalist can "begin the business of living" (107). Almost as if attempting to flesh out her vision of life in which "the urge to destroy is a creative urge" (92), Eric Packer then proceeds on a frighteningly rapid path to self-destruction, betraying his wife, seducing one of his loyal bodyguards and shooting another, and finally virtually throwing himself into the path of his better-armed archenemy, a man who has been stalking Packer through the whole novel. A lack of morality, even about the evils of capitalism itself (Kinski "grins evilly" as she speculates about Packer being murdered by anarchist protesters who throw bombs around his limo) is the hallmark of her creed (92). Packer follows this creed to his ultimate demise. Ironically too, when the ruined man daydreams vainly of the kind of funeral he most wants, he imagines the presence of his other great lovers there: his African American bodyguard Kendra Hays, his chief financial officer and single mother Jane Melman, art critic Didi Fancher, and last but not least his estranged wife Elise Shifrin. Vija Kinski is not there, and therefore perhaps his

attachment to her is as superficial as the implications of her complex theoretical viewpoint are.

Therefore, we must raise the following questions: In seeing DeLillo as
the Great American Postmodernist, are critics "really seeing" his work as
opposed to the "photographers of the barn" discussed in *White Noise*? Are
the multiple references to postmodernism in these novels enough to truly
make DeLillo a postmodern novelist? On the subject of DeLillo's work
before *The Names* (1982), critics refer to DeLillo's more light-hearted sat-
ires to show a mocking of many standard contemporary schemes of making
logical order of things. For example, rock and roll is mocked in *Great Jones
Street* (1973), the story of megastar Bucky Wunderlick, who retreats from
society to release his great masterpiece album only to have to deal with
doubts about how the music came about. Is it is or a facsimile constructed
by some cult who brainwashed him? Similarly, *End Zone* (1972) pokes fun
at the world of college football, with its protagonist halfback Gary Harkness finally unable to experience the game as giving his life any sense of
relevance. These early novels do not raise the kinds of doubts about postmodernism that can be raised in later novels like *Cosmopolis*. But Kinski
is not the only theorist we meet even in the earlier fictions. Beginning with
White Noise, for example, as with postmodern theorist Vija Kinski we can
cite the effect of Murray Siskind as an estimation of the value of purely
relativist, speculative theory. To demonstrate, even though Murray serves
central character Jack Gladney as the voice of such theory through much
of the story, as with Vija Kinski, he seems to vanish at the denouement of
the tale. His final words to Gladney in the tale "Kill to live" (*White Noise*
291) are just as destructive as Kinski's effect on Packer. In a completely
fatal self-immolating bend of irrational foolishness, Gladney engages a drug
pusher who has seduced Babette, his wife, in a vengeful gun battle. The
denizens of pure postmodern theory just don't seem to be very helpful to
DeLillo's central characters! Rather, they tend to exercise a corrupting influence when the naïve characters act on their hollow theories, because the
words of the "theory guru" tend to release the protagonist from any sense
of moral responsibility in a world that cannot certainly be said to exist.

Yet scholars like Duvall and Green raise a good question. Does postmodernism not serve as a useful lens for skeptical social critics like the
author himself in examining the social causes of historical misdeeds like
the JFK assassination? That may be so, but my last rejoinder to those who
might suggest DeLillo as any sort of "pure" postmodernist or champion
of the allegedly enlightening powers of a purely relativist view involves the
example of Jesse Detwiler. This character from *Underworld* is yet another

postmodernist from the DeLillo canon, a "waste theorist whose provocations had spooked the industry" (*Underworld* 285). As with Vija Kinski and Murray Siskind, the postmodern theorist here appears primarily to satirize popular theory, rarely examined as closely in published writings about DeLillo. Skeptical Nick Costanza Shay, with his insightful views, quickly skewers Detwiler as a cultural leftover of the avant-garde of the sixties: "He'd earned a brief feverish fame in the chronicles of the time, part of the strolling band of tambourine girls and bomb makers, levitators and acid droppers and lost children" (287). Jesse's scheme to turn garbage and nuclear waste into a tourist trade for major urban areas (Nick is a waste manager by trade) is a farce worthy of the eccentric faculty of the College-on-the-Hill in DeLillo's comic novel *White Noise*. Like Kinski and Siskind, Detwiler touts the "mandate of the culture," only here it's "Consume or die," sounding a great deal like Murray Siskind's cultural mandate "Kill to live" noted in *White Noise*. But Nick is not sold on the idea of a" Plutonium National Park" and rather sees Detwiler as a "waste hustler, looking for book deals and documentary films" (287).

Though postmodernism stresses the relative equality of truth values such as "art" versus "garbage" or "cultural mandates" as opposed to "moral right and wrong," a complete equalizing is not credible in Nick's point of view. As we saw in our reading of *Cosmopolis*, Vija Kinski's thoughts, signifying the thinking of postmodern theory, leave in their wake chaos in the life of main character Eric Packer. Here, instead, Detwiler has a similar negative impact on Nick's relationship with his coworker Simeon Biggs (278), or "Big Sims" as he is called, for some time into their talk Biggs is insulted by Detwiler's reference to Sim's knowing the name of the "the white man's horse" (287), which is the Lone Ranger's horse Silver. Later Nick and Sims experience some ethnic tensions and fight, and Nick also cheats on his wife Marion following Jesse Detwiler's exposition of his theories and ideas. In sum, there are many reasons for not labeling DeLillo completely postmodernist or as a "postmodern author." For one, Nicholas Branch's status as a reader who fails to find a definite answer to the mystery of JFK's assassination in *Libra* does not necessarily mean that indefinite or relativistic readings of DeLillo's novels are to be prioritized or favored. Instead, in *Libra* the reactions of the characters (like Beryl Parmenter) to a historical event suggest that DeLillo would recommend an emotional engagement with real events instead of a postmodernist's cool analyzing of events in history as an artificial "text" of sorts. Moreover, when postmodern theorists appear as characters in other novels, such as Murray Siskind of *White Noise*, Vija Kinski of *Cosmopolis*, or Jesse Detwiler of *Underworld*, their theories are generally presented in an unflattering light by DeLillo, satirized as absurd and portrayed as leading to negative moral and personal consequences when the protagonists listen to the suggestions these characters' pontifications imply. So to state this in more sophisticated theoretical terms, simply because DeLillo's fiction may be historiographic does not necessarily mean that it is also primarily postmodern. Other literary categories come into play as we seek to contextualize DeLillo within his genre.

The second major literary style frequently evoked when critics analyze DeLillo is literary modernism. Modernism is defined as a revolutionary artistic movement beginning at the turn of the 20th century but actually not impacting American literature until around the end of the First World War. Modernism was the dominant style in American fiction until around 1945 with the end of the Second World War. The increasingly murderous and grotesque use of technology during warfare, along with the decline of traditional values like monogamy and sexual fidelity in relationships, inspired a sense of loss, alienation, and despair portrayed in modernist literature. Examples of other modernist literature will be discussed as we treat DeLillo as a modernist, responding to the readers and critics who treat DeLillo basically as a modernist.

Furthermore, there are other stylistic features and philosophical tenets that characterize modernist literature and its various offspring. A break with tradition was primary; modernists like James Joyce and T. S. Eliot thought that the history of Western culture was morally bankrupt and that traditional was no longer able to lead us to any sort of good progress. Styles such as surrealism, the portrayal of dreamlike or hallucinatory structures in art, and absurdism, humorous and bizarre representations of the human condition emerge in modernists' work (think of Monty Python's film satire of the Christian story *Life of Brian,* in which the crucified Brian on his cross whistles a catchy tune called "Always Look on the Bright Side of Death"). Another factor in the modernist style of fiction is a narrative technique known as "stream of consciousness," which is a structure mimicking the random flow of disconnected thoughts within an individual's mind. The associations made within that mind show the character's psychological state. Clearly, this is found in DeLillo's work in many places, such as the absurdist humor of *White Noise* or the clear portrayal of Oswald's mind in *Libra*. Another modernist literary earmark, borrowed from modernist artist Marcel Duchamp, who once took a common urinal and transformed it into a piece of art he called "Fountain," is the inverting of the usual relationship between high art or cultural pieces and the commonplace, discarded things or garbage. The message in this inverting is to find beauty in that which most discard as worthless. In terms of language, this idea that things that high-culture artists find worthless are really the most valuable is also important. As far as language goes, it means that slang or dialect language is frequently used in modern fiction. As noted in my chapter on Italian American culture, vernacular, or the common slang of the people, is important in DeLillo's work. A final element of modernism to note here is that some modernists felt the power of moral traditions could be rediscovered or renewed by their art in its return to mythic or other ancient, pretraditional sources. For many reasons, especially because of some concern for art's ultimate moral impact, critics sympathetic to modernism hit closer to the mark in their work on categorizing DeLillo.

A different gathering of the Cambridge critics argue that DeLillo's work tilts more toward modernism than postmodernism. Phil Nel's "DeLillo and Modernism" is a valuable essay in this campaign. Nel provides evidence to support his case that DeLillo uses John Dos Passos as a model for a "newsreel" style interpolation of Secret Service and police walkie-talkie background "chatter" to present the final moments of the Kennedy shooting (Nel 15–16). It is correct to note that this use of an alternative media form aligns DeLillo's work with that of Dos Passos in the modernist style. Nel goes on to say that Dos Passos does this in accord with the modernist idea to utilize "the speech of the people" (16). However, Nel does not note that the language of the people of many modernists (not just Dos Passos) is frequently an ethnic dialect or local slang accented in many instances in James Joyce, T. S. Eliot, and DeLillo's *Underworld*. Without bringing in too many examples to divert us from DeLillo, when a character from a short story in James Joyce's *Dubliners* walks into O'Neill's and says to the bartender, "Here, Pat give us a g.p. like a good fellow" (*Dubliners* 71), someone aware of the Irish local vernacular would know (and Joyce's description could teach us) that he is asking for a glass of porter, which is another name for a dark beer. T. S. Eliot, better known for sophisticated allusions, also brings in the slang and dialect-laden speech of working-class Brits, wives of First World War veterans in his own masterpiece epic poem *The Waste Land*. In the second part of that poem, a woman discusses her conversation with a friend in a dialogue spiced with informal grammar and slang. "It's them pills I took to bring it off," the friend says, probably referring to an abortifacient—these had been known for hundreds of years, though their use was uncommon (Eliot 1). So important was the idea that lowbrow dialect was as artistically significant as upper-class art that Eliot considered titling his poem, "He Do the Police in Different Voices," with this possible title being a reference itself to a dialect-speaking character in a Charles Dickens tale.

In all, the speech of the people is presented in modernist literature not only by the alternative media patterns novelists Dos Passos and DeLillo deploy but also by slang, informal idioms, ethnic accents, and the like.

Finally, *Underworld* is stuffed with dialect, vernacular, and ethnic representations of language that signify the language of the people, the working poor. In my analysis of DeLillo's treatment of the Italian American Bronx, I've noted how DeLillo spices up his presentation of Nick Costanza Shay's past through the heavy use of Italian vernacular and/or Italian American dialectical terms like "Tizzoon" (768), "scucciamente" (695), and others. Therefore, if we make a case for DeLillo as a modernist fiction author, we must also examine his extensive use of such "speech of the people." Further, it would be a mistake to think the Italian Americans were the only ethnic group whose speech is woven into the fabric of novels like *Underworld*. DeLillo's African American characters also debate the morality of the nuclear arms race in a New York bar, stopping to listen to an impassioned street preacher who connects racism and militarism by noting the government's failure to build bomb shelters in Harlem: "They're putting shelters out in Queens all right. They're sheltering Wall Street deep and dry. A-bombs raining from the sky, what are you supposed to do? Take a bus downtown?" (353). Like other modernist authors, DeLillo's use of the speech of several ethnic groups tends to highlight the serious issues of the day, such as racism and atomic war in *Underworld*, the post-traumatic stress disorders of the post–World War 1 generation in Eliot's *The Waste Land*, or James Joyce's treatment of the issues the Irish face in *Portrait of the Artist as a Young Man* or *Dubliners*. Nel's work is more reliable in this light than that of postmodernists.

Patrick O'Donnell adds that in *Underworld* DeLillo dramatically expands the modernists' artistic vision of waste or garbage as art. O'Donnell notes how Nick Costanza Shay looks on Simon Rodia's Watts Towers, which is a famous modernist artwork literally made of trash by an Italian immigrant, and feels a sense of "loss of family and nation" (O'Donnell 118). Yet the remarkable thing is that despite even committing adultery, Nick never really does lose his wife and family, remarking on the survival of his children and their families in the nuclear age. DeLillo evokes Eliot's famous allusion to the mythical phoenix with a clever pun on the characters' home locale of Phoenix, Arizona. However, I would agree with O'Donnell and John Paul Russo (Russo 227) that Nick loses touch with his Italian American identity as he becomes part of American society. Perhaps, though, Nick also finds some sort of inspiration in Rodia's success at making an arrangement of garbage, something Nick himself cannot do with nuclear waste, a permanent poison out of which Detwiler's ridiculous "Plutonium Park" can never made. Unlike Simon Rodia, Nick's diabolical radioactive medium precludes him from creating as beautiful a thing as the Rodia towers and exiles him from the "innocent anarchist vision" (*Underworld* 276), which O'Donnell claims DeLillo aligns with the Italian American artist through Nick's point of view. Furthermore, through differing readings of Nick's other symbolic vocation as textual narrator one could posit a contrasting reading that he is a success like Rodia in terms of the arrangement of subjective detritus of his own experience, and transforming this into the astute and insightful dietrologia we will see emerge in Nick's character as an aspect of DeLillo's very creative response to that crucial cultural representation tackled in his art: the male mob stereotype (see chapter 5 of this book).

In addition to this, DeLillo's look at Rodia in *Underworld* raises the question of the role of the artist in relation to civilization, that perhaps illusory modernist/elitist vision of culture that imagines itself to be not only better than the detritus but also above the poor who live therein. Here is where DeLillo breaks from modernism and its occasionally elitist sense of the artist as cultural savior. O'Donnell refers to the hope of *Underworld* being the same as "the Eliotian possibility that...the technology producing the objects that kill us is the same technology that can produce the objects that cure us" (118). For one thing, the only technology receiving a favorable presentation in *The Waste Land* is not mechanical industrial technology attacked by both Eliot and DeLillo at all but rather the intelligent craft of poetry, which Eliot was trying to renew, literally to create an entirely new style of poetry from his enlightened position of one with a vast knowledge of Western literary traditions. In DeLillo's *Underworld*, recycling is certainly valorized as a morally good use of technology. But as with most of Eliot's negative sensibility regarding the mechanized monsters it has unleashed, "All technology refers to the bomb" (467) for DeLillo. Recycling is necessitated by technological evil. It's hard to avoid the idea that O'Donnell imagines DeLillo to posit the same idea about the role of the artist that Eliot did earlier in his own equally scathing poetic attack on technology found in *The Waste Land*. Notice that Nick's muse for his reflection on Rodia in relation to his father Jimmy Costanza does not issue from the top down of the artistic structure but from below. Nick sees Rodia "in torn overalls and a dusty fedora, face burnt brown, with lights strung on the radial spokes so he could work at night, maybe ninety feet up, and Caruso on the gramophone below" (276). Here, rather, the artist pulls inspiration from the cultural ground socially and symbolically below, the ignored Italian voice of Enrico Caruso. And the gramophone, that negative image of promiscuity in *The Waste Land*, is fictionally recycled in service of the good, as Nick draws on this recorded voice to put his father's sins into a proper perspective. To recontextualize personal history is thus to fulfill one definition of the moral role of the artist.

My suspicion that both modernist and postmodernist critics have over-looked DeLillo's vision of the role of the artist found in the *Underworld* and elsewhere is further confirmed by Marc Schuster's reading of the role of the artist in his recent book on DeLillo titled *Don DeLillo, Jean Baudrillard, and the Consumer Conundrum*. Schuster claims a difference between the vision of the artist in society in Baudrillard and that vision offered by DeLillo in his novels, namely that DeLillo offers a hopeful faith in the power of the individual subject to "alter the ideological framework of society" (Schuster 145). But he offers no adequate textual evidence from the novels as proof of this faith. His choice of proof is the example of *Underworld*'s "Moonman 157," a graffiti artist offering a possible example of resistance to an ideological and social problem. Simply put, this social problem that Schuster labels "the Consumer Conundrum" in his 2008 book I called the commoditization of culture in my 2005 article on Don DeLillo published in the *Greenwood Encyclopedia of Multiethnic American Literature*. Art-ists and their works are commoditized and sold as a product: think of Bill Gray's hearing the racks of novels in a bookstore screaming "Buy Me" (*Mao II* 19). Resisting such commoditization, Moonman's graffiti relies on a kind of shock value that Shuster's most quoted theorist feels is the power of art to liberate us from unspeakable pressures, to cause "radical revolt" (Baudrillard 78 as qtd. in Schuster 142) against the powers that bring about the evils we saw in *Cosmopolis, Libra,* and *Mao II* and say to the world, "I exist; I am," in Baudrillard's terms. Moonman 157's efforts to "hit a train" and thus "get inside people's heads" with his colorful and nonconform-ing words of paint are successful in creating this shock value. But despite Ismael Moonman's potential to do great things, Schuster does not prove that Baudrillard's vision of the artist's role as purveyor of Baudrillardian "irruptions" is necessarily DeLillo's also. For one thing, Moonman's violent "irruptions" of graffiti do not bring about for him the kind of radical revolt Baudrillard discussed, nor do they even get him individual recognition, fame, or any sort of power to transcend circumstances of class and race. When we see Moonman 157 later down the road of his life, he is home-less and destitute of all things save a bevy of disciples to follow his graffiti path—we will return to that scene later—but here we see that for DeLillo, Baudrillard's vision of the artist's role does not pan out. Shock value is not enough to nurture Moonman's artistic career or vision. In chapter 7, I will return to Moonman's ultimate moral and artistic fate as we see again the figure of the individual artist in light of a moral responsibility not only personal but social.

In further defense, Schuster points to the artistic rebirth of Klara Sax, who was married to Albert Bronzini and had an affair with Nick Costanza Shay when Nick was young. But Schuster limits Klara's artistic transcendence to a vicarious appreciation of "onscreen self-appreciation" (Schuster 149); in other words, she achieves great social change simply by appreciating a masturbatory movie scene. Marc Schuster ignores the fact that like Nick, when she sees the Watts Towers (*Underworld* 492) she has a second and far more profound moment of epiphany at the sight of refuse transformed into art. Like Nick also, Klara is moved by the fact of Rodia's being an Italian American immigrant and thus transcending his original position. Furthermore, where Nick sees innocence in Rodia's work, Klara is thrilled by the independence the work represents. Of course for Baudrillard and his later followers such as Schuster, the conditions by which such subjective independence can exist are impossible. According to them, the commodization of culture has "grown to such mammoth proportions as to enslave the heretofore dominating class as well" (Schuster 6). Though Schuster's untested intuition is correct insofar as Don DeLillo *does* provide counterexamples to postmodernists' hopeless determinism, it is no surprise that he does not find the right ones. This is because most critics have ignored the vast and rich cultural fields in which the author places such counterexamples, most notably Italian American culture and the Catholic Church of post–World War II America (see chapters 5 and 6 of this book). Here both Schuster and O'Donnell seem to err on the side of making another great writer or a postmodern theorist more important than DeLillo's text, each looking at the tower from only one side, so to speak.

Modernist critics of DeLillo do not all shift the balance this way, however. Hitting closer to the bull's-eye, Mark Osteen focuses on the role of the artist very specifically in his article "DeLillo's Dedalian Artists," in which he draws upon examples from *Mao II* and *The Body Artist* to argue that the artist's duty is to strike a balance between isolation or "exile" (Osteen 137) and "an embrace of social engagement" (149) and thus not to completely isolate oneself to the point of detriment as does Bill Gray. His title is drawn from Stephen Dedalus of James Joyce's *Portrait of the Artist as a Young Man*, who is at points isolated and at points not so. One question that arises from reading Osteen's recent piece is how the detrimental effects of isolation are different for artists than they are for ordinary human beings. Recall that high modernism, as I point out with Eliot's case, frequently imagines the artist as a sophisticated technician, a cultured student of poetry descending (in Eliot's case literally into an insane asylum) to save the art, the medium, from above. This view of the artist's role, though perhaps accepted in some elitist circles, significantly excludes nonartist figures like Eric Packer of *Cosmopolis* and DeLillo's Oswald of *Libra,* who suffer exactly the same detrimental effects Gray does, the same failure of the art of reinventing the creative self (exactly the goal of Stephen Dedalus in his successful flight to freedom). Each suffers the same collapse into the unspeakable that threatens to subsume artists like Lauren Hartke, Stephen Dedalus, or Klara Sax. For DeLillo, these collapses or failures are the waste of important human beings, for like Ismael Moonman, who lives on a literal garbage heap in the South Bronx, each is at least a potential artist. The similarity of the impact of isolation differentiates DeLillo's idea of an artist from the high-culture modernist idea that the artist is of special origin. To Ismael, the artist on the street, the modernist artist may appear to be a member of an elite group or some Icharean fallen angel, attempting to mythologize himself or self-subsume like Packer into some immaterial disembodied or digital image on a spy camera. Here is where Osteen is right: DeLillo's artist must be concretely, socially engaged. And for DeLillo this artist could be poor, an Italian "immigrant," or anyone, a fact modernist critics like O'Donnell, Nel, and Osteen do not engage in enough or at all in some of their work. Again, their work is highly insightful and opens doors to deeper appreciation of the work, but only these crucial cultural surfaces can yield a complete sense of the writer's vision.

To further differentiate between the purely modernist idea of an artist and DeLillo's, we need to ask a second question raised by Osteen. How should we define what this specific "social engagement" ought to be for the liberation of? Once again, we are looking at the moral force of the roles DeLillo presents to us. DeLillo casts as a moral imperative to us, his audience or readers, who must also be his "cunning collaborators" for this revolutionary and liberating "effect of echoes" (Osteen 149) to occur. Returning to *Underworld* with its successful and potential artists for the moment, is Klara Sax's memory of her first traumatic teenage experiences with sex, double-dating in a parked car with Rochelle Abramowicz (*Underworld* 399) an echo of the proper kind of social engagement? Or running around at parties with Broadway press agent Jack Marshall, who smokes and drinks too much and is "on the perennial edge of dropping dead" (391)? Neither of these appears to be the proper type or form of social engagement DeLillo is advocating in any of his novels. In fact, in contrast to the artist being some sort of spiritually or socially empowered person a priori,

DeLillo advocates the opposite idea: the artist as victim of the same social forces impacting everyone else, and even more in need of the kind of social engagement that transcends racial and class boundaries. That artists are impacted by the same social conditions that reduce Bill Gray or Packer to ruin is clearly shown by three *Underworld* examples of Lenny Bruce, Klara Sax, and Ismael Moonman. As artists, all seek some sort of transcendence to that epiphany an artist may experience as independence, like Klara does, or as a return to innocence, in Nick's case. Lenny Bruce, the countercultural Jewish American comedy who was censored for transgressing so many of the social mores of the early 1960s, represents to the greatest extent that Baudrillardian "shock" effect. DeLillo uses the alternative media form of transcribing into *Underworld* a monologue Lenny delivered on October 24, 1962, in San Francisco. In the middle of his irreverent comic performance, Bruce imitates a "duck and cover" victim of atomic attack, crouching beneath his raincoat into the fetal position, and shouting, "*We're all gonna die!*" (547). He thus reveals himself to be just as impacted by the nuclear arms race as his audience feels themselves to be. Secondly, Klara's problems with relationships with men impede her progress in her career, experiencing the same social oppression as others would. Clearest of all is the example of Moonman, whose poverty and social deprivation appear more extreme than that of the other artists referred to in the novel. How does one help figures like the Moonman transcend his circumstances and share in this sense of independence?

Osteen's call for social engagement finally calls to mind the fact that DeLillo's artist-characters do not operate in a hermetically sealed world; crucial surfaces must be involved. The type of heroism needed to turn the destructive impulse into one more creative is moral heroism. Before we close the case of Ismael Moonman, there is one final critic who is one of the few to take on the moral dimensions of DeLillo's work. Stephanie Halldorson, in her book, *The Hero in Contemporary American Fiction: The Works of Saul Bellow and Don DeLillo*, considers DeLillo's work in light of moral questions and heroism, albeit in juxtaposition to another novelist. Halldorson does not, though, find any moral heroes in DeLillo but rather "assumed heroes" who, as opposed to doing anything in a set narrative, simply sets up the conditions by which acts of heroism might be performed and thus the hero will "finally, return" (Halldorson 177). But Halldorson's examples are not DeLillo's *best* proof of moral heroism, or moreover as I suggest, of moral heroism as a necessary part of support for the artist in his or her struggle to transcend. She provides us with Jack Gladney, who, though he accepts his fate and comes to the realization that "one arbitrarily chooses" stories of religion or other stories to give rise to heroic action, finally fails in her analysis of *White Noise* (143). Another "assumed hero" is photographer Brita Nilsson, who by cowering under gunfire and completely unable to assert herself at all over the totalitarian manipulator Abu Rashid is yet able to create the background conditions for heroic action (177). How is it possible that 20th-century American fiction could be thus devoid of authentic heroes? It is because, as it is for the other postmodern critics, no one can escape the "blatant manipulation of the impulse to the heroic narrative" and thus "there is no space, no time, no image that could any longer represent 'authenticity' in America" (161). With simulated postmodern heroes on the back of every cereal box, real heroism, according to Halldorson, is gone. But the problem with this analysis is that in her creating the idea of DeLillo's "assumed hero," Stephanie Halldorson does not treat *Underworld* and thus is in no position to answer the Moonman question. Good and evil actions that would make the difference between a hero and a nonhero are not defined.

NEITHER MODERN NOR POSTMODERN: NEOREALISM AS AN APPROACH TO *UNDERWORLD* AND TO DELILLO'S ARTISTIC INFLUENCES

Neither modernism nor postmodernism really applies as a label for DeLillo's work. As shown, neither the relativity of the postmodern outlook nor the occasionally elite-driven vision of the artist evoked by some modernists captures the moral force of DeLillo's vision that is the author's sense of right and wrong. A crucial piece of the critic's puzzle that is missing is an earlier approach to popular literature shunned by contemporary critics but still essential to correct understanding of DeLillo's work. Realism was an approach to writing popular at the time of Mark Twain's *Adventures of Huckleberry Finn* and that continues to be so popular not among academic critics but by anyone who judges a book or film by how accurately it represents "real life" or the everyday world we see, hear, touch, and live in every day. Mimesis comes from a Greek term meaning imitation, and in this light it means that literature as popular art imitates life. From this view of art, we can better capture DeLillo's vision of the artist in vital social engagement with DeLillo's version of the hero, as opposed to the mere "assumed hero" of Halldorson. The only two characters from beyond the dire poverty of "the Wall" who come to visit Moonman are the Catholic nuns in *Underworld*, Sister Alma Edgar and Sister Grace Fahey. Their interaction with the impoverished graffiti artist, himself the "fragile purveyor" (Schuster 140) of cultural resistance, is meaningful on several levels. They reach out to him, distributing charity to the people he lives with, and he helps them to distribute their food and feed the hungry. When Esmeralda, a young girl whom Sisters Grace and Edgar were trying to save, is killed before she has a chance to leave the Wall, Juano, one of Ismael's followers, paints a graffiti angel in tribute to Esmeralda. The boy must hang from a rope to complete his artwork. Grace, with her usual passion, tries to inspire Ismael to find the killers. But her presence reminds him more of his duty to younger artists like Juano: "It's all I can do to get these kids so they spell a word correct when they spray their paint."

"Who cares about spelling?" Gracie says.

Gracie's comment is a reminder of what Moonman should care about, not the technicalities involved with the art, but the people. Moonman's teaching of his people should unite an activist's compassion for the weak and those who suffer the greatest. This is the particular kind of social engagement the artist needs, to be reminded of what is most important. Though Ismael, Grace, and Edgar are too late to save Esmeralda, their collaboration could save others like the budding artist Juano. Artists of all media like Ismael Moonman need to connect with those proficient in the art of charity, like the sisters, so they in turn can shun isolation and in turn give charity themselves. Further, even Alma Edgar does eventually seek out and embrace Ismael (*Underworld* 823) after she becomes more compassionate. Thus with the artist and the activist in a mutually supportive social engagement, the isolation plaguing figures like Bill Gray can be cured. So the artist's role is interactive with other parts in DeLillo, particularly the part of moral heroes. Moral heroes remind artists of their responsibility, and the artist in turn spreads the grace the hero gives to the community. This collaborative model provides the chance to transcend one's circumstances, though it does not omit Moonman's personal responsibility for acting on his chances. Collaboration between the individualist artist and the socially engaged activist is critical in DeLillo; if Bill Gray had had associates more concerned with the social good than with personal gain, he might have survived the tragic dénouement of *Mao II*. This representation of the artist socially engaged with the activist is both crucial to an understanding of DeLillo's concept of the role of the artist and a proof of the accuracy of the label of mimetic realism to his work. In the world outside the text, the author is known for such engagement as when he advocated for the cause of artistic freedom for Salman Rushdie. Within the mimetic realist tradition, these sorts of social commitments are more commonplace than not, going all the way back to American realism's heyday as the most popular literary style, roughly 1865–1910. Harriet Beecher Stowe, author of *Uncle Tom's Cabin*, wrote newspaper columns supporting abolitionist views, which her novel also embraced. Her one-time neighbor in Connecticut, Samuel Clemens, or Mark Twain as he is known, also was a staunch advocate for abolition and the rights of Chinese immigrant laborers, even in a few cases sponsoring scholarships for African Americans. So in imitation of social ties between art and social action, DeLillo's work is more clearly defined.

One counterpoint to my contention that neorealist aspects of DeLillo's fiction trump the postmodern might be that the conditions of life, postmodern in nature, are the subject of DeLillo's work. That is the case of many Cambridge critics who discuss DeLillo's representation of "a thoroughly postmodern, dehistoricized America" (Duvall, "Introduction" 7). However, if real conditions are postmodern, and DeLillo is simply representing them as such, he is a mimetic realist. Like Grace Fahey, DeLillo's earlier literary influences reveal a preferential option for treatment of the poor. Mimetic realism is his tribute to an earlier author, Nelson Algren, who was an influence on Don DeLillo. The fact of this influence is demonstrated by several factors, including a comparison between fictional work by the two authors and by a recent public appearance at the Steppenwolf Theater by Mr. DeLillo. Focusing on the fiction of the two writers, Nelson Algren created several patterns of symbolism and action that we can recognize as influential. For one, Algren's narratives dealing with characters who are down and out frequently show a blurring of the lines between legitimate and illegitimate authority—the poor and suffering frequently experience both kinds of authority as one and the same in collaborative effect.

An example is found in Algren's short story "A Bottle of Milk for Mother," which is a story about a gang leader who is accused of mugging and murder, or "jackrolling" as it was called in 1920s Chicago, where the story takes place (Algren 73–90). This main character, Bruno Lefty Bicek, presumes that his position in the interrogation room is more secure than it is because he is well acquainted with a Chicago city alderman. What he does not know is that this same "alderman "is the brother of the aggressive police captain Kozak, who is interrogating Bicek for the murder. Bicek believes in a kind of magical power of authoritarian names and does not know that he has been deceived. The alderman's politically powerful name "alderman" outweighs the value of knowing the man's actual name. In fact, just as with DeLillo's "Lee Harvey Hidell Leon Alek true-blue Oswaldovitch Oswald" in the novel *Libra*, Bicek identifies himself and is identified by others under a confusing cloud of names. When the Captain wants to gain his trust, he calls the suspect by his familiar boxer name "Lefty" (76).

When he wants to intimidate the prisoner with interrogation techniques, he orders him around by calling him "Bicek" (86). Like Oswald, Bruno Lefty Bicek is literally trying to make a new name for himself, to legitimize his brute strength; he regretfully thinks, "Why hadn't anyone called him "Iron Man Bicek or Fireball Bruno for that matter?" (75). Again, a clear resemblance to DeLillo's version of Oswald. Also, by evoking the power of names, Algren's text shows a thematic influence on DeLillo's *The Names*. On that note, the issue of the power of a secret or original language comes up in this same short story. Lefty feels he can ease the situation by telling the police that he "talked polite-like in Polish in his ear" (78) during the alleged mugging. Nor is Lefty Bicek alone in his faith in the power of a native tongue; the victim of the crime is said to holler "m' lody bandyta" (78), which is a Polish expression for young bandit. Lest we conclude that Algren himself was Polish and thus some sort of ethnic model for DeLillo's use of Italian American language and cultural symbols, this is not the case. Rather, Algren prefigures DeLillo's use of ethnic language and mimetic realism as an author of fiction, with reference to an authentic and realistic use of language. Again, like Lee Harvey Oswald in *Libra*, Bicek may have acted alone or may be the patsy for a gang or conspiracy activity. In any case, he is presumed guilty, as Kozak begins the interrogation with, "Let the jackroller tell us how he done it hisself" (73). In his multiple and conflicted attempt to name himself, and in his helplessness before powerful figures who thus blur the line between legitimate and illegitimate use of their authority, Algren's Bicek appears to resemble DeLillo's Oswald in more ways than one. The power of "naming" and the struggle of the subject to self-define are central in the work of both authors.

Furthermore, another way that the realist writing of Algren resembles elements we see in DeLillo is the power of the erotic relationship. In the conclusion of some of Algren's short stories, we see a male and a female remain together in a love bond, which means more to the couple than their financial situation. Examples abound throughout the anthology *The Neon Wilderness*, whence readers can draw their own comparisons. To name two examples, in "Stickman's Laughter" (Algren 65–72) gambler Banty Longobardi drowns his sorrows in the arms of his partner; in "He Swung and He Missed" (157–164) Rocco and Lili do not seem to mind her having lost a bundle gambling that he would win the last fight of his career, a dive he almost did not take because of his pride. When the relationship between the lovers is broken at the end of an Algren story, there is a sense of all being lost, like when in the story "Depend on Aunt Elly" (47–64) unfortunate convict Wilma (Algren's characters frequently lack last names) leaves her fighter/boyfriend on the verge of making it big and the man feels "as though the bottom had dropped out of something inside him" (64). For both DeLillo and Algren, bad omens prevail in the lives of those male protagonists who abandon their partners, while for those whom erotic love smiles upon, such as Nick Costanza Shay from *Underworld*, material loss does not seem to matter. Nick was a collector who had the prized baseball that Ralph Branca hit in the 1951 pennant game between the New York Giants and the Brooklyn Dodgers. He's pleased to remain married to Marion, while Eric Packer loses the love of Elise Shifrin in *Cosmopolis*. This is not to say that the main point of DeLillo's work is that "love conquers all," although that is one possible interpretation of these Algren works. But traces of Algren's use of eroticism are present in DeLillo as well.

If these similarities between the writers in terms of the themes of authority and romantic love and structures evocative of the naming power of language do not convince readers that DeLillo is a mimetic realist in the same way Algren is, my recent experience is here added as proof. Recently, Mr. DeLillo gave a dramatic reading of Nelson Algren's dramatic works and a brand new previously unpublished short story at Chicago's Steppenwolf Theater for the occasion of the 100th birthday of Algren. Martha Lavey, Willem Dafoe, and other talented actors took part as well. As a special gift to all those who attended (myself included), Don DeLillo did publish a short memoir of his own personal experience knowing that Nelson Algren was in the program.

What was clear from Don DeLillo's reading was that he had a tremendous understanding of and sensitivity to the subtleties of Algren's passionate treatment of the American poor. What was also clear was that the two American writers had been friends, spending time together one summer in New York at a beach cottage. So these facts as well demonstrate that it is likely that DeLillo, with his compassionate treatment of the poor and clear portrayal of social injustice, especially in *Libra* and *Underworld*, may well have been strongly influenced and inspired by Algren. At any rate, beyond postmodernism and simple modernism, the idea of mimetic realism also shines through Don DeLillo's work.

Neither postmodernism nor modernism fully defines DeLillo's work. Even if only in imitation of 21st-century life's appalling postmodern state, there is mimesis occurring in these novels. From the devastating portrayals of evil in *Mao II*, *Libra*, and *Cosmopolis* to the confrontation of media stereotypes and inspiring renditions of urban missionary work in its collusion with art in *Underworld*, art imitates life. Since this mimesis all takes place in language, the powerful vision of language introduced with suspense in

The Names and satirically in *White Noise* grounds hope for some greater good, a potent moral force of this author's work. When David Cowert, postmodernist, suggests that the real curse of postmodernity is "the universal recursivity at the heart of a symbolic Order always already at a remove from the Real" (Cowert 160), what else can that "Real" be than DeLillo's works of language thus engaged in morality. Imitating his human imitations of actual good, like Arthur and Gracie, readers living DeLillo's work as well as reading Don DeLillo can heal this "remove" between the way things *are* and how they *ought to be*. In short, the moral force of Don DeLillo's work is to inspire us all to truly live "responsibly in the real" (*Underworld* 82).

_____ *Chapter 2* _____

Intimations of a Moral Vision
in DeLillo's Early Novels

Despite the postmodernity of their narrative structure, consistent intimations of the artistic/moral vision that will emerge in his major late-career
novels recur in the texts published before DeLillo's breakout success: *Americana, Great Jones Street, Ratner's Star, Running Dog,* and *Players*. All the
novels feature consistent use of antiwar imagery. Beginning this negative
treatment of the violence of war and its aftereffects is *Americana,* where
antiwar images and scenes foreshadow many later treatments of war's
attendant evils. Continuing this theme is post-traumatic stress disorder as
presented in *Libra,* war-ravaged settings and scenes of action in *The Names*
and *Mao II,* and finally *Underworld*'s extensive treatment of the Cold War,
Vietnam, and weapons of mass destruction. Another major moral issue
we will note involves a preoccupation with resistance to the contemporary mediated attack on the subject as this issue comes up in *Great Jones
Street* and *Ratner's Star* especially. A lesser-known work, *Ratner's Star* also
evokes a critique of late 20th-century capitalist appropriations of theoretical sciences and their application as technology. To readers today, a third
intimation of DeLillo's later moral vision is discovered when one analyzes
his 1970s-era treatments of terrorism in relationship to capitalist econom-
ics in two other early novels: *Players* and *Running Dog*. Overall, though,
given the fact that DeLillo's oeuvre is dominated by the presence of the epic
novel *Underworld,* easily overshadowing any one other novel, *End Zone*
must be reserved as the most enlightening in terms of its focus on the moral
issue closest to the major theme of *Underworld*: that of nuclear weapons
and ultimate nuclear warfare. As one reads through the entertaining and

evocative early novels, one can establish a base for a better appreciation of DeLillo's more widely accepted later works.

Readers of *Americana* may not be inclined to view this work as making or containing any sort of moral statement whatsoever. David Bell, the antihero with the conflicted heart, sets out to break with most if not all of the conventional social, moral, and sexual mores of middle America on his road trip set in the late 1960s and early 1970s. A large part of his experiences are centered on a very dated glorification of sexual liberation, a period-appropriate pursuit of breaking all sexual inhibitions to lay the groundwork for creative transcendence of personal limits of self-expression. He seeks out his muse, a Native American/Irish woman called only "Sullivan." Eventually, he will find her and fulfill his desires as they complete a creative project together.

Bell's philosophy would be compatible in this sense with the by-now discredited *Playboy* philosophy or policy but was still a cultural novelty at the time of *Americana*'s release. But the appearance of absolute sexual/moral relativism in DeLillo's implicit themes is deceptive; in fact, a highly negative treatment of the violence of war and its aftereffects is a pronounced theme in this first novel. Implied here is not so much an "anything goes" rejection of all morality but rather an ethical statement specifically against war.

To begin outlining the plot and relevant treatment of war, the protagonist David Bell undertakes his journey to find his artistic vision, to complete the avant-garde film he has set out to make in defiance of his television network boss. Bell's original series, *Soliloquy,* consists of videotaped monologues dedicated to one person's point of view, one person speaking into the camera without censorship or editorial intervention. His series faces cancellation at the hands of his supervisor Weede Denney, who as his name implies is a corrupt and toxic person, choking off Bell's creative growth. Weede is only interested in profit for the corporation. He does not care about anything else. This is revealed in the sequence where Bell's series is cancelled when one of the sponsors complains that it was not profitable enough: "Chip Moerdler over at Brite Write said it wasn't selling any ball-point pens" (70). When Ted Warburton, the employee thought of as the conscience of the company, objects on behalf of David and his show, Denney's response displays the supervisor's crass materialism and failure to see the value of the more subjective and personal truth Bell is pursuing through his use of the subjective camera: "You can't argue with a sales chart" (71). As the novel's title indicates, conditions such as greed infuse the whole of American society, DeLillo's proper target. So the formation of ethics or morals in American culture is viewed primarily as hypocrisy, stylized as part of a script Bell later will write as he walks off his job at the network. A woman says to her man back from a business trip, "What's fascinating about people like you is your blazing sense of morality. Your devotion to the concept of a place for everything and everything in its place. When you get right down to it, that's what morality means to a moralist. It means shoot to kill but not in a hospital zone. You might wake the patients" (304).

So for its superficial status in the narrative, American morality is basically hypocrisy, and war is a major instance of such hypocrisy. Throughout the novel, anytime war is presented, it is presented in a disturbing and consistently negative fashion. The opening scene finds Bell escaping from an unpleasant party interrupted in the bathroom by Prudence Morrison. The two aren't doing anything in there but talking, and Pru wants to boast of her brother's military actions in Vietnam. David is not necessarily interested: "The war was on television but we all went to the movies," he reflects (5). What is negative here is, for one, that Pru's comment about her brother's experience of the war directly reflects David's feelings about the party: "you can't tell the friendlies from the hostiles" (5). Bell has elicited a mixed reaction from his friends and acquaintances at the party because his date, B. G. Haines, is African American. Despite the fact that this is the relatively liberal early 1970s, Pru makes an openly racist remark about B. G. to David Bell in the bathroom, criticizing him for dating someone not white. Implicit here is the message that social conditions stateside mirror those overseas in war and that racism and unclear alliances plague the American situation at home and in Vietnam. War, hatred, and racism emerge in this first reference to Vietnam, which in the early 1970s evokes all these associations. Although a small scene, this encounter presents the negative portrayal of war that runs throughout the novel.

Even in the bizarre cast of characters that make up Bell's coworkers, we find references that evoke this antiwar theme. By far the most interesting figure is Ted Warburton, who is not only defined as the conscience of the network but is also its "Mad Memo Writer." Leaving anonymous notes all around the office, the "Writer's" job is largely to provoke controversy and challenge Bell and his crew to think critically about what they're doing. Warburton is a postmodern character, a double for DeLillo's own criticizing of American culture through writing. Criticism of contemporary American technological means of warfare and the social conditions these means bring about is implied in the Mad Memo Writer's quote from St. Augustine, "And never can a man be more disastrously in death than when death itself shall be deathless" (21). Images of such "deathless death" become a part of the treatment of warfare later as the novel unfolds.

David Bell's journey is presented n terms of sexual freedom, but what repulses him about the "vision of sex in America" is that it is couched in terms that are too violent: "that montage of speed, guns, torture, rape, orgy and consumer packaging" (33). In DeLillo's America, sex has begun to resemble modern warfare. One of the many emotional traumas Bell's family endures is his sister Mary eloping with a character, Arondella, who appears to be a gangster from Mary's account of the business trips her lover mysteriously takes (163). What's stylized about DeLillo's portrayal of this relationship, a second juxtapositioning of sexual love and violence, is the pun about the phrase David Bell uses when discussing Arondella with his sister Mary, remarking that their father objects to Arondella's being "in the rackets" meaning living a mob lifestyle (163). Earlier in *Americana*, the Bells' father had virtually ordered David to destroy his other sister Jane's romantic suitor in a game of tennis, to "run his ass ragged" (151). This game of "rackets" is presented in terms nearly as savage as Arondella's potential gangland activities. Likewise, both references to the "rackets" shorten the distance between illegal and legalized violence, the (presumably Italian American—see chapter 5) criminal mob, and American capitalism, the advertising industry David and his father serve. This further juxtaposition raises one question (among many) of what constitutes legitimate and illegitimate forms of violence in American society.

For now, the focus of the criticism of violence in *Americana* is best found in references to war. Some of these criticisms emerge when David Bell finally does get to make his avant-garde film. He joins forces with amateur actress Carol Deming, who jokingly answers her phone, "North Atlantic Treaty Organization" (225). Like NATO, David's film is an attempt to deal with American postwar realities. We learn that Carol is dealing with many issues including a possible incident of abuse by her father, who speaks "softly in the darkness of war and death" during the incident, associating the violence of war with perversion (228). She does not resolve her issues but proves useful to David in the process of filmmaking; her soliloquies or monologues allow him to give voice to his memories of his sister Mary, and to a lesser degree, to those of his ex-wife Meredith. Carol desecrates the state of American warfare in her off-screen talk with David, referring to patriotism and war as "killing the pig-eyed and the slope-headed" (226). This critique coupled with her victimization seems to characterize her as one who can see the truth but is powerless to do anything about it, internalizing her insights as a source of her acting ability.

Beyond relatively minor characters like Carol, David's core group of fellow travelers also reveal a critical presentation of contemporary war and its violence. Bobby Brand, one of Bell's film crew who does a scene with Carol, exhibits a constant state of post-traumatic stress disorder resulting from his prior military service. Brand cannot function very well because his memories of Vietnam torment him: "Inside my head the action is constant" (252). His speech to Dave is laden with memories of attacking civilians, like shooting a man riding a bicycle and firing off "cans of nape" (252).

Bell's putting him in the film opposite Carol highlights the fact that Brand is also victimized in his suffering PTSD. Like Carol, Brand is fairly disempowered, and like the jilted man he portrays in the indie film Bell shoots, he really cannot accomplish much in the plot of the narrative. Bobby Brand's deep-seated disorientation is another formative portrayal of war's destructive impact; even his name is an advertiser's pun on the American "brand" of postwar experience.

In addition to Bobby Brand's PTSD and some other passing references to illegitimate violence and war interspersed throughout the novel, *Americana* also includes a brief selection from a shortwave radio "shock jock" to whom Bell is listening as he attempts to get some sleep in the camper-top vehicle the ragtag film crew calls home. The voice is transcribed into the text directly from radio speech (DeLillo will also mirror the radio medium as a narrative style in *Underworld* by transcribing the University of Madison's WIBA covering an anti-Vietnam rally). This voice again mocks war and highlights its violent impact. The voice, which only calls him or herself "Beastly," sends up a mock prayer to the bombers of the Strategic Air Command: "And lead us not into annihilation but deliver us from rubble, for thine is the power and the power and the power, forever and never, oh man" (234). The wild speech of "Beastly" reminds Bell and others of the ultimate threat of nuclear war, with the ideas of "annihilation" and "rubble" and also the line "forgive us our strontium," which evokes the strontium-90 residue of early aboveground nuclear testing in America turning up in cow's milk. All in all, the violence of war is highlighted as it initiates a backlash effect against the original perpetrator, whether it is Brand's being haunted by the memories of what he has done or the airwaves resounding with residue of the reality of the omnipresent threat of nuclear violence.

The political critique of war becomes interior and personal in the overall structure of *Americana*. David Bell himself emerges as a character wrestling with his own social and sexual history: the problems of his mentally challenged mother, who died of cervical cancer (300), and his father's aforementioned issues, as well as his own past with episodes of sexual violence. The reciprocity of the impact of war permeating the narrative thus is essential to a thorough interpretation of *Americana*'s structure as it emerges through social and personal dysfunctions. Sexual and wartime violence are both characterized as reciprocal.

When Bell meets his foil in the character of Glenn Yost, World War II veteran and advertising executive, the plot of Bell's coming to terms with both personal demons and his need to make a social statement with his film heat up. Yost is a negative opposite to Bell, who instead of reacting to the moral contradictions posed by the extreme violence and sexual aberrations he has witnessed paradoxically ignores them, forcing a normal functioning as a dishonest template over continued cooperation with the system. Like Bell, Yost is an advertising executive, but unlike *Americana*'s narrator he feels no remorse nor sees any moral issue in the work he performs. Yost seems to perceive a mistake in the typical 1970s advertisements dealing with "the more depressing areas of life—odors, sores, old age, ugliness, pain" (272). He calls these emotional appeals to a common sense of physical pain and empathy "the anti-image," speaking derogatorily of "Madge...suffering from irregularly" and so forth. Yost's mistaken belief that the consumer "never identifies" with the suffering protagonist of these commercials belies a lack of faith in compassion and an overemphasis on power and might: "We have exploited the limitation of dreams. It's our greatest achievement" (271). Signs of human weakness are a scandal to Yost and his world, as an entire commercial must be reshot due to the unattractive visual presence of one extra, a "small shrunken old man" (274). Glenn Yost rejects the suffering of the diverse human subject David Bell is searching for with his soliloquies; rather, Yost is content to participate in the deception advertising is famous for, the same "preempting the truth" (274) that allows war to persist as an evil in society. The final confrontation between Yost, who lives in a of banal conformity with his innocent wife and high school basketball star son, and Bell takes place over the fact that David captures Yost's testimony of his experience in the Bataan Death March in the Philippines in 1942, one of the most atrocious war crimes in history. Yost had been part of a mass surrender to the Japanese during which Americans were forced to march unceasingly without pause or provisions. To attempt to help a fellow prisoner was tantamount to a sentence of death. The popular version most Americans would be familiar with of Bataan would be from a John Wayne film about the incident. But Glenn Yost has really failed to come to terms with his experience; although he is more stable and higher functioning than Bobby Brand, he seems now to take the denial of compassion forced upon him in the war as an advertising social norm in the present moment of his life. Speaking of his experience in a tough, John Wayne–like war hero voice, he reveals no trace of remorse or lingering pain, using description like "But it really wasn't too bad" (294) as he presents unspeakable horrors of mass beheadings and other torture he reveals to Bell. Yost's memories build up to his own being forced to dig mass graves and what should have been a shocking event: a young, indigenous boy being buried alive, attempting to rise out of the ditch. Yost stops his story without telling whether he obeyed the guard forcing him at bayonet point to bury the child anyway (298). Throughout, he expresses no remorse, calling the child "the little wog" (298) as he relays his soliloquy of war to David Bell. The only sign Yost exhibits of any long-term disturbance he may be experiencing as a result of his participation in the war is his injured eye, which he cannot control. His eye jumps around, and in an impressionistic and eclectic aside, Bell comments, "Fellini says the right eye is for reality and the left eye is the fantasy eye" (293). In a fairly transparent symbol, the eye could be said to represent Glenn's suppression of the moral conflict he experienced in the Philippines, fantasizing that the war "really wasn't too bad." To sum Yost's experiences up, the unspeakable horror of burying the boy alive forms an image hearkening back to the St. Augustine quote in Ted Warburton's memo: "When death itself shall become deathless." Yost's repression of his memories causes a failure of moral distinction, moral consciousness of the difference between human and animal death. Because he could no longer feel, he now embraces fully advertising's deceptive assaults on humanity in its vulnerable state.

Continuing the theme of war's aftermath, Bobby Brand describes how his crew would relax after attacking the enemy. They would then play a game called "Godsave," chanting irreverent pseudo-prayers like, "Godsave the women and children I vaporized this morning" (280). When three of the five men are killed in action, Brand keeps mindlessly chanting, "Godsave God." Similar to Joseph Heller's *Catch-22*, Brand's testimonial in *Americana* is a dark satire of American mainstream religion and the sanctification and moral blessing it attempts to give to war.

While Yost suffers a moral failure, Brand's breakdown is more psychological. He cannot hold down a stable position or stable relationships. David Bell must leave these men behind in order to find closure for his film project and move on in life. As Bell is leaving Glenn Yost's home, the man shoots him a look of sheer hatred "hints of cold deacon fury…that furious cold light damning my soul" (318). Perhaps the reason David Bell has become so despicable in Yost's eyes is because his filmmaking inquiries into the veteran's past have forced up images the man does not want to deal with.

Yet both Brand and Yost could be exonerated from their imbalances and moral blindness because, as veterans, they are also victims of wartime violence, an interior or psychic violence primarily. But DeLillo's *Americana* saves the worst example of American religious jingoism and bloodlust for last: the perverted pleasure-zealot Clevenger, the last strange to give David Bell a ride, most baldly and boldly asserts a twisted faith in "the name of the Christ of the dogs of war" (328). This phrase comes from before Bell meets Clevenger. As Sullivan delivers her symbolic soliloquy of attempting to moderate a family feud between her father and her uncle, she speaks of the image of Jesus Christ in two contrasting ways, as the gentle Jesus and as "Christ the tiger" (300).

DeLillo's contrasting representations of Christianity connect the treatment of religion and violence. The author's images represent that Christianity is commonly evoked as a rationale for warfare, and this is precisely the prowar mentality Clevenger evokes in his rant to David Bell: "We're too soft and too sweet and we got to bear down on all those people that blaspheme our Christian nation with their catcalling and their gibbering like an Islamic sect from out of the motion pictures. We got to blitz them, friends" (366).

Clearly Clevenger presents a religious/extremist warhawk's view, one that is the heart of the problem. Despite Clevenger's claim that "Keeryst Jesus was not a stranger in his own land" (366) that is not only how the historical figure of Jesus Christ died but also how David Bell has proceeded through the novel, collecting subjective narratives to reveal the American conscience in the Vietnam era. But Bell graphically defeats him via escape. What he saves here is not a friend but the rough cut of his film, his artistic vision set against the mainstream American cultural glorification of war.

To simplify, this negative treatment of the violence of war and its aftereffects is a pronounced theme in DeLillo's first novel. It is also one to which he will return frequently, in the post-traumatic stress disorder suffered by the author's version of Lee Harvey Oswald in *Libra*, the flight of Matt Costanza and his fellow B-52 bomber crew in *Underworld*, and the war-ravaged settings and scenes of action in *The Names* and *Mao II*, not to mention *Underworld*'s extensive treatment of the Cold War, weapons of mass destruction, and many other attendant issues. Therefore, to see *Americana* as DeLillo's announcement of central antiwar concerns that will drive later novels in a first major work of fiction, as many critics have, is an accurate insight. Though Bell's Freudian triumphant escape via a kind of sexual liberation is a motif dated by our standards, an antiwar ethic emerges from the plethora of viewpoints that are assembled in the novel. Readers naturally see an ethical relativism in those varied viewpoints; however, *Americana* represents the first emergence of a moral imperative against war that can be read in later works.

Antiwar themes are only one major intimation of the moral issues that will recur in the later novels DeLillo wrote after achieving great fame and critical acclaim. Another significant issue is DeLillo's recurring preoccupation with individual resistance to contemporary mediated attacks on the personal subject. Addressing the impact of such attacks in his article, "DeLillo's Dedalian Artists," Mark Osteen argues that the rock star protagonist of DeLillo's *Great Jones Street*, Bucky Wunderlick, stands as a negative moral example for artists of a lack of balance between taking time for privacy and public engagement: "Artists must both engage their society, and maintain a critical detachment from its blinding glare and deadening buzz" (Osteen 138). While all this may be true, my claim is that Bucky may have learned his lesson, punishing though it may be, and that there are suggestions that though he appears beaten down in a final Icharean descent from rock stardom, another Wunderlick comeback is not absolutely impossible given the details of the conclusion of *Great Jones Street*.

The novel is the story of rock superstar Bucky Wunderlick, who walks out in the middle of a commercially successful tour to pursue privacy in a "time of prayerful fatigue" (*Great Jones Street* 19). But his hedonistic lifestyle and nearly irrational immaturity prevent this from happening. Bucky's nonstop touring and partying have led him to the point of nearly complete mental breakdown: while on this breakneck tour, he inexplicably and without justification screams in the face of an old woman in a wheelchair and then seems to become hysterical himself, alternately laughing and crying (36). He returns to the dilapidated apartment of his groupie girlfriend Opel Hampson on run-down Great Jones Street. He is pressured to release his coveted "Mountain Tapes," a set of unadulterated acoustic recordings Bucky made in his hideaway anechoic-chambered mountain studio (23). He is thus pressured by nefarious and obese record company manager Globke. When he refuses to cooperate, his situation deteriorates. Meanwhile Opel has taken a job as an illegal drug courier, getting mixed up in a plot of the Happy Valley Farm Commune to manufacture and market a super powerful mind-altering drug stolen from the U.S. government and originally designed "to brainwash gooks or radicals" (58–59). She has unfortunately become the bargaining agent between this sinister underground commune and an equally criminal scientist called "Dr. Pepper," whom Opel considers "without a doubt the scientific genius of the underground" (59). Bucky and Opel throw a wild party reminiscent of Jay Gatsby's occasions on East Egg in F. Scott Fitzgerald's *The Great Gatsby*. Unbeknownst to the couple, they are observed by Dr. Pepper and his Happy Valley minions at the party, as they believe they can use Bucky Wunderlick to obtain the drug. In fact, Bucky may even have had it in his possession if Opel mixed her packages up. Bucky parcels up his time between Opel, the Transparanoia Record Company, their lackey Hanes, and his upstairs neighbor hack writer Eddie Fenig in a general state of stoned malaise and obnoxious resistance to Globke. Opel finally dies of neglect and a hard lifestyle. But before dying, she had mailed the tapes to Bucky in a plain-brown-wrapped package that was similar to the package with the drug Dr. Pepper is after, which is alternately referred to as "the package" or "the product," just as Bucky's music is (171). The record company hires Happy Valley goons to raid the Great Jones Street apartment building to get the Mountain Tapes, and Bucky learns they have been stolen. He meets Hanes, who is carrying the drug Dr. Pepper wants, on the subway train. Despite having been charged by Pepper to get the drug from Hanes, Bucky does not take that package from the young man. Globke then invites the singer/lyricist to a dinner party where he proposes another breakneck tour schedule and mass marketing of the tapes, now being pressed into LP form (200). Bucky departs in his usual cavalier and obnoxious manner, but he is pursued by Happy Valley thug Bohack. They credit Bucky as their spiritual inspiration. Bucky is finally captured and taken to their bleak inner-city living quarters, where Pepper and his malcontents, possibly even at the behest of Transparanoia, inject Bucky with the mind-altering drug, which takes away his powers of speech and language formation. This effect finally grants Wunderlick the peace and isolation he craves (264). Furthermore, in an act of criminally insane revenge, Dr. Pepper and his misguided band plot to blow up the recording studio in Cincinnati, destroying both the records and Bucky's priceless original Mountain Tapes. It is not entirely clear if they succeed. As the novel closes, the drug wears off, and we leave Bucky in the decrepit neighborhood reflecting on his "double defeat" of failing both to make a comeback drawing upon the Mountain Tapes and also of failing to find perfect wordless isolation in his chemically induced muteness. However, he may yet "return to whatever is out there" (285).

Clearly, his relationship with Opel is abusive, a by-product of the violence and confusion swirling about the two of them. When Opel returns from a long plane trip with an airplane cold and tries to take a hot bath in her own apartment, an oblivious Bucky walks into her tub without even bothering to remove his grimy street clothes. Even though it is pretty clear that the obnoxious rocker is feeling happy and secure in their relationship (as he says, "We lived in bed as old couples rock on porches, without hurry or need" [55]), an awareness of what Opel actually needs does not enter into Wunderlick's blissful view of their bond. When the unfortunate Opel later dies, the damage she has suffered to her self-esteem is revealed. The groupie who has wandered into a very destructive arrangement with a deadly crowd describes herself as, "Luggage. I'm luggage. By choice, inclination and occupation.... But I don't like that word very much. Lug-gudge. Heavy brutish word for a delicate thing like me" (91). Ironically, Bucky realizes that her death has come as "a result of unrelenting neglect" (122), but instead of seeing the moral connection between his own mistreatment of her and this death, he considers it to be "natural."

Domestic abuse is not the only tragic social effect associated with rock and roll that DeLillo portrays in *Great Jones Street*. Substance abuse, more culturally accepted in the world of early 1970s rock and roll than in many other cultural settings, has rendered Bucky analogous to the symbol DeLillo presents to paint the rocker's character—his dead telephone. As we will also see in *End Zone*, the symbolic use of a singular cultural artifact, frequently an instrument of technological communication, reinforces themes presented in the form of characterization: "The business normally transacted is more than numbed within the phone's limp ganglia; it is made eternally irrelevant. Beyond the reach of shrill necessities the dead phone disinters another source of power" (31).

This description of the telephone of course represents the character of Bucky himself "more than numbed" by his desensitizing lifestyle involving drug abuse. Studied as an object of analysis in relationship to other characters and situations, Bucky Wunderlick reveals if not literally "disinters" sources of social power. At this highly sexist point in time (the misogynistic culture of early 1970s rock, with the Rolling Stone's tune "Midnight Rambler" as one instance to support my claim) gender is one of those sources of power. In part a self-created victim, Opel Hampson is united with Bucky in this drugged-out "dead telephone" state of consciousness. The two of them partake in a destructive journey that can be characterized as highly analogous to the dead phone's "descent into total dumbness." As with the broken telephone connection, this descent involves both parties in what we can only call their abusive relationship. The gender power dynamics disinterred by this objective examination of their relationship can be shown to be related to the irrationality of the rock and roll lifestyle, the "relentless neglect" Opel is made to suffer in her socially defined role as groupie. Numbed by the bond between them, Opel is finally reduced to terminal dumbness, foreshadowing Bucky's later fate at the hands of Happy Valley.

Moreover, trumping both gender oppression and substance abuse in destructive power, it is rather the market processes of commoditization that prove to be the demise of the artist or creative person. Bucky has no creative control over the recordings he makes for Transparanoia; hence his music becomes a depersonalized and mindlessly reproduced "product." Trying to avoid explaining himself further to the press, Bucky jests, "Transparanoia markets facsimiles" (24), as if the record company was making clones of its artists and managers in commodifying their work. More specifically, this illustrates that this commoditized, reproducible product is indeed the effect of not only Bucky's self-recording of his own music (he also jokes with Opel during a meal that he wishes they had "Live strawberries instead of strawberries on tape" [83]) but of his participation in his commercial contract with Transparanoia. DeLillo will return to the theme of the effect of the marketplace on the artist in his later work, *Mao II*, when the character of photographer Brita Nilsson, staring at Warhol-style reproductions of the faces of Russian public figures, states her belief that "it is possible to fuse images" through which the artist's high personalized and creative life force is transmitted to the reader, rock audience, or viewer of visual art. Bucky's own facsimiles are used in *Great Jones Street* to ruin him.

When Globke makes off with the Mountain Tapes as the "dog boys" of Happy Valley ransack the apartment building where Bucky lives, we begin to see Bucky's final Icharean descent nearly to its nadir of total dumbness, where Opel winds up. Transparanoia's greed acquires transparently criminal overtones, as this interaction between Globke the manager and Bucky the managed indicates: "You walked off the goddam tour, Bucky. You took away my action. We needed product, see. You were failing to deliver product. Product is something that matters deeply. . . . Enormous sums of money were involved in your disappearing act" (186).

His tone is quite menacing, and the encounter resembles closely Wunderlick's other menacing encounters with underworld figures like Bohack and Dr. Pepper. The reader can easily appreciate the paranoid mindset Bucky suffers from in which Tranparanoia Records and the Happy Valley commune have conspired against the rock star. No matter, given the fact that he very well could have permanently lost his lyric-making abilities because of his kidnapping and poisoning, Bucky Wunderlick has learned his hard lesson, reaping the unfortunate results of what he has sown in extreme vanity, substance abuse, and an immature and obtuse outlook on life. If we read the novel as closing with the Mountain Tapes destroyed and his last chance at a productive life gone, *Great Jones Street* forms a portrayal of how commoditization can completely destroy the artistic spirit.

However, there are other possibilities. Largely because the work is also a novel about rock and roll and the complex relationship between music and language, a truly meaningful interpretation of *Great Jones Street* involves more than the theme of the Faustian bargain between the artist and the marketplace. As the title of this book indicates, the moral implications of every aspect of American culture that DeLillo's work portrays is of great significance and force, and here in *Great Jones Street,* as Opel puts to Bucky prior to his transformation at the end of the work, "Evil is movement toward void and that's where we both agree you're heading. It's your trip" (88). Indeed, Bucky is heading toward evil, an unspeakable and deathly void throughout most of this narrative. DeLillo's continuous thematic reference to unspeakable evil, particularly in later novels like *Libra, Mao II,* and *Cosmopolis,* is of course intimated here. But the question remains as to whether or not the evil discussed in *Great Jones Street* is simply a matter of the irrationality found in rock and roll as the cultural form the novel satirizes. In one example of the music described as so much sinister irrationality Bucky speaks of Opel being drawn to the "brute electricity of that sound" (*Great Jones Street* 12). Further evidence is found in Bucky's incident with the old woman in the wheelchair; his weird and noisy assault on her seems to reflect the "evil drift" of this protagonist's character. In an included "Superslick Mind Contracting Media Kit," which relates pieces of the Bucky Wunderlick Story "in news items, lyrics and dysfunctional interviews" (95), Bucky tells one of his interviewers that "we mash their skulls with a whole lot of watts.... Nobody can hear the words because they get drowned out by the noise; which is only natural" (104). Once again, this comment aligns rock and roll with the ultimately inaudible irrational and incommunicable final void of evil. It is significant that Bucky refers to his megadecibel assault on his unfortunate audience as "only natural"—the same terms he used to refer to the death of Opel, for which he shares accountability. All in all, these descriptions point to rock and roll as aligned with unspeakable evil.

One can also differentiate, though, between brutally loud rock and roll as a commoditized and therefore corrupt product and the broader issue of music as a form of language. Returning to Bucky's account of his art and its impact on Opel, just because the music (and by extension, limited references to the nonspoken or even extra-rational in philosophical or literary language) exists "beyond the maps of language" (12) does not necessarily mean that it is purely evil or "brute electricity." In fact, this description by Bucky of music is one of the most important passages in DeLillo's entire oeuvre (see chapters 5 and 6), as it will be discussed in five of his best-selling and most celebrated novels. This is because Bucky Wunderlick's seemingly simple-minded description opens up a central metaphysical and moral question of the nature of the unspoken. Is it a transcendent good or an unspeakable evil, or to some degree both? His major novels will deal very thoroughly with this question and its ethical implications. Here, however, the idea is that music functions as a form of language, itself certainly a serious issue in all of literature. To the degree that music participates in verbal language or any kind of artistic communication, such as lyrics, it cannot be an unspeakable evil to the writer. To resolve the issue of music if not the multinovel treatment of the problem of the unspeakable, we should examine the idea of a possible comeback for Bucky, my abovementioned qualification of Mark Osteen's argument.

Unlike Icharus, Bucky does not make a complete descent into the unspeakable void. The idea that Bucky could potentially make a comeback, or better yet, achieve some degree of mental or moral improvement as a result of his torturous and potentially fatal experiences, is based upon an intimation of the theme of language's transcendent power to which we will return in *White Noise* and in *Underworld*. Basically, the antispeech drug wears off, in essence returning to Bucky his lyric-making abilities. There may be some improvement in the laughable quality of his best-known lyrics "Pee Pee Maw Maw." Bucky's concept of language has been altered by his victimization. Prior to his being kidnapped and drugged by the evil minions of the Happy Valley Farm Commune, Bucky has an ignorant view of the signifying process inherent in language. Simply because he is bored, one day he fantasizes about shouting out the window, "Hey fire, fire!" Ignoring completely the communicative power of language constituting the immorality of the act of pulling a false alarm, he predicts the only response he'll get will be to have a bunch of firemen respond to him in a low whisper, "Water, water, water" (29). Wunderlick simply does not comprehend the power of the process of language in how people act in respond to the material facts the words correspond to and thus signify. But this changes after his bout with Dr. Pepper and his mind-altering drugs.

As Bucky recovers, he appears to exhibit a new respect for the signifying power of language. He hears a street vendor call out, "RED YAPPLES, GREEN YAPPLES, GOLDEN YAPPLES!" and compares this cry to a religious call for prayer at a mosque. His usually keen powers of description are finally focused to display a more sensitive awareness of human relationships in a structured landscape. Finally, he sees the ethnic color of his neighborhood in greater detail, "the women pinned in little windows, forty years flowing through an isolated second…their true lives taking place in a European pastureland.…The oldest immigrants lived in tower blocks" (259).

This narrative voice displays a powerful ability to create new lyrics, as if Bucky has gone from "dead telephone" consciousness to a new connectivity with the reality and needs of others in the linguistic environment. Arguably, a Wunderlick comeback is not at all impossible, and what is more important, a power of language to potentially bring the subject beyond his circumstances is indicated. Above and beyond this vital intimation of the problem of the unspeakable and the transcendent power of language in *Great Jones Street*, another intimation is found in terms of the treatment of the women in the novel as victims of sexism in clearly antiwar terms, as a post-torture Bucky describes another groupie, Skippy, as having a face like "one of those children found after every war" (262). The treatment of a mediated attack on the modern subject is continued as DeLillo moves from a send-up of rock and roll to a lengthier treatment of fame and theoretical mathematics in his next novel.

Ratner's Star concerns the adventures of William "Willy" Terwilliger, also known as Billy Twillig, who at 14 is the world's youngest recipient of the Nobel Peace Prize in mathematics. Willy has been called upon to use his mathematical talent to translate a signal coming from deep space, a communication believed to be coming from aliens living on a planet orbiting distant Ratner's star. Along his way he encounters many bizarre characters in the employ of Space Brain, a giant multinational conglomerate housed in an enormous cycloid-shaped structure housing a V-shaped support with several rings inside, adjacent to a field of myriad radar dishes aimed at the cosmos.

But the mathematical language celebrated and capitalized upon by the characters in *Ratner's Star* is devoid of language's emotionality. These scientists, engineers, and capitalists idolize theoretical math as the language "most independent of our perceptions and most true to itself" (48). Yet as the novel winds along its obfuscating and nonlinear path, one wonders about the true nature of math in its universal applicability to human experience. Troubling any existence of pure math is the power of capital throughout, exhibiting its tendency to harness pure mathematical, logical, or scientific theory to create unwieldy technologies and the thoughtless bureaucracies that control them.

One aspect of the social dynamics of the novel that is troubling is Billy's moral innocence in contrast to the depravity and bizarrely irrational behaviors he sees and experiences in the Space Brain complex. Billy's continuous encounters along the way take advantage of the protagonist's social and erotic discomfort as they seem to want to weave him in to their bizarre professional schemes and use him as a virtual captive audience. Despite the bizarre behaviors occurring all around him, Billy maintains his innocence and dedication to substantial research throughout his time at the corporation. Late in the novel, one of Billy's endless parade of interchangeable supervisors, William Softly, articulates the position Billy seems to play in the minds of the other characters in the novel. While most of the other scientists and engineers seem to have their own personal ambitions regarding the project to receive the message from deep space and communicate with the life forms that may be sending it, Billy proceeds with his calculations and desire to work driven purely by the desire to really know the meaning of the message and by his real enjoyment of mathematical calculation. As this character Softly puts it, "we absolutely need him" (317), and refers to Billy as a moral center for their theoretical research group: "His intransigence speaks against us.... We need him to balance things. He's the listener, the person we need to judge what we do" (317). Because Billy is not perverse or overly ambitious like so many of his colleagues, his ethical state of goodness counterbalances their personal corruption, especially in the case of Softly and his particularly morally shallow staff. Part of the drama of the story, then, is whether Billy will survive his employment at Space Brain with his money and his morals intact. In terms of the structure of the narrative, Softly's disingenuous pegging of him as the moral center also forms a postmodern commentary of how the protagonist is generally the center of moral concern in any fictional text.

To aid him in surviving this test of integrity, Billy has his memory of the compassion and affection of his working-class family as it is presented in the Bronx setting of the novel. In particular, his mother Faye provided him with much loving support: "Many times Faye and Billy stayed up until 2 or 3 in the morning drinking coffee and watching old movies on TV" (27). For his part, Billy's father, known as "Babe," drinks the old 1970s beverage Champale, impersonates baseball pitchers, and expresses his dissatisfaction with their lives in many ways. But for all his vitriol, he obviously loves and takes pride in his talented son with Billy's acceptance into many prestigious colleges. With this supportive childhood to draw moral strength from, the crazed and unethical personalities who loom as an endless parade of supervisors cannot finally turn Billy's character bad.

To continue, the staff at Space Brain demonstrates an environment of insanity and absurd immorality that drags Billy down. Ratner, the scientist for whom the star is named, simply wants to talk to Billy and have the youth bring him flowers. He seems to be searching for a disciple for his theories of unspeakable reality (220). But this bizarre character must remain in a plastic bubble or his face will collapse; thus, he receives a series of Botox-like injections via technicians who work on him through plastic gloves much like those used by the nuclear-weapon handlers in DeLillo's later novel *Underworld*. Another significant tangent readers can follow reading Ratner's medical condition through the advantageous lens we have of DeLillo's later work sets up a significant moral critique of how technology acts as a filter through which we subjectively interact with or "face" the world, so to speak, but for our purposes here Ratner's infatuation with Billy is dysfunctional and one of the many obstacles would-be authority figures place in his path. To bow to their infatuated whims is no less than to compromise the moral integrity forged in Billy by his supportive mother and to a slightly lesser degree by his father.

Despite Ratner's inappropriate behavior, two other adult authority figures overshadow the scientist with their ridiculous antics. Orang Mohole (179) is a reclusive "man of ambiguous pigmentation" (179). Addicted to brain medication, or "greenies," his theory of "Moholean relativity" makes the truth of Billy's investigation much more difficult to obtain. He claims that there is no planet and that Ratner's star is an illusion of perception and actually "a binary dwarf. One red star, one white star" (179). Thus Billy has no aliens to investigate, and his message issues from a place Mohole calls "the value dark dimension," an image of indeterminacy and also phenomenological relativism suited to Mohole's "ambiguous pigmentation." Here nothing can signify anything. But this relativity cannot cover up the fact that Mohole is sexually perverted and repeatedly tries to tempt underage Billy into his strange orgies (188 and again on 198). So his "Moholean" phenomenological relativity is a metaphor for moral relativism that here treats the morally value-dark state of the strange crew of the aptly named Space Brain.

Thirdly and worst of all is the grotesque Robert Hopper Softly, deformed so that his oversized head and genitalia dwarf the rest of his body (261). It is Softly who misleads Billy into thinking that he will be given more creative freedom under his tutelage, betraying the youth's trust (178–179). As Billy begins working for Softly, the project and the facts about it change so extremely that Billy's task becomes a confusing-to-impossible one. The original project is diverted and becomes overshadowed by a new underground project called "Logicon Minus One"—the attempt to create a computerized software language with which the scientists can communicate with the alien life forms, presumably issuing the message if indeed they exist. For Billy, this is a useless and distracting project because of the motives of the individuals involved. Because Robert Softly is distracted by constant sex with his temporary partner Jean Venable, the project ultimately fails and the whole kit and caboodle is satirically transformed into a bat guano pit by a suspicious Honduran cartel. One may well ask how this ridiculous denouement can be interpreted in light of Billy as some sort of moral hero. Or for that matter how the problematic themes of technology, subjectivity, or moral vision are resolved. The three figures here, though—Ratner, Mohole, and Softly—certainly do form an immoral set of adult authorities against which Billy must steel himself to maintain his integrity.

Furthermore, there a few different ways to answer these broader thematic questions. For one, DeLillo does not seem to be making a negative statement about the field of theoretical or of applied mathematics generally. At one point, the quest for all forms of scientific truth is described as "an effete form of assassination" with the "corrective dagger...slipped between our own meatless ribs" (193). This violent imagery would seem to imply that math and science are a violent form of communication, but DeLillo brilliantly interjects some references from the actual history of mathematics, showing that the discipline can have a human soul. When he meets Myriad, the wife of one of his colleagues, taking a walk with her baby in a carriage (256), she inspires Billy to reflect on Evariste Galois, the brilliant but socially outcast 19th-century French adolescent mathematician. Like Billy himself, Galois could not find acceptance in society, his groundbreaking work on algebraic equations all but forgotten at the time of his death during the unstable early years of the French revolution. Published 24 years after, Galois's theory revolutionized algebra (*Evariste Galois* 1–2). Thus his example serves as both a positive and negative model for Billy; on the one hand to trust his own original thinking, and on the other not to get swept up in the violent social passions surrounding him.

Another theoretical mathematician who was subjected to social oppression and whom Myriad invites Billy to reflect upon is Srinivasa Aiyangar Ramunajan. This fin-de-siècle Indian mathematician faced hardship and discrimination not due to his age but rather to his ethnicity. When his original and highly distinctive work brought him a scholarship at Madras College and a subsequent visit to Trinity College in Cambridge, he struggled with accommodations to his strict vegetarian diet and with suspicions that a poor man from a British colony could not be capable of high achievement in theoretical math. Unlike the unfortunate Galois, Ramunajan did achieve some recognition in his lifetime (University of St. Andrews 1–7). Our third in Myriad's allusive triumvirate of highly ethical and admirable mathematicians is Sonja Kowalewski. This pioneering Russian 19th-century feminist mathematician struggled with gender oppression just as Ramunajan dealt with ethnic discrimination and just as Galois had to cope with his youth and the political violence of the France of his day. Sonja was unable for many years to find a university teaching position because of her being a woman, as women were not allowed to become university lecturers in 19th-century Russia (Holt 14). So for Billy these three ethical heroes serve as inspiration for him to stand up to the immoral pressures brought on by authoritative villains like Ratner, Mohole, and Softly. Furthermore, for the reader these historical references justify the discipline of mathematics as potentially liberating, not because of the technical power of math itself to give people technological control over matter and therefore wealth but because of the people whom it ought to serve. Myriad's reminder to Billy of math's human side refocuses the reader on Billy's moral struggle and also broadens the thematic scope of *Ratner's Star* to include intimations of DeLillo's wider moral vision of more global issues.

To continue, this broader scope includes DeLillo's general critique of militarism, capitalism, and technology that continues throughout this novel and intimates the moral vision more fully articulated in later novels such as *White Noise, Libra,* and *Underworld.* References in passing remind us of the social context that the bureaucratic dupes of Space Brain routinely ignore in favor of the technological control they lust after. Chief of Security Kyzyl's monologue to Billy includes one such passing reference. Kyzyl describes the torture and persecution of native populations very euphemistically, in a scientific or mathematical language. He was involved with a mysterious project "tagging" indigenous populations, which sounds like branding cattle or other animals for experimental use (*Ratner's Star* 189). Kyzyl uses euphemisms and vague references to his actual actions on the project: "We utilized no force or prereaction sweeps except as they applied... and never inflicted as we say incommensurate pain. Pain inflicted had to be equal to the threat to our persons" (189). These vague references to pain inflicted are troubling, begging the question of what right Kyzyl had to be "tagging" these peoples in the first place. His project sounds like an imperialist invasion, as the peoples fight "with their teeth and feet" while Kyzyl and his compatriots sit in "armored vehicles" (189).

But the vague description of the precise actions they undertake puts the moral condemnation of imperialism into a indefinite or "value-dark dimension" evoking again the moral relativism of Mohole: Kyzyl cannot see the immorality of what he is doing, putting him in a category of perpetrators of violence like Glen Yost in *Americana* as he regrets his violent acts during the Second World War. Moreover, in this surreal reference to the violent use of military technology, a hint of moral condemnation shows through the ambiguity of Kyzyl's reflections. Moving on from the critique of militarism and technology in *Ratner's Star* to a critique of the capitalist system that fuels the use of technology during wars of occupation, the presence of the group of financiers who buy out the project, or "Consortium Hondurium" as they are called, sheds light on how the profit motive determines the most socially determinant uses of sciences. In a significant passage, these bat guano wizards start sending Billy a series of mail-order contests and surveys that appear to solicit information from him in a strange 1976 style of phishing. For example, on a quiz card he receives that is emblazoned "Pay then Play" (297), Billy is asked whether some children have to be "coaxed" (or) "hoaxed" into playing certain games (296). Though superficially just an innocuous word choice quiz, the Consortium Hondurium is trying to find out if Billy has become cynical or still can process information ingenuously. Their relentless pursuit of Billy's identifying information is one expression of capitalist profit motives at work.

Another is formed by the passing references that are contained in the denouement of the novel in a symbolic passage. DeLillo in a narrative second-person voice appears to address broad philosophical questions as we approach the end of Billy's travails. DeLillo returns to the theme of mathematics as an abstract system distinct from its human compassionate side as we saw in the references to Galois and the other pioneer mathematicians elsewhere in the novel. Epistemological and ethical relativism appear to be flawed as the narrator addresses the reader in the second person, discussing how mathematics is "what the world is when we subtract our perceptions" (432). Theoretical science's requirement that the observer doubt empirical evidence, its false promise to "unsnarl us from our delimiting senses" (431), has the unfortunate consequence of quelling the compassionate ethical conscience, the heart of the reader or observer. The mathematician, or rather the technocrat, impassively observes the "grieving man's belief in the everydayness of the absolute" and is unmoved by the reality of families who "sleep on pavement" and of "children stealing to live" (431). Human compassion or our emotional identification with the realities upon which math bases its calculations "is the ethic you've rejected" (431). One gets the idea that the use of math by technocrats is what is being condemned, not the compassionate mathematical narratives of Galois, Kowalewski, and Ramunajan. In shutting down human compassion, the capitalist abuses science's requirement that we "deny the evidence of our senses" (87). The love of pure math for humanity's sake (shown in the admiration of the three worthy mathematical heroes) is corrupted by the cold outlook of the technocrats, best exemplified by the portrayal of the scientists of Space Brain, exempting of course the innocent Billy Terwilliger.

Yet despite this sin of abstraction, the narrator goes on to imbue the presence of math in the world with even more imagery suggesting the realities of human compassion and human suffering. Math can play a role in tallying up the sheer numbers evoked in the human misery runaway technology has created, and in light of this fact, the narrator continues these indirect references to horrendous contemporary global conditions. The narrator laments, "With burial grounds full, people deposit bodies in shallow graves, bared by local dogs" (433), referring to the numeric inequalities consisting of starvation and mass death in "map-blue China." Rather than a pragmatic use of mathematical and scientific theory to prevent these unnecessary deaths from world hunger (the reader is reminded of "children with begging bowls...begging for a cracked fragment of biscuit...eating crumbs to live" [430–432]), these abstract systems are instead channeled into our fantastic obsession with astrophysics, life on distant stars, and the need to communicate with such life as demonstrated in *Ratner's Star*.

With these more serious themes presented at the symbolic level, the novel begins to exhibit a profound impact. The end result of all this technological abstraction is potentially disastrous. Divorcing math from the human experience of materiality and emotion functions easily as a moral escape route; the Space Brainers routinely ignore the consequences of their actions, whether those actions be mindless sex or mindless reception of intergalactic transmissions or endless drilling into a gigantic hole in the ground. Brief reference to global conditions evokes prophetic warnings of calamity, though not as specifically as later novels such as the tragic *Mao II* or the prescient critique of the American stock market we find in *Cosmopolis*. In *Ratner's Star* one detects a prophetic moral intimation in these words: "The bottom is falling out of space." Billy intones this in his typical cavalier and dismissive fashion, yet none of his false bravado can fully blunt the impact of the content of his exchange with Softly about typical emergencies at Space Brain and its underground annex Logicon One: "Mounting international tensions...states of precautionary alert...maximum arc situation awareness" (281). In a language now evocative of the later disaster warnings that taunt Jack Gladney in 1985's *White Noise*, the well-known mechanism of simulated disaster reinforces the potential of ignoring the material consequences of the technical projects that morally abstracted calculations take on in the novel. Later works by DeLillo of course address the destructive impact of technology more pointedly, problematizing again the idea of a cavalier and detached mathematics on the landscape of American culture circa 1976, a proud year of celebrating the Bicentennial and the Apollo moon landings.

Billy's plot, however, resolves some of these themes on a more positive note. Though Softly's attempts to dominate him become more treacherously severe, he will in the end hold together his moral innocence and profound love for the mathematical work he does. Thickening the twisted plot of the novel, Softly cruelly feeds the Nobel Prize Committee privileged (and partially false) information about Billy's work, causing the young mathematician to experience the diabolical danger of the loss of his identity through the corruption of the system around him (306–307). But at the very end, Billy is saved by a deus ex machina; an anomalous zone of Moholean relativity sweeps him up and away on a tricycle from the Honduran Consortium, the despairing Softly, and the bat guano pit their corporation has become (438). This takes place after Billy manages to redeem his scientific reputation by correctly interpreting a mathematical puzzle, which gives the correct time of the anomaly. Here the "value-dark" (181) dimension takes on a positive spin in an existentially relativist sense; if all that exists in a postmodern physicist's landscape is random and fundamentally a matter of chance, why shouldn't Billy's morals and integral self emerge intact from a technocratic morass? Though it may be tempting for the reader of later DeLillo novels to read the transcendent tricycle ride in light of Wilder's death-defying crossing of highway bypass traffic on a tricycle in *White Noise*, I might take issue with so doing. For one reason, the later ride in the context of *White Noise* forms a commentary on the American cultural tendency to attempt to defy death and the fear thereof (also seen in Jack and Barbette's ingestion of Dylar, the anti-fear-of-death drug, and Orest Mercador's attempt to break the Guinness world record for remaining in a cage full of live snakes) as opposed to a comic victory. In this case, Billy's random transcendence is not a warning to his parents to wake up to the material and moral consequences of living recklessly as it is with Wilder. Rather it is an attempt to (successfully) escape a world where all the adult figures live recklessly. Given the discrepancy in age between the two characters (Billy is 14 and Wilder is only 2), the contrast between the two uses of the tricycle ride in DeLillo's work seems appropriate. Furthermore, the fact that the novel is written in the science fiction genre (which DeLillo later referred to as "pretentious") can account for this magically transcendent twist of plot; no such magic occurs in the more realistic *White Noise*. At any rate, the deus ex machina insures that Billy's journey as the protagonist of the narrative ends successfully.

Even though *Ratner's Star* evokes many significant themes, including the power of history, a sense of mystery, and the moral problems involved with technology, the novel does not do so quite as successfully as DeLillo's later longer novels, such as *Libra* and *Underworld*. The subplot lines are not as tightly connected, minor characters and situations appear in a distracting fashion, and finally the two main experiments involving Space Brain and Logicon One are not united by the novel's denouement. Yet the novel remains a good read for those interested in observing how DeLillo first introduces these important themes. Moving to *Players* will bring us to a moral intimation of startling significance for our times: the notion of modern terrorism.

For DeLillo's follow-up to *Ratner's Star*, the author made some wiser choices in terms of structure for plot and character. Rather than choosing exceptional protagonists like rock star Wunderlick or boy genius Terwilliger. DeLillo shifts to a very typical bourgeois childless cohabitating couple, Lyle and Pammy. The plot of *Players* is far simpler as well, and thus readers can access a better focus: bourgeois decadence and domestic terrorism are related in terms of cause and effect. On the other hand, the most significant aspect of *Players* relative to the later DeLillo works is how this brief text evokes many issues and patterns to which DeLillo returns, especially in *White Noise*. These include the impact of television and moreover the use of erotic infidelity as a motif conveying an atmosphere of sociopolitical tension. Infidelity's deceit, its pervasive mood of instability, and the general chaotic disruption it yields in its wake is here used for the first time in the DeLillo "canon" of novels as an apt image to represent the chaotic dynamics of terrorism. By staying with the minds and emotions of only a few characters, DeLillo is able to more accurately convey treatment of important themes.

One sees a range of techniques on display in this novel. For one, the novel begins with an evocative prelude. The novel opens with a scene inside a 747 of a small group of passengers watching an in flight film of a group of golfers suffering a surprise attack on their green by a roving band of terrorists. The film is accompanied by odd music from the piano bar, suited to a Buster Keaton style silent film. The passengers resemble main characters that populate the main narrative. There is a couple who appear to be "wearing each other" (*Players* 4). These two resemble the central figures, Lyle, a naïve stockbroker, and his partner Pammy, who works as a counselor for "grief management" at the World Trade Center in the North Tower (the novel takes places in the 1970s). On the 747 is also a gay couple corresponding to same-sex lovers Ethan and Jack in the main plot; Jack works with Pammy, and the two will have an affair. On screen, the action of golf serves as an illustration of bourgeois capitalist decadence, a major issue in *Players*. The golfer's clothes are described as "so strident they might serve as illustrations of the folly of second childhood" (9), and DeLillo's witty attack on this sport does not stop with the clothes. The game is described as an "anal round of scrupulous caution and petty griefs" (9–10). As the audience of the film watches the golfers "being massacred," they take a certain "sardonic delight" (9–10). Their cavalier indifference to the fact that they could just as easily be the bourgeois players since they are rich enough to afford to travel on a jumbo jet with piano bar and in-flight film is shared by Lyle, Pammy, Ethan, and Jack.

To further the parallel between the prelude and the film, just prior to the denouement Pammy, Ethan, and Jack actually do stop to watch a golf game. The sexual decadence and ennui marring their lives lays them open to a kind of terrorist infiltration, especially in Lyle's case. Through his infidelity, Lyle will become connected to Rosemary Moore, his paramour who leads him away from Pammy and into an actual roaming band of domestic terrorists who plot attacks on the floor of the Stock Exchange and assassinate his fellow broker George Sedbauer. During the movie, one of the golfers tries to escape the knives and guns of the approaching killer in a cart, just as Lyle will try to escape his association with the domestic terrorists by traveling. But a young woman with a machete hacks him down, and the terrorists take the green, led by a capped leader appearing as "liberation's bright angel" (9–10). All of this action will be seen to prefigure plot events as they unfold in *Players*. Capitalism with its inherent corruption lays the grounds for terrorist activity just as infidelity leads to self-dissolution in the lives of the two main characters, Pammy and Lyle. The two will each suffer a self-induced emotional destruction brought about largely through the bonds they form in infidelity.

One phrase that DeLillo employs very poetically is the reference on the first page to an "implied bond" between the travelers on the 747 as between all film audiences when a movie begins. *Players* is a novel much about the implied bonds between not only couples but also between individuals within the political-economic system, rebels and capitalists. When we first see Pammy and Lyle, we realize that the couple's relationship is headed for a fall. Their lovemaking has become routine sex; Lyle resents having to perform and "service her," and after they are finished all Pammy wants to do is eat pizza in a corner alone, to "stuff herself with junk" an act de-eroticizing intercourse symbolically (35). They quarrel and only seem happy when entertaining Ethan and Jack. Lyle has clearly begun to take her for granted as his obsessions with television and pornography have dulled his mind in its efforts to interpret the evidence of his senses. He will fail to escape the terrorist plot unfolding around him until it is too late. We see Lyle abusing Pammy when she brings him fruit, and he refers to the fact that the produce she buys tends to "shrivel up like fetuses" (33), a slam on the lack of fertility in their relationship or "implied bond." Pammy reveals the fact that she is losing her moral center when she talks about the sound of the word "Maine" as her "moral core" (20) and kills time with Lyle drinking and socializing with Ethan and Jack; getting still drunker, she adds, "I don't think I can stand the idea of tomorrow" (20).

The emptiness of all their lives is also signified by the symbol of the "Mister Softee" ice-cream truck, an early appropriation of a consumer product for use as a symbol by DeLillo. Every evening, filled with ennui in their apartment, Lyle and Pammy hear "the cranked out mechanical whine" of the passing Mr. Softee ice-cream truck. Their mythological figure is completely emasculated and paralyzed: "He can't get up. His flesh doesn't have the right consistency. He has no genitals" (36). Made of ice cream, the figure is debilitated, like DeLillo's later Dylar-crazed addicts in *White Noise* or like Lyle as he wastes away watching porno on late-night television. This mythological Mr. Softee serves as an early foreshadowing of the use of consumer products by DeLillo in a symbolic send-up of the American consumerist lifestyle that we will find in *White Noise*; literally a self made out of consumer product. DeLillo here attempts to address consumerism in its impact on identity. Lyle and Pammy are made anxious by the annoying sound of the white Mr. Softee truck. Since Mr. Softee represents an imaginative manifestation of the moral, physical, and spiritual corruption that will take the couple eventually, their anxiety is perhaps an expression of the subconscious fear that they themselves will self-destruct due to morally bankrupt lifestyle choices. In the later work *White Noise*, we'll see a similar bourgeois fear in the lives of Jack and Babette Gladney.

Furthermore, looking at the couple as individuals, Pammy is one example of that self-centered and materialistic lifestyle DeLillo condemns in *Players*. As mentioned, her relationship with Lyle is at a dead end, and so is her job. As Lyle drifts away from Pammy and into a new relationship with a new employee, Rosemary Moore, Pammy begins to drift toward the more attractive half of our gay couple, Jack Laws. Jack and Pammy commiserate over the meaninglessness of their working conditions in grief management, indicting the profit motive as a reason why their work is awful: "Per diem rates for terminal illness counseling? So if it drags on, forget it, we got you by the balls?" (42). From a simple commiseration they progress forward, as Pammy chooses to go vacationing in Maine with Ethan and Jack while Lyle is making more and more time with Rosemary. When the three go away for this vacation, Jack starts to show interest in Rosemary; he wants her to pay more careful attention while he shares his goals in life (142). Pammy pursues him even though she knows he is in another relationship, seeming to care more for her own needs than for his. When the two finally consummate their mutual attraction, Jack is anxious that his lover Ethan will discover this act. Jack's behavior becomes increasing skittish, and finally he becomes depressed. Rather than do the right thing and be forthcoming, Pammy selfishly wants to continue to sneak around, leading Jack further into depression. Finally, Jack commits suicide by self-immolation (198), causing both Ethan and Pammy extreme grief. There are many ways to interpret his behavior; however, one is a judgment on Pammy for her selfishness. Too late is it revealed to her that the three of them on vacation have been living in a state of mutual "disloyalty, spitefulness and petulance" (177). Later, the emotional toll of all this will devastate Pammy herself. Finally, to further reinforce the artistic trope of the prelude, Pammy, Ethan and Jack are found watching a golf game just before the latter's suicide (198), equating them directly with the happy-go-lucky irresponsible travelers mentioned therein.

Thus far, it would seem that the consequences of American self-absorption are primarily interpersonal or romantic. But as we shift the focus from Pammy's erotic dalliances to Lyle's equally disastrous and also politically treacherous misadventure into the path of the domestic terrorists, DeLillo's treatment includes infidelity as a literary trope for the chaotic dynamics of terrorism. Lyle's obtuse and impervious mind is completely unable to process logical connections. As such, it is completely representative of the political ignorance of the American bourgeois class. That his mind is thus representative is indicated by his colleagues who believe that working "in a roar of money" gives them the "vestigial right" to ogle women during their lunch hour (13). Clearly, Lyle's sense of self is grounded in his economic or class status; hence his habitual checking of his pockets for tokens of capital-based identity: change, wallet, and keys (26). His class-based obtuseness will lead him into a great deal of trouble.

Not a very perceptive soul, Lyle also habitually fails to add up the evidence of his senses, just stumbling his way into the arms of Rosemary Moore, who is the longtime associate and presumably lover of J. Kinnear. Kinnear is the de facto leader of the domestic terrorist collective. Stubbornly, Lyle fails to heed repeated warnings even from the terrorists themselves that he is headed for trouble (102, 179). Consumed with lust for Rosemary, even to the point where he stalks her repeatedly after work, Lyle eventually achieves his sexual goals with her. Yet he is completely oblivious to the fact that Rosemary is playing him for Kinnear's sake; she never reaches orgasm but rather lies disinterested like a "drugged child" while Lyle fantasizes post-coitus that he has made her "groan with pleasure" (91–93). So dense is Lyle that he cannot even pick up on the political implications of his position. When one of his colleagues, George Sedbauer, is killed by the terrorist organization, another Wall Street broker tells Lyle that the killer is of interest to a friend from Langley, Virginia. Our obtuse broker is seemingly unaware of the fact that the locale "Langley" signifies that this friend is a CIA agent and that therefore both Sedbauer's murder and Lyle's own romantic involvement with Rosemary are linked to a major terrorist organization worthy of note by the agency. DeLillo's treatment of the faithless-lover-as-terrorist-dupe links the disruptive quality of infidelity to the chaotic dynamics of domestic terrorism. Lyle's jejune and irritating obtuseness is representative of the typical American bourgeoisie in their stubborn refusal to see themselves as a source of oppression. Rosemary was bait for Lyle and George, compromising their identities on Kinnear's behalf; Lyle could not possibly take less heed of the consequences.

Granted, Lyle does attempt to turn informant for the government, spilling the information that he knows to a gruff agent from an unidentified group who only identifies himself to Lyle as "Burks" (128). But he does not seek protection for himself nor is offered any; in fact, to obfuscate matters even further, he subsequently tells Kinnear of his becoming an informant. When Kinnear remarks that he himself also once was an informant, Lyle's confusion is complete, and he can no longer tell which side either Kinnear or Burks is on (145). This sheer political chaos is inherent in the unpredictable violence of the terrorist act. To attempt to figure some of this mess out, Lyle asks Marina, another member of the subversive group, what will become of J. (145). Her reply, that the leader figure probably "will be killed" but that it is "not an urgent matter," could just as well apply to Lyle himself. For his part, Burks's brusque treatment of his informer ("I could tell you to eat shit off a wooden stick" [130]) could be prompted by Lyle's irritating manner of seeking to be treated as Burks's equal. Burks emerges as a "corruptible cop" figure much like the early-20th-century Chicago cops Nelson Algren populates his own gritty Chicago streets with, figures DeLillo could have possibly been influenced by as a younger writer (see chapter 2 of this book). In all, Lyle's naïveté in not demanding perfection is at fault for his failure even as an antiterrorist informant.

Despite the protagonist's excessively foolish disregard of his own life in pursuit of sheer erotic pleasure with Rosemary (and later with Marina), Lyle is not assassinated at the close of *Players*. Rather, he suffers an extreme form of male disempowerment, a gender-role reversal that falls short of castration but nonetheless can be seen symbolically as emasculation. To underscore this, in the swinger's world DeLillo portrays in 1970s Manhattan, men and women do not play equal roles. Here, Pammy is left with Ethan and Jack, who do not exactly give her an advantage in the games of sexual "one-upmanship" Lyle, on the other hand, has already acquired a reputation as a womanizer before he commences his conquest of Rosemary. The male oppressive figure (we've seen Lyle abuse Pammy early) has a wider field on which to play, while Pammy's quest is determined more by his neglect of her needs. Yet, like the Mr. Softee man of ice cream, Lyle's power relative to his gendered advantage will soon melt away.

Wasting another warning on the bourgeois American, J. Kinnear informs Lyle that the late George Sedbauer had been passed on literally from Rosemary to Marina Vilar, an older and more aggressive domestic terrorist in their inner circle (119), a move Kinnear calls a "sort of promotion" with Lyle finally slaking his sexual thirst on Marina as well (187). Significantly, though, this was not his choice in a world in which men make all the important choices and women are (were) either secretaries or grief managers. And this loss of autonomy does not stop with sexual choice. Acting too little and too late, Lyle dials the contact number he has received from agent Burks, giving further information about a planned bombing of Wall Street and a description of the bomber Luis Ramirez. It would appear that Lyle is provided with a perfect escape, flying out to Toronto in a 727. But Rosemary arrives unexpectedly to meet him, signifying a renewal not of their erotic "implied bond" but rather his inextricable bond into the terrorist network. He learns too late of her scheme to seduce men to give J. access to their identities with relevant security information: "You've been with him for awhile," the now-powerless Lyle asks her (197). In their final scene having more gratuitous hotel room sex, this negative gender-role reversal is made symbolically complete by Rosemary's acquisition of a plastic penis "hardened to her body" (197). As we last see Lyle, he completely lacks any sort of personal decision-making power his culture associates with masculinity, awaiting "detailed instructions" for any future move he might make. He cannot do anything without J.'s knowledge and is thus in a chronic condition of permanent fatal danger—death seems inevitable for this pawned plaything. In contrast, now Rosemary has complete power and "knows his soul," while Lyle is rendered a figure "barely recognizable as male" (212).

It is important to realize that DeLillo is not buying into the myth of male superiority in Lyle's disempowerment but rather critiquing it through violent reversal, a terrorist-like turning of the tables on a situation of hierarchical violence.

Lest the contrapuntal thread of Pammy's story be lost, she suffers an emotional dissolution no less personally devastating than Lyle's extralegal entrapment. Not yielding Jack's secrets to the last, she has nowhere to go to manage her own profound grief at her lover's death. She is finally severed from her emotional center as Lyle is stripped of his phallic power, grieving not at the death of Jack, whom she passionately desired, but rather letting a TV movie serve as a placebo for emotional reality. The movie is about a middle-class man "whose life was quietly coming apart" by his connection with racketeers. This media-within-media, like the in-flight film, forms an ironic echo of what is simultaneously happening to Lyle. Only this artificial ritual can make Pammy feel "awash with emotion," although it does not restore her sanity. In a Dylar-like state, Pammy's power to distinguish between television and reality has melted away, and DeLillo readers can easily recognize formal intimations of major themes in *White Noise*. We last see her looking down the corridor of grim fate as Lyle does, in front of a flophouse for "transients" into which she seems destined to fall.

In all, the emotional chaos concluding *Players* evokes the political turmoil resulting from terrorist activity, and although DeLillo does not pursue the treatment of the group's politics to the extent the reader might wish him to, here the violence of terrorism is best theorized as governed by this mad thought of Kinnear's: "The only worthwhile doctrine is calculated madness" (108). Finally, the prefigurations of *White Noise* we see in the earlier and less-well known work *Players* make the book significant for a study of the overall development of DeLillo's work. Even the latter book's rejected title, *Panasonic*, is evoked by the repeated motif of the whining sound the Mr. Softee truck makes and the anxious "m" sound Lyle is last heard humming in his hotel. This apocalyptic view of the failure of the American individual at the hands of the terrorist will be continuing in the next DeLillo novel, *Running Dog*.

Among the novels written before DeLillo attained his highest level of commercial and critical success, *Running Dog* is the most tightly told story, meaning that by the conventional standards of American popular fiction, the narrative conforms to the reader's expectations for the kind of suspense, action, erotic interludes, humor, and binary gun fights where one hopes the proverbial "good guy" will be victorious. At one point, Nadine Rademacher, the part-time actress and erotic partner for our would-be "hero" character, Glen Selvy, remarks that their escapades are "turning into a Western" (*Running Dog* 186) and the comment has that post-modern "fourth-wall" breaking effect of making the reader feel as if the character is addressing her or him directly. However, *Running Dog* is by no means a Western.

Rather, to sustain the argument that DeLillo's early work prefigures his later treatment of important issues in social ethics, having *Running Dog* as the successor to *Players* allows the reader to glean an answer to one of the most significant unanswered questions arising in the prior novel. As Lyle from the prior work is confessing to Burks and later to a character known only as "Burks-2" (who is masquerading as an anticapitalist protester) even the reader can be confused when trying to determine what side the agents are on. In short, for both *Players* and *Running Dog*, DeLillo portrays the complex relationships between terrorists, American anti-insurgent forces, espionage, and counterinsurgencies as the diabolically convoluted mess that they really are. Or as Moll Robbins, the writer for the magazine, puts it: "These goddamn bastards. Who were they and what did they want?" This next novel furthers DeLillo's treatment of the issue of the idea of insurgent terrorism as a by-product of capitalism that we have seen in *Players* as well as the general critique of other aspects of capitalism in *Great Jones Street*, *Ratner's Star*, and *Players*. Furthermore, the novel is a definitive treatment of post-Vietnam era problems such as the postwar life of veterans and the state of America's left-leaning radicals, their culture, and media outlets in the aftermath of the war's end (the phrase "Running Dog" is both a satire of the magazine title *Rolling Stone* and an insulting name hurled at American forces by the North Vietnamese during that conflict). Of greater significance is another prescient characterization of the dog-eat-dog dynamics of the privatization of American military forces and its impact on any late-20th-century social stability apparent in postwar culture. Mafia leaders, left-leaning exposé journalists, corrupt politicians, veterans, and mercenaries are all reduced to a level of equivalent amorality, setting up a need for the philosophic search for meaning informing in his next novel after *Running Dog—The Names.*

Without revealing too much, the main plot of *Running Dog* concerns pornographer/art-collector Lightborne's discovery of the existence of a film believed to be a pornographic movie made by the Nazi inner circle during Hitler's last days in his bunker beneath the Reich Chancellery in falling Berlin. The story has numerous twists and turns as a corrupt senator (Lloyd Percival), a reporter from hip left magazine *Running Dog* and her editor (Moll Robbins and hard-drinking Grace Delaney, respectively), one single-minded Vietnam vet with a crystal clear focus and accurate aim to match (Glen Selvy), a yuppie super-wealthy pornography mogul (Ritchie Armbrister), and one major mafia captain (Vincent "Vinnie the Eye" Talerico) all hotly pursue the acquisition of this film. Complicating the plot is the fact that mercenary Earl Mudger and his private paramilitary organization Radial Matrix also have a stake in the project and are very actively trying to wipe out his rival Selvy. What unfolds ought to be read in the original without my unraveling any of DeLillo's well-wrought suspense for readers' pleasure.

One highly recognizable theme in *Running Dog* is the notion of insurgent terrorism as a by-product of capitalism and its imperial policies in other lands. One of the paramilitary figures is a Vietnam veteran, Selvy. Glen Selvy is himself a renegade from the Radial Matrix that Mudger commands as his own private army and fiefdom. Wanting to terminate Selvy, Mudger brings in two former North Vietnamese rangers, Van and Cao, to achieve his bidding (119). These pursue Selvy relentlessly through the American landscape, their resettlement connected to a mysterious third insurgent forming a three-person terror squad. American actions in Vietnam come back to haunt both Selvy and Mudger here as they both have unwittingly unleashed violent forces at home as well as abroad.

One of the important aspects to note in this work is DeLillo's critique of the post-Vietnam left-leaning media, most particularly of the 1970s. By "left" I mean here the denizens of mainstream rock-and-roll journalism and the culture of opposition of Vietnam and associated causes, such as more permissive standards regard pornography, that were highly popular after the American withdrawal in 1975. However, I would absolutely not align DeLillo with the generally perceived opposite of the left either. In fact, some representatives of that particular organ of the American body politic are subjected to DeLillo's stylized and ironic satire here as well. Perhaps it is best to focus on yet another prescient quotation, this time from privateer Earl Mudger in reference to the information age: "Devices make us pliant. If they issue a print-out saying we're guilty, then we're guilty" (93). He was referring to information technology and the manner in which information-gathering systems inspire paranoid guilt in modern people. For Moll Robbins and her editor Grace Delaney, the term "device" and the powerless compliancy it leads to can just as easily be seen to refer to the implied and necessary collaboration between investigative journalists and members of the established power structure. Moll's need to pursue information leads her into very dysfunctional trysts with Glen Selvy and nearly with Mudger and Senator Percival as well. Fortunately, the last is preempted when the doddering politician falls asleep! Moll discovers Percival's secret collection of erotic art (79–80) hidden in an inner house-within-a-house. However, she cannot interest her editor Grace to run the story of the collection, and she is disempowered, made pliant. Unbeknownst to her, Grace is sleeping with a party interested in controlling the flow of information about Percival and his collection. This is Arthur Lomax, who is connected to the senator through a secret branch of American intelligence money laundering called PAC/ORD. Lomax is also tied in to Mudger and Radial Matrix. Ultimately, Grace puts the facts together too late as it is revealed that Percival is connected to the disappearance of an ancient erotic art collection. She loses her lead into the story because Grace would be likely to see it squelched (215).

Grace Delaney for her part is also compromised in terms even more immediately correspondent to Mudger's insight. Because Arthur Lomax has access to Grace's income tax information, including some negative reports of fraud, he can blackmail and intimidate her into cooperation with any of PAC/ORD or Radial Matrix's schemes and in essence completely render the left-wing investigative impact of her magazine worthless. Their countercultural punch has been reduced to an infantile fascination with profanity, as Moll states, "We say 'fuck' all the time" (21). When *Running Dog* was published in 1978, the release of the Pentagon Papers and the scandal of Watergate had sensitized the American public as to the power of information to change destructive conservative policy, but here DeLillo warned even progressive critics of the establishment of their "pliancy" via Grace Delaney's technologically induced plight. In ways in which few foresaw in 1978, DeLillo's *Running Dog* prefigures the abuse of spyware in violation of human rights by many governments around the globe.

If the American left has been rendered pliant through its dependence both on the devices of information technology and its complicity with the powers that be, aggressively reactionary forces in society have fared no better by the conditions portrayed in *Running Dog*. H. Glen Selvy, DeLillo's rendition of the "strong silent type" of American cinematic hero personified in cowboy or hard-boiled detective protagonists like those portrayed by Clint Eastwood or John Wayne, serves as a measure of how even the toughest on the right can be rendered pliant to destructive forces in society by the devices of their training. Despite Selvy's heroic actions, he is a troubled character overreliant on his training at Marathon Mines, the special grounds for Radial Matrix mercenaries. This training has rendered him obsessive-compulsive, a symptom of post-traumatic stress disorder. All of his attitudes and behaviors, from the idea that "shaving was an emblem of rigor" to his self-imposed rule to only have sex with married women (81), demonstrate this pliancy to the devices deployed by training. He jests with his lover Nadine that his Native American name would be "Running Dog" (160), typifying himself as the American imperialist soldier of the mocking label. Like a Pavlov-trained dog, Selvy has no apparent consciousness of the power of free will and choice; as he says, "Choice is a form of disease" (192). This symbolism is reinforced later when Richie Armbrister reflects on his own dogs that they are "good dogs…Trained in simulated combat situations" (195). Selvy allows his training to control everything from how he grooms himself to his self-imposed rule to sleep with married women only. That he is not quite the man he appears to be becomes revealed in ironic ways, from Nadine's healthy appearance and attitude about sex annoying Selvy (182) to his ultimate conclusion that the purpose of all his training at Marathon Mines was simply undertaken to prepare him for a violent death (183). Selvy, like his one-time romantic partner Moll Robbins, can also be seen as a pawn of his own devices.

DeLillo's representation of the problems of the paramilitary devices in American society goes beyond Selvy's fate. In contrast to Selvy, who simply suffers one tragic flaw, Earl Mudger shows monomaniacal tendencies that bear a frightening verisimilitude in comparison to the adventures of privatized mercenary groups in 21st-century America, such as Blackwater/Xe. The dog-eat-dog dynamics of the privatization of U.S. military forces are revealed as Mudger pits his resources against Selvy. A veteran of Korea and Vietnam and a "long-term contract employee" (75) of the CIA, Mudger has become "in love with profits," a mercenary worthy of inclusion in today's worst paramilitary organizations. Lloyd Percival's comment that Mudger is "completely autonomous" with government and private entities both "afraid to move against him" (75) calls to mind former president Bush's failure to criticize Blackwater's killing of civilians in Iraq in 2007 (Lee) or the recent spate in the privatization of the U.S. forces in both Iraq and Afghanistan. As with the gendered treatment of Selvy, Mudger's interactions with Moll, whom he appears to try seduce, clue the reader in on the depths of the character's dysfunction. He virtually kidnaps her and takes her to his isolated ranch compound, run like a private fiefdom. He interrogates her as to Selvy's identity, with an increasingly menacing tone: "Tell you what…this is so much fun, I'd do it for nothing." (91) Mudger kept a private zoo in his "feudal barony" (84) in Vietnam. Now, his American domicile resembles the compound of Colonel Kurtz in the film *Apocalypse Now*. Mudger fails to win over Moll or intimidate her into revealing any information, and their next encounter occurring as Mudger has disguised himself as a cab driver taking her to her apartment building is even more frightening as it degenerates into his screaming curses at her (172). The mere fact that he would employ enemies of the U.S. government, Van and Cao, to simply do his bidding in the attempt to terminate a rival reveals the depth of Mudger's evil intent and disregard for the worst possible terrorist consequences. Social stability seems impossible given the predominance of the element represented in the character of Earl Mudger. He stands as the catalyst of the mercenary morality that runs rampant over the events of *Running Dog*, and once again American life tragically seems to imitate DeLillo's art.

But paramilitary privateers are not unique in this regard. As a negative moral force, profit-seeking murderous intent renders the America of *Running Dog* a moral "value-dark dimension" to refer back to *Ratner's Star* again. The journalist, politician, veteran, mercenary, and Mafia man are all reduced to a level of equivalent amorality as regards the legitimating of violence in society. Enter Vincent "Vinnie the Eye" Talerico, about whom I will have more to say in chapter 5. Talerico is one of the stock Mafia characters who occasionally emerge in such novels as *Americana*, *Libra*, and *Underworld*. The question of whether or not DeLillo, an Italian American writer himself, evokes this stereotypical image in such a manner as to reaffirm or to combat such bigotry against Italian Americans will be discussed in that later chapter. Here, the effect of Talerico on this narrative is to open up broader questions of the legitimacy of violence in the United States. In an empty parking lot under cover of darkness, Talerico and his wingman face off against Richie Armbrister and his man over the location of the secret Hitler film. It ends with Talerico's man being shot. Given the fact that the battle could have gone either way, Armbrister and Talerico are put on an equal moral plane. Moreover the Italian American Mafiosi are not even the first to pull a gun. As he flees the scene, it is left to Talerico to philosophically reflect on the problems of working in "acquisitions" in "a part of the U.S. where everybody owns a gun of one kind or another...Cowboys" (207). The Mafiosi's philosophy seems to sum up the mercenary attitudes present in each walk of life portrayed by the characters from the journalists to the paramilitary and finally to outlaws. DeLillo's use of the Mafia stock character here significantly levels the moral playing field since it is commonplace to consider such a person completely immoral and to in contrast consider journalists, art collectors, and the military to be morally superior to the Mafiosi since the former acquire their wealth through legitimate means. But DeLillo shows the phenomenon of *acquisition* as the problem; the common interest that each character in his or her field has in being the first to get their hands on the Hitler piece overrides the veneer of moral respectability. All of these social functions are reduced to the level of criminal behavior by the legitimization of violence in society. In sum, Talerico's presence in the narrative serves to signify Arthur Lomax's comment that "the logical extension of business is murder" (76). As will be discussed in chapter 5, the presence of Talerico as a mirror image of mainstream white American figure Richie Armbrister illustrates Fred Gardaphé's 2006 sociological insight that "the Italian-American gangster makes a perfect 'other' (to mainstream American figures) by virtue of his connection with a tribal culture that does not play the game of capitalism according to the rule of law" (Gardaphé 11).

The problem here, notwithstanding the larger issue of ethnic representation, is that the narrative and symbolic statement formed in *Running Dog* offers us little, if any, grounds for hope. Like the later novels *Libra*, *Mao II*, and *Cosmopolis,* the prospects for American life to change for the better, especially through creative acts of self-expression—like, for example, Moll Robbins's writing—are quite bleak. Philosophically and ethically as well, humanity does not fare well in the slice of life we have seen DeLillo portray in the darkly acquisitive America seen here in *Running Dog*. These matters are not worth the effort, and H. Glen Selvy reflects as his nail-biting adventures draw down to a close that "people came up against themselves in the end. Nothing but themselves" (224) when embarking on the philosophical quests for goodness and truth heroic "Western" struggles like Glen's are meant to represent.

Fortunately, DeLillo was not quick to abandon such quests on his own part as a novelist. His next five novels, spanning from 1982's *The Names* to 1997's *Underworld* present the reader with a profound examination of the moral nature of humanity particularly as regards the notion that the American artist may have some role in the moral betterment of social conditions surrounding her or his work. In *The Names* and *White Noise*, one finds a focus more on the medium of language itself, while other novels from the period return to the American landscape to grapple with issues of morality and art. While Selvy's journey ends, the reader's best adventures are yet to come.

Standard conventions like the Western action-based plot are trumped by the writer's fidelity to his emerging ethical vision.

DeLillo's second novel, *End Zone,* sustains brilliantly the antiwar theme we see introduced in *Americana* in the form of a brilliant central metaphor with nuclear war as the tenor and football as the vehicle. Through the perspective of main character Gary Harkness, a waning college football star obsessed with the terminology and imagined consequences of an all-out nuclear exchange, we see how postwar American culture founded

on the faith in nuclear dominance to ensure domestic security dehuman-
izes its inhabitants through blunting any interior sensitivity regarding the
dignity of other's lives or even life itself. Additionally, the studies of other
characters reinforce this paradigm of nuclear dehumanization. As the narrative winds up to its tragic conclusion, the impossibility of ethically delimiting the postnuclear holocaust landscape is made abundantly clear in the
final war games Gary enacts both with his gridiron buddies and with his
nuclear strategy professor, Major Staley. With its tightly controlled plotlines
and flawless consistency of imagery, 1972's *End Zone* brings the horror of
nuclear weapons and the culturally reflective violence of sport home to the
reader powerfully, setting the stage for the deeper moral exploration of the
nuclear issue we find 20 years later in *Underworld*.

To begin, the interior perspective of Harkness is deployed to introduce
the central metaphor of nuclear warfare as football. Harkness begins to
experience football as reflective of the desensitization inherent in the ethics
of mutually assured destruction. Following in the footsteps of his father, a
frustrated would-be player for Michigan State, Gary begins to experience
a strange lack of motivation as he plays football first for Syracuse and then
for Penn State. The repetition and lack of distinctiveness in practice after
practice begins to render Gary disoriented and unfocused on football as
such, even though he says his life means nothing without the game (*End
Zone* 22). For the discontented yet bodily engaged Harkness, football, especially in his stint at Penn State, becomes mindlessly repetitive: "I tripped
on the same step on the same staircase on three successive days" (19).
Gary's emotional commitment to the game becomes only superficial and
then subdivided into an obsession with nuclear weapons and warfare. The
terminology he uses to speak of nuclear war shows a psychic move in an
unspeakably evil dimension: this character realizes that the sheer size of the
mass destruction an all-out atomic exchange would cause is so great that it
makes the "language of the past world wars become laughable" (21). But
instead of feeling horrified, Gary finds in contemplation of such holocaust
"pleasure...a thrill almost sensual" (21). Gary's lack of moral outrage at
this imagined spectacle of "people diseased and starving. Two hundred
thousand bodies decomposing on the roads outside of Chicago" (21) could
arguably be said to show up the moral outrage readers should feel by virtue
of its omission. One should add that Gary does not reject compassion in
favor of perverse pleasure suddenly; he experiences a serious depression
at his failure to assimilate the horrendous idea of nuclear warfare and its
"rationality of irrationality" (21). The failure to wrap one's mind around
this unthinkable nuclear horror becomes a diabolical blunting of sensitivity

even unto death: Gary feels or at least exhibits no remorse when with two other players he tackles an Indiana safetyman resulting in the safetyman's death: "He died the next day and I went home that evening" (22). Such a disregard for human life, essential both in the contemplation of nuclear attack on an international "opponent" and in at least the rhetoric of football (at one point Harkness's coaches instructs Gary and his teammates to "pop, pop hit those people…drive them back till they look like sick little puppy dogs squatting down to crap" [37]) demonstrates that the ethics of mutually assured destruction permeate the dominant culture of American football as rooted in American nuclear dominance. Remorse at the Indiana safetyman's death, like depression at the prospective of the failure of deterrence, is simply not appropriate to the grunting game—better to relish the dehumanizing prospective of reducing the opponent to "crap." Gary's perspective, deteriorating in human sensitivity, unites the destructive ethics of the game of football to that of nuclear omnicide.

When not on the gridiron, the form of entertain Harkness and his friends participate in reinforces this blunting of sensitivity toward or regard for life found in the other two games that occupy Gary's mind. They play an informal game called "Bang, You're Dead" (33), during which the players ambush each other at odd locations around campus and make shooting noises at the opponent with their hands in the shape of a gun and replicate a killing complete with the best possible pantomiming of death. This pantomimed murder ritual, with a "massacre" (37) taking place in the early days of play, represents another misguided attempt to place the contemporary reality of death into perspective. It becomes another depersonalized, if playful, mindless way to "hit" or "kill" regardless of the consequences. As with Gary's psychic numbing toward life ultimately manifesting itself in the Indiana safety's death, Gary again begins to deny the material consequences of what he is doing while playing the game of "Bang You're Dead":

> One afternoon, shot from behind, I staggered to the steps of the library and remained there, on my back, for several minutes…. I felt the sun on my face. I tried to think of nothing. The longer I remained there, the more absurd it seemed to get up. My body became accustomed to the steps and the sun felt warmer….Taft Robinson was sitting on a bench not far away, reading a periodical. For a moment, in a state of near rapture, I thought it was he who fired the shot. (33)

Here, Gary finds the enactment of his own personal death as perversely pleasurably as his imaginings of a nuclear holocaust ("a state of near rapture"), but he is in a state of dangerous passivity. Feigning death is a dysfunctional means for him to attempt to come to grips with the thought of death. For his part, Taft Robinson is the only African American football player at Logos College, and Harkness was charged by the president of Logos College (called only by her late husband's name "Mrs. Tom Wade" or just "Mrs. Tom") to help Robinson feel comfortable at Logos (it is still 1972, and we are in West Texas). So Gary is dangerously passive here, disregarding any consequences or impact his behavior might have on his relationship with Taft. Furthermore, Taft might not feel very comfortable as the only black man in a West Texas college shooting game even if the game is merely pretend. Beneath the pretention is once again a denial of the reality of death; or as Gary puts it, the attraction of "Bang You're Dead" was that "it enabled us to pretend that death was a tender experience" (34). Such disregard is of a piece with the attitude of the players toward the death of the Indiana player and with the denial of the horrific consequences of attack essential to the proliferationist, prodominance nuclear strategist.

DeLillo's tracing of a gradual desensitization toward the value of life and accompanying denial of death in Gary Harkness's psyche finds reinforcement in the description of several intrapersonal and interpersonal processes involving other characters close to Gary. Mina Corbett, his girlfriend, attracts Gary's attention by her interest in science fiction and her orange dress emblazoned with an enormous mushroom cloud. Mina deals with issues of her weight and society's standards for female beauty. Initially, she is completely unwilling or unable to cope with these, as she tells Gary that she accepts herself exactly as she is but also protests his compliments and refers to herself interiorly as a "sloppy emotional overweight girl" (67). On the other hand, Mina takes control of her life, her attitude, and her weight, rejecting fully the process of how society would define her identity rather than continuing to hide her feelings of inferiority relative to social standards in her obese state. She loses 25 pounds and basically tells Gary to stop being so needy, but he is hesitant to embrace her positive changes. But Mina is not daunted; she intends to go on with her life with or without Gary. In contrast, Mina does not become desensitized as Harkness has or allow herself to be defined by the dictates of society. In a similar way, Taft Robinson also rejects society's definition of himself, quitting football to pursue his studies partly because he is uncomfortable with the racial tensions he finds at Logos in West Texas.

Picking up on the onus Gary is given to help Logos become more integrated "because [Gary] was a northerner" (6), Gary fails in this regard due in large part to the cultural violence imbuing *End Zone*, which is rooted in the nuclear arms race as DeLillo presents that violence. Racial tensions, introduced somewhat comically in the novel, are presented as structurally similar to the culture of the arms race and nuclear violence. The revered president of Logos College, Mrs. Tom Wade, is hilariously and "accurately described as Lincolnesque...tall, black-browed, stark as a railroad spike" (6–7). Irony is embodied in the fact that the novel is set 100 years after the close of the Civil War, yet America is still not only divided by these tensions but utilizing violent games as a means to achieve racial integration. Like Lincoln, Mrs. Tom does not survive to see the result of this experiment. The parallel between racial and nuclear tensions that DeLillo is illustrating (and that will reemerge in *Underworld*) unmistakably emerges early in Gary's failure of integration. While Gary and Taft sit together eating with the team during dinner, one of the team's offensive captains, right tackle Moody Kimbrough, very emphatically reprimands Robinson for simply wearing sunglasses, striding toward the two men's table in a threatening manner (26). The chilling scene ends in a trade of punches between Kimbrough and Harkness as the latter defends the lone African American player's right to self-expression, with Robinson sitting by having his dessert like a civil rights–era protestor at a lunch counter. In the culture of holdover Civil War–era racism, a palpable aura of violence looms between races, with chaos about to break out at any time. Later, in *Underworld*, we will also find this juxtaposition of oppositional imagery of black and white with the tense polarity we associate with nuclear issues such as fission or global conflict. Here in this novel, the fight scene is evocative of the permanent threat of destruction present in the nuclear philosophy of mutually assured destruction.

It is this looming, predetermined reality of nuclear death and destruction that overshadows a simple discussion of football or even of racial and gender politics in the aptly titled *End Zone*. Rhetorically, the nuclear shadow is seen in the manner of speech deployed by the Logos football coaches when lecturing the players about team strategy: "We use the aerial game here to implement the ground game whereby we force their defense to respect the run" (27). This description of Logos's offensive pattern bears a striking similarity to the use of nuclear deterrence or aerial WMDs to accomplish American objectives on the ground, be they military or political. This rhetoric of football becomes a completely appropriate language to use to describe nuclear omnicide.

However, the problem of nuclear destruction raises profound philosophical issues with language itself. This is revealed when Gary goes to visit the professor of the AFROTC courses he has been auditing, Major Staley, a veteran of the Nagasaki atomic bombing. The two begin a philosophical dialogue, during which the problem of language is evoked: "Major," states Gary, "there's no way to express 30 million dead. No words" (85). Because the evil of nuclear omnicide is unspeakable, Gary states his conspiracies belief that "certain men are recruited to reinvent the language" (85). Major Staley defends himself as not enjoying the prospect of discussing this mega-death but that his duty is to present the language of the prospect of nuclear war objectively, so that people know what they are facing (85). Staley's response begs the question Gary's next comment raises to the effect that "the problem goes deeper" than simply the reinvention of language (85). This dialogue will prove vitally significant in future DeLillo works, since the idea of an unspeakable evil will be alluded to in many ways. The dialogue signifies *more* than just those limitations and therefore mere reinvention of language will prove woefully inadequate to solve the "problem" these men discuss. As Major Staley puts it, "Weapons technology is so specialized that nobody has to feel any guilt. Responsibility is distributed too thinly for that" (86). It is the impact of the weaponry involved, though, and the language used to describe it that make an intimation of moral responsibility via the very language inescapable despite Major Staley's blind faith that responsibility is distributed too thinly. In response to the major, Gary is both right and wrong in a sense; the words "thirty million dead," or later on their dialogue "milk, children and thyroid cancer" or "twenty-four hundred genetic events per four hundred thousand people" exposed to nuclear attack would receive express the impact of nuclear war with a pretentious scientific objectivity. But they cannot permit the morally sensitive listener or reader to put the unthinkable horror into perspective. Staley and Gary's philosophical conversation paradoxically illustrates a significant point from the great Cambridge philosopher Iris Murdoch about the language of science and technology as they "seem to undermine our ordinary language and its 'naïve' truth values" (Murdoch 199). Staley's insistence on objectivity and precision in describing nuclear omnicide undermines on the one hand morally based truth values that would dictate that we feel the horror that blocks a technically precise visualization of the nuclear holocaust. But Gary, on the other hand, prompts Major Staley to move forward in his efforts to conceptually embody in words this same inconceivable evil, undermining for his part ordinary language's adequacy in shocking us with what it can reveal to us of the potential nuclear debacle. That moral sensibility of language that Murdoch outlined and that Major Staley would stun us out of with technological objectivity (a quality of scientific language DeLillo will also respond to in *Ratner's Star*) escapes the AFROTC professor. Gary is too dense and confused to fully appreciate the moral force of language either.

So the problem does indeed "go deeper" than the issue of the inadequacy of plain ordinary language. But to quote Murdoch, technology such as Staley's only "seems" to undermine the moral power or "truth values" of language as it is absorbed. Gary Harkness will not be able to solve this deeper problem by going to Major Staley to learn what "nuclear war...might be like" (86). Therefore, though the shadow of nuclear destruction raises epistemological issues, the moral imperative it raises is even more important.

If ordinary language is appropriate to evoke the omnicide horror that no language can fully envision or express, it seems fitting to ask why DeLillo should choose football as the vehicle for his central metaphor to paint the nuclear wasteland. I would argue that one possible answer to this reasonable question (the game of baseball will be the central focus of DeLillo's later novel *Underworld*) lies in the symbolic ramifications of a cultural artifact that exists outside of the world of the novel *End Zone*. This is not to reduce the novel to an extended artistic response on DeLillo's part to one Pentagon artifact, but it is fair to unpack the literary tropes the writer inevitably uses in terms of concrete material historical conditions, as these emerge so frequently in the later novels *Libra*, *Underworld*, *Cosmopolis*, and *Point Omega*. All of the key nuclear weapon launch codes, a direct radio link to the Strategic Air Command, and a strategic playbook known as "the President's Decision Book" are carried by a high-ranking military aide who never leaves the side of the president of the United States in a valise known as "the football" (Weapons of Mass Destruction WMD 1). The idea of this "nuclear football" is evoked when Gary's teammate Bing Jackman senses the essence of the football they are throwing and kicking around:

> "I sensed knowledge in the football. I sensed a strange power and restfulness.... The football knew that this is a football game. It was aware of its own footballness."
>
> [Gary responds:] "You went ahead and kicked the ball."
>
> "Naturally," he said. "That's the essence of the word. It's a football, isn't it? It is a *foot ball*. My foot sought union with the ball." (*End Zone* 37)

Jackman falsely associates rational consciousness (a sense of awareness) with the football in response to his own experience of the essential or nominalizing power of language—the "essence of the word" gives to the Logos player's football "its own footballness." But this same nominalizing power of language of "the word" is given to the separate reality of nuclear warfare through the cultural metaphor of "the nuclear football," which

names the president's portable central command center. The cultural artifact does indeed extend consciousness or knowledge as there literally is
computer software programmed into the "nuclear football" a consciousness involved with destructive opposition, making the cultural metaphor
suitable for extension into what we see in *End Zone* as a fundamental similarity between the two games.

If what could be a simple coincidence between the real-life "nuclear
football" currently being carried around behind President Obama and
DeLillo's central choice of metaphoric elements in this novel is unconvinc-
ing, the manner in which the game of gridiron football unravels for Harkness provides more evidence of the similarities, showing that this novel is
about nuclear omnicide as opposed to simply being about the mind of one
somewhat obtuse college athlete. Such unraveling occurs when another of
Gary's teammates, Jim Deering, brings a football to the parade grounds
for an impromptu game. This game begins simply and gently enough as a
simple touch football match, but gradual disregard for any system of rules
accumulates as the men tough out snow-covered conditions. First comes
a tolerance for general incompetence, as no one starts to care if fumbles
occur or if players fall in the snow. Then the hits grow harder, injury is
ignored, and Gary begins to enjoy being smashed down into the snow.
Blocks become harder, referees are absent, passes and laterals outlawed; in
short, the game becomes reduced to simply its own nucleus, its innermost
"primal impact" or "violent action" (193). At Logos's parade grounds,
ethical rules become irrelevant, violence increases, and the injuries these
rules were designed to prevent occur more frequently (193). Thus does
the civilized game of football unravel into an essential and uncontrollable
violence. As occurs with the novel's raising of epistemological issues, philosophical questions of morality become raised by the violence imbued into
End Zone's portrayal of American culture. But can nuclear war strategy
really be critiqued through this lens of Harkness's experience of this game
of "nuclear football"?

Turning once again to Major Staley, the novel's spokesperson for America's post–World War II nuclear strategy (a version of which is still in place
at the time of this writing), we see a parallel between the unraveling of
the structural and moral limits on violence in the game of football and
the ridiculous impossibility of imposing such limits on nuclear violence.
Staley paints an unreal projection of the future for Gary during which
there will be wars kept "as relatively humane as possible...we agree to
use clean stuff" (81). This picture of the use of so-called clean nuclear
weapons such as neutron bombs and depleted uranium, etc., disregards the

destructive nature of these weapons. Staley augments the rosy picture of a limited exchange by using euphemistic language such as "strictly counter-force" (81). This doctrine of limited exchange is as arbitrary as the game of impromptu football in the snow, and the theme of "nuclear football" implies a comparison between the two unlimitable games. Later in the nar-rative, Major Staley plays a crude form of war game with Gary Harkness in a hotel room (219). Using very transparent acronyms for major world powers, such as NORKOR (for North Korea), COMCHIN (Communist China), and AMAC (the United States), it only takes the two players 12 short steps taking merely three hours to get from a limited "counterforce" exchange (the game equivalent of an American 6th Fleet aircraft carrier suffering small damage from enemy aircraft arms fire), to the final destruc-tion of Washington DC, New York, Los Angeles, and major Russian cities, all wiped out by multimegaton omnicide ICBMs. At the climax of this imagined carnage, the major's telephone rings and he is terrified "for a long second," as if the border between terrifying fantasy and reality have become temporarily blurred. An evocative erasing of limits allows the reader to complete the parallel between the snowbound football game on the parade grounds and what the war game reveals about real nuclear war-fare. Because the weapons are so powerful and the outcome of conflict so unpredictable (the major refers to his simulated nuclear war as "a scenario premised on futuribles" (220), nuclear war is as unlimitable as the primal violence the Logos players inflict on each other at the Parade Games. Sys-tems of rules, limitations, and "clean game" scenarios are equally likely to unravel into sheer chaos and primal, violent destruction in both cir-cumstances namable as "nuclear football." Thus quoth the major: "The humanistic mind crumbles at the whole idea [of nuclear warfare]. It's the most hideous thing in the world to these people that such ideas even have to be mentioned" (81). This atavistic destruction of humankind, Gary Harkness's obsession, and the major underlying theme of *End Zone* can finally be summed up ironically enough by Staley: "The big danger is that we'll surrender to a sense of inevitability and start flinging mud all over the planet" (80).

Finally, *End Zone* trumps earlier novels in terms of the foreshadowing of later DeLillo treatment of moral issues. Nuclear warfare, in its unspeak-able scale, trumps the issue of media's attack on the individual, and it also trumps the treatment of conventional terrorism introduced in these early novels. What I have not reiterated in this chapter is of course one other clear issue prefigured in these novels; as readers must notice, the concept of an unspeakable evil and some very evocative references to a battle taking place in language are interwoven into DeLillo's prose regarding the struggles of the contemporary subject both in a personal and social form. Such an issue must be tackled in smaller pieces, so the next issue to uncover involves a certain faith in the power of language as it is treated in DeLillo's next two works, *The Names* and *White Noise*.

_____ *Chapter 3* _____

The Names and *White Noise*:
A New Faith in the Power
of Language

One of Don DeLillo's major concerns as a writer is the power of language. Words and the use of them mark us as a unique species. In his first two novels of great reputation, the theme of language and its power is introduced for the reader's consideration. Both these novels, the first of the impact of the Iranian hostage crisis on the life of a risk analyst and the second of a toxic waste disaster comically portrayed, invite us to reflect on an important question. Language can possibly provide a way out of catastrophe in our troubled times. Will the healing power of words be enough in the face of the kind of disasters our century has shown us, whether surprise acts of terrorism or unexpected environmental disasters? These questions are considered in the two novels beginning with *The Names*.

Considered by the *Atlantic Monthly* to be the first of five of the "essential" novels of Don DeLillo, *The Names* received strong reviews in journals highly respected in the literary world, such as the *Los Angeles Times Book Review* and the *New Yorker* magazine. Particularly significant is the *New Yorker*'s use of the word "frightening"; this indicates that DeLillo's tale of American businesspeople in the late 1970s and early 1980s in Greece and the Middle East struck a chord with its treatment of the political tensions typical of this time and place. In this chapter, we will see DeLillo introduce several important themes that he sustains in several of the major novels represented in this book. *The Names* criticizes American capitalist practices as it points out how American predatory loans overseas arouse anger in foreign countries. Another important motif is DeLillo's portrayal of how personal relationships, in this case marital relationships and cases of adultery, have a political significance as well. Tension in the bedroom leads to social instability and conflict. DeLillo here also examines the causes of terrorism deeply through his examination of the interactions between the American capitalists and the Greeks as well as through frequent references to the Iranian hostage crisis of 1979–1980. Here we find that terrorism is associated with a variety of causes, including a people's need to assert their own self-identity as a nation, combined with an American ignorance of the host country's language and culture. A fundamentalist expression of religion is also brought to light in *The Names* as a potential cause of terrorist activity. Finally, though, the more positive theme of the power of language to provide a way out of catastrophe is introduced in this first essential novel. But the question of whether that healing communicative power finally will save America from terrorism is left open at the end of *The Names*.

The Names is a murder mystery/adventure novel narrated by James Axton, an American freelance writer and insurance risk analyst working for a firm connected to big oil companies and other corporations. Because he is involved with protecting American assets overseas, he must also stay connected with and stay informed of American intelligence actions and volatile political situations. Crises like the taking of the hostages in Iran affect his clients' ability to do business and thus James's ability to insure them. James's cohorts include banker David Keller and his new young wife Lindsay, the Maitlands, Charles and Ann (who is one of the many women with whom James has an affair), Dick and Dot Borden, and many other American traveling investors and those with a stake in the volatile governments dotting the landscape of Middle Eastern nations. When the Americans go out to dinner, Ann strikes up a conversation with a Greek native, Andreas Eliades, who explains at length the issues the Greek host country has with American multinational corporations and banks involved in predatory loan practices overseas (*The Names* 53–60).

Eventually, the pressures of his high-risk job and constant travel destroy Axton's marriage to Kathryn, an archeologist, and endanger his bond with their nine-year-old son, Tap. In anger Kathryn once attempts to attack her husband with a potato peeler. Kathryn's mentor and supervisor on her dig in Greece, Owen Brademas, has been spending a great deal of time with the mother and son. Tap has begun to develop a bond with Owen, which threatens James. Despite some attempts at reconciliation, Kathryn plans to take a new job at the British Columbia Provincial Museum and take Tap with her (137).

After she departs, James joins avant-garde filmmaker Frank Volterra on a fact-finding mission about the Names cult, about which Volterra wants to make a documentary. James is assessing the risk this cult forms for his clients. The cult murders innocent persons with common household tools, choosing targets so that the victim's initials match the location of the murder. Axton will help his old graduate-school friend gather information about their common interest.

Axton arrives at Yemen en route to Amman, Jordan, to meet Volterra. George Rowser, Axton's supervisor and fellow political analyst, discloses the myriad deadly dangers their intelligence corporation is facing in the volatile political climate overseas formed in the wake of the Iranian hostage crisis. But they press on, ignoring the obvious risk. James opens an office in North Yemen. On their way to Amman, Axton and Volterra arrive in Jerusalem. Axton chats with Del Nearing, Volterra's traveling companion, who does not appear to have any idea what is going on in the Middle East. Volterra brings James to a restaurant where a series of informants eventually brings them into contact with the cult. When Axton, Nearing, and Volterra set out to Amman, Axton learns that Amman is set on seven hills and that Jebel is the word for "hill" in the relevant Arabic language. With a sense of mounting horror, James figures out that "Jebel Amman" has the same initials as his own name, "James Axton" (158). Therefore he realizes that he could be the cult's next victim. When Owen Brademas returns to James's office, he confirms significant details about the cult's modus operandi: the victim's name was Michaelsis Kalliambetsos, and the village of his assassination was Mikro Kamini. While discussing this, James finds out that Brademas has been in contact with cult members, heightening the danger to them both.

Father and son reunite as Tap and James cross a mountain range called Taygetus in the Greek Peloponnese and drive into a nameless town (181). Axton gets out of their car to ask at a café for directions to a hotel and a bathroom. The response he gets is frighteningly cold. James and Tap see a terrifying landmark suggesting that they are getting closer to the cult: a ten-foot fallen boulder, red in color, with the Greek words "Ta Onomata," meaning "The Names" (188). But they depart safely, and James runs into David and Lindsay Keller once again at the Hilton, searching for recognizable traces of American culture, Axton poses a repeated question reflecting the group's central concern: "Are they killing Americans?" (193).

Following up on informants' information, James gets a chance to meet a member of the cult, Andahl, who waxes mysteriously about the motives for the multiple murders these killers commit. Couching their conversations in spiritual terms, the cult spokesman claims to be "working at the preverbal level" (208). The power to name an unnamable or ineffable evil seems to be their goal: "Extreme, insane, whatever you wish to call it in words.... Inevitable and perfect and right" (208).

Axton's next stop is a break in the investigation: a party at Dick and Dot Borden's, the stereotypically perfect American couple who host purposeless drinking parties. After traveling to Rhodes, Axton meets the Kellers at the beach where Lindsay is watching David take a "punishing" night swim. Here David reveals his condescending, bourgeois views of the host countries he does his banking in. This conversation can be contrasted with the next one Axton has with Andreas Eliades, when the Greek decries American injustices toward other countries. Axton meets up with the Kellers, and this impromptu dinner group is joined by Roy Hardemann, another American businessman who gets drunk and obnoxious. Hardemann and Keller start arguing. The group attempts to send their passed-out drunk, uninvited guest on a plane to Tehran, a virtual death sentence in this post-hostage-crisis setting. However, they can't get him out of his car seat (265).

Axton goes looking for Owen Brademas. The two share a story of Owen's final encounter with the cult. They discuss Owen's past and how religious fervor had drawn him to the cult. We learn that Owen's upbringing in the farmlands of Kansas—the violent sermons of the hellfire and brimstone preacher of his family's prairie church—have rendered him vulnerable to the dangerous religious extremism of an angry nation. Brademas reveals how he met the remaining cult members of the Greek cult: Avtar Sing; the woman, Bern; and Emmerich, the leader of the group. Owen receives none of his desired spiritual enlightenment from his talks with Emmerich, who asserts only that killing is the most significant thing the cult does. Crouching in thatched silos, Owen hides with the other cult members and tries to care for Bern, who is vomiting blood in her self-imposed starvation, Owen sees the meaningless evil of the Names murder, making himself complicit as a silent witness. A stoning of a man whose name matches Sanskrit letters appears in the cult's mad war against any attempts to name an unnamable God.

As the novel draws to a close, James Axton feels satisfied that he has survived and assessed the risk. However, as a shock ending, David Keller is shot in the shoulder by a totally different and new evil group presence, the Autonomous People's Front, more of a terrorist group than a religiously labeled mass-murdering cult. This revelation, plus Axton's sharing with the reader the pages of Tap's rough draft in which he describes Owen's stressful experience with the Kansas preacher (335–339), shake up the resolution of violence at the end of the plot.

Marital relationships in *The Names* take on a particular significance in light of the political conflicts discussed in this text. The breakup of James and Kathryn's marriage provides a poignant tension in the early part of the novel. Owen Brademas, as mentioned above, interferes with their time together as a couple. James will only tell us that Kathryn feels a "fondness... a warm regard, whatever a woman feels" (19) for her older mentor. Owen lingers while James perceives his ex-wife undressing for bed in the next room (17). He will not let the former couple be alone together. To complicate these character relationships even further, she announces that her future plans are undecided. She does not demonstrate much affection for Owen at the beginning of the novel (33), but then she tells her husband that she does not want marriage "ever... to anyone" (33). The fact that she really feels passion for neither man at this point may indicate that Kathryn's true passion simply is for knowledge; she is described by her husband as having "the look of the girl in the family album who asserts her right to calculate the precise value of what is out there" (27). Too much anger has passed between them. Thus separation for the sake of her career is chosen.

Owen Brademas is a tragic, forlorn figure (19). His character manifests a restless curiosity toward knowledge, but without a focus. A self-described "man who has given up on himself," Brademas is a "wanderer" who feels a perpetual "soft awe" (276). His presence in the story signifies the theme of language, especially the unrequited love. He reads meaning into his archeological relics as the student of literature investigates the meaning of symbols. He connects the idea of relationships with the notion of investigations into language. Brademas refers to his work as a "form of conversation with ancient people... riddle solving to a certain degree. To decipher, to uncover secrets, to trace the geography of language" (35). This passion for searching out value has been lost, and Owen fails in his attempt to recover it. His infatuation proves to be his undoing. His talks with cult leader Emmerich do not enlighten him; the man only asserts to Owen that killing is the only significant thing that the cult does. The cult has declared a mad war, or so Emmerich reveals to Owen, over any attempt to name the ineffable God. Owen's quest is disastrous. In fact, Singh even calls him a member of the cult as Brademas's observation of the Sanskrit killing has drawn him into a silent and passive complicity. Brademas reports the murder to no one but James. Fortunately for Axton, Owen, now complicit with the cult, cannot replace him in Kathryn's and Tap's lives: "Whatever he'd lost in life-strength," reflects James Axton, "I'd won" (309).

Axton feels jealousy over his wife's relationship with Owen Brademas. He has had affairs not only with a woman named Antoinette (68), prompting Kathryn's fit of jealous rage, but also with Ann Maitland, wife of his friend Charles. The numerous adulterous affairs that occur in *The Names* cause much tension, even anger, and finally, acts of violence. When James has an erotic tryst with a banker's wife, Janet Ruffing, she appears to be less than willing, but he prevents her from escaping (230). This episode forms a tense situation. The potential for anger and violence is shown when James encounters Charles Maitland after his tryst with Janet. Charles has been told of Axton's prior affair with his own wife and reveals that he knows Janet Ruffing's husband. Maitland then tensely refers to the fact that he's heard about the "interesting" evening when Axton met Janet and thus may know of that affair as well. Charles's jaw tightens. Axton wonders if the men are "fixed in some near symmetry of friendships and adulteries" (240). To paraphrase English romantic poet William Blake, it's a fearful symmetry. Jealous rage could break out between the two men at any time, as it did when Kathryn attempted to stab James Axton with a potato peeler. In all, these chaotic adulterous affairs break down the social stability of the characters' lives.

Erotic and social tension feeds the political tension of the characters' situation. When the little clique of American capitalists attempts to put a passed-out Roy Hardemann on a plane to Tehran, they do so at the prompting of David Keller. Keller is angry at their rude comrade after Roy fights with David in front of Keller's beautiful new young wife Lindsay. A pattern in *The Names* forms of the older man leaving his wife for a new woman, fairly commonplace in couples like the Kellers, James and his numerous conquests, and possibly even Frank Volterra and Del Nearing, who also tempts James to sexual conquest. Given the Greek setting of the novel, the ancient story of Helen of Troy comes to mind, where the taking of the beautiful female hostage Helen catalyzed the violence of the Trojan War. As we will see, such hostage crises propel the thematic structure of *The Names* as well as the characterization DeLillo deploys.

The themes of international oppression, terrorism, and the power of language in the face of such historically destructive forces operate dramatically in *The Names*. History forms a very significant context for DeLillo's fiction. As we discuss the troubled marriage of James and Kathryn as a metaphor for the signifying power of language, we will see that the question of just how powerful words are against these forces is opened up but not conclusively answered. So *The Names* becomes the beginning of our quest with DeLillo, an investigation into language's power and mystery. Along the way, we'll interpret and investigate DeLillo's analysis of the reasons behind terrorism and how those reasons connect with the fanatical impulses we see sometimes in religion. In her article "The Language of History: Don DeLillo's *The Names* and the Iranian Hostage Crisis," Anne Longmuir states that DeLillo has "plotted," or structured, this "novel against a historical intertext" which is of course the Iranian hostage crisis, the 1979 taking of the American embassy and the 52 hostages in Tehran. As she reveals, "the political ramifications and historical circumstances" (Longmuir 105) surrounding the book form an important context or set of clues against which we will interpret the novel.

DeLillo's symbolic presentation of this theme starts out with James's reluctance to climb the Acropolis, a setting chock full of historical significance. Note how the author will blend classic and modern historical intertexts: James does not want to visit or climb this ancient peripheral defense of Athens, despite peer pressure from his friends to do so. Athens is a symbol of Western Civilization and cultural values. During the 5th century B.C.E. while Greece was at war with ancient Persia, the Persians famously burned the Acropolis. Persia in ancient times was the name of modern-day Iran. Throughout the novel, James Axton makes several references to the concurrent taking of U.S. hostages in Tehran. One can read the reference to the Acropolis as a setting symbolically here. Like the burning of the ancient Acropolis, the taking of the American hostages in Iran represents hostility toward a foreign country present in a nation by the native people.

But why does DeLillo focus so much on the Iranian hostage crisis as a theme that will govern the structure of *The Names*? As Eliades indicates, it is America's unwanted intervention in the affairs of other nations that arouses the ire of others. This theme is reinforced by James Axton's insights about, "the colonialist theme...of exploitation, of greatest possible utilization" (266). Speaking for his own native land of Greece, Andreas Eliades refers to predatory lending practices in Greece and Turkey. His criticism is insightful:

> This is interesting, how a U.S. bank based in Athens can lend money to Turkey...they are the southeast flank and there are U.S. bases there and the Americans want to spy on the Russians, okay. Lift the embargo, give them enormous foreign aid.... You approve loans from your headquarters in the middle of Athens. But the documentation is done in New York and London. Why is this, because of sensitivity to the feelings of the Greeks? No, it is because the Turks will be insulted if the agreements are signed on Greek soil.... You structure the loan and when they can't pay the money, what happens? You have a meeting in Switzerland and you restructure. Athens gives to Ankara. (59)

Eliades's argument is essentially that America's economic intervention in Greek and Turkish affairs has caused Greece to be exploited by predatory loan practices. Eliades's protest against this exploitation of his native land is comparable to the argument of the Iranians who resented America's political intervention in Iranian affairs by propping up the shah. Eliades and the Iranians could say, as he does, that "our future does not belong to us. It is owned by the Americans" (236) even though that means of ownership is through predatory loans on the one hand and the puppet government of the shah on the other. So in *The Names*, the extensive references to the hostage crisis show the event as caused by the people aroused by intervention, reinforcing the theme present in the historical reference to the Acropolis as well.

DeLillo further shows that these practices of unwanted intervention and exploitation of these countries by Americans results in confusion as it interferes with the processes associated with representing another people's national/ethnic identity. Anne Longmuir notes that social and literary theorists have long been aware that representation, or the act of identifying or naming a thing, has "hitherto been a prerogative of the West" (Longmuir 112) With the uprising of the Iranians, Western dominance over language, representing others or "naming" them as another unwanted cultural intervention, is disrupted. The intervention is made morally acceptable in the world and in *The Names* by the fact that James and his American colleagues are completely unaware of their foreign surroundings, the cultures, the peoples and the languages these peoples speak. So here is raised my central question: what are the relationships among the power of language, good, and evil? Language has the power to justify moral or immoral acts, and this power is shown in DeLillo's work.

One example of myopic disorientation is James continually asking the question "Are they killing Americans?" (45) when he inquires about a few foreign countries. He and his friends only care what happens to Americans. Moreover, James can't speak Greek, and many of the Greeks he comes into contact with know no English, so he cannot gain awareness through communication: "He didn't know a word of English. My Greek was so tentative and insecure I began to wish I could avoid the man" (102). World dominance has led to a willed ignorance of other languages. As James wanders around a Jordanian airport, he laments, "I didn't know the names of things" (138).

In fact, the prevailing attitude among James's comrades about the culture and language of their hosts is best expressed by Charles Maitland and David Keller. Maitland's way of dodging communication is to claim to "learn the language, but not to let them [the native people] know" (41). His rationale for this is based in the same ethnocentric viewpoint driving the interventions mentioned above: "One does business in English" (42). Charles is desperately trying to hang onto American dominance over language in the form of the power to name all business. Additionally, David Keller is so disrespectful to his host culture as to rename an Iranian Shi'ite ceremony of mourning "Chain Day" and to throw a party, ignoring the mourners outside shouting "Death to the Shah" as he laughs and drinks with his friends (65). Keller also speaks out revealing his ignorant disdain for the native cultures and languages he's involved with, calling the societies he does business with "my countries…huge tracts of economic and social and political wreckage" (232) that he ought not to miss. Representing the views of indigenous peoples, Eliades is not impressed with how Americans depart from their monolithic views only when their political or economic dominance over another country is disrupted by a crisis: "Americans learn geography and world history only as their interests are damaged in one country after another" (58). So the willed ignorance of world culture shown by Maitland and Keller as the insular nature of American speaks a language justifying bad actions.

DeLillo also goes in depth on the subject of terrorism, predicting a world "steeped in calamity" where "bombings will become commonplace" (330). In contrast to how many feel, *The Names* paints terrorism as the attempt to reclaim those means of representation or self-naming. "Ta Onomata," the cult group for which the novel is titled, perhaps cannot truly be called a terrorist group, but they understand the power of names as "an opening into the self" (210). The Iranian students who held the hostages in exchange for the return of the shah claimed that the United States had held their country hostage for several decades, struggling to assert their identity as a nation.

Continuing DeLillo's treatment of the complex causes of terrorism and the need for national autonomy over identity is also clearly suggested as a cause or motivating factor behind terrorism by the name of the terrorist group that is responsible for the final shooting, "Autonomous People's Initiative." This group wounds David Keller with a shot to the shoulder (325). The choice of Keller as a target can be traced to his exploitative perspective on the native culture, just as the Ta Onomata's modus operandi can be traced to initials of people and places that match. Beyond terrorist group labels, we note that *The Names* explains why the terrorist act is essentially untraceable. Looking at the shooting of Keller, we see that because so many nations desire autonomy the perpetrators of a terrorist act have anonymity; Axton and friends *suspect* Eliades, but it could have been anyone cheated by Keller's American predatory loan practices. Against this historical and narrated backdrop, the confusion of national/ethnic identity resulting from a restructuring of another nation's identity, such as with Greece/Turkey, Palestine/Israel, and most recently with Iran and Iraq, can have disastrous results. DeLillo puts forth in *The Names* that terrorism is one such result.

Further and unfortunately for the Western world, religion is not here presented as a reliable response against terrorism but rather as a cause. This theme is best articulated in *The Names* by the character Owen Brademas. Axton tells us that Brademas equates "the nightmarish force of people in groups" with "the power of religion" (276). Religion, it seems, is not a benign use of words all the time. Religious "delirium" (276) makes people more vulnerable to the influence of charismatic cult leaders like Emmerich. As Owen and James approach their final encounter with the cult, the words of pandemonium increase as DeLillo describes through their eyes the "madness of priests," "human surge," "trampled bodies," and the like. Although Brademas will try to control events around him by becoming part of this experience of religious mass hypnosis, Axton, and by extension the author DeLillo, casts a cautious, skeptical eye upon the theme of religion in *The Names*. As we continue to read the major novels, DeLillo's presentation of religion will shift and change but will frequently return to the idea of religion as a negative social force.

The author himself has some insight to offer into this point in his own nonfiction essay titled "Silhouette City, Hitler, Manson and the Millennium" (344–352). In this, DeLillo argues that "there is an element in the soul that creates in us a need to know the worst about ourselves" (345). It is precisely to this dark impulse that the leader of the Ta Onomata cult precisely speaks when he says that the cult kills for the experience of a "frenzy of knowing "(*Names* 211). While it is true that Ta Onamata is not performing political terrorist acts, their need to kill springs from this impulse. DeLillo further claims that it is this impulse that is expressed collectively in fanatical religiosity as in the Crusades, Nazi German apocalyptic visions, and today's millenarian cults such as one at a 224-acre compound raided at the Missouri-Arkansas border (350). Add the nationalist political need to identify oneself, which we see in the Iranian kidnappers and in post 9/11 events, and the idea of a driving force behind terrorist acts is very recognizable in this story. Though the "religion" of the terrorist shooting of Kellerman by the "Autonomous People's Front" is one of worshipping freedom, this fervor has been transformed. The artist's desire for personal freedom has been supplanted by the more destructive impulse. The attempt on Kellerman is easily comparable to the narrated historical events of Islamic terrorism we see in *The Names*. So the author's insight qualifies the premise of Paul Maltby, who claims that "DeLillo is more likely to endorse his character's beliefs (as in religious beliefs) than to dismiss them" (510). Simply to have a religious belief does not guarantee that all is well in DeLillo's worlds. As in Owen Brademas's experience of running in fear from the charismatic Kansas preacher, the use of language's power can be for good or evil even in religion.

However, an overriding theme in *The Names* paints a somewhat brighter picture. The sinister fundamentalist impulse one sees in both politically terrorist and nonterrorist cult crimes does not fully dash the hope one might find in the power of language. Writing soon after the 9/11 attack in December 2001 in *Harper's* magazine, DeLillo's praise for New York City reveals this hope, "The city will accommodate every language, ritual, belief and opinion" ("In the Ruins" 40). Terrorist attacks cannot banish hope from language; hence its power. Following up on this, James Axton, narrator of *The Names,* reflects, "The river of language is God" (152). Passion for language fires up Axton's quest as he finally turns the all-consuming "need to know" against the cult itself toward the close of the novel. There are times when Axton does express a stronger desire to learn about native languages and culture. His openness to and respect of language's power will prove very helpful to him as he is able to assess the cult and survive harm in ways other characters cannot.

So for an analysis of language's power, critic Paul Maltby states that the optimistic romantic view of language is operating in the novel, referring to the "visionary power" of language in *The Names,* which works to "invest the world with some order of deep and empowering meaning...[and to] reveal human existence in significant ways" (502). For an example of this visionary power, he refers to a scene in *The Names* where James and Katherine go out on a pier in Greece and James really enjoys their conversation: James is "lighthearted, brilliantly happy...knowing the real meaning of every word" (*The Names* 32). However, disregarding the context of this scene, Maltby has neglected to note that James and Katherine seem to be on the verge of a reconciliation and James even refers to her here as "my wife," even though later they will separate again. While Maltby compares this scene to a later one in *White Noise,* he misses an important component of DeLillo's treatment of the theme of language. This visionary power does not simply come easily, dropped into someone's lap as in the *White Noise* scene where Maltby discusses Jack Gladney simply listening to his daughter talking in her sleep and experiences the same reaffirmation James does here as far as the critic is concerned. One has to work to attain this level of experience; this "pure nomenclature" (Maltby 502) is not something without a nonprimal context, an active learning process. So like the couple trying to put their marriage back together, one must work to unlock the power of language, an important idea in *The Names*.

To continue, one must follow the couple's relationship to its logical conclusion. Unfortunately for Maltby and others who would embrace a completely optimistic reading of *The Names*, James and Katherine do split up, leaving work yet to be done on their marriage. It is agreed that Kathryn will leave her archeological dig to take a good position at the British Columbia Provincial Museum (*The Names* 133). As they part ways, their marriage is shown to be a metaphor for the signifying power of language. Some linguists commonly use the terms "the signifier" to refer to a word as an active agent invoking a reference to some object, and the "signified" as that thing which the word represents, an object in the world. For our purposes here, the signifier can also be a narrator of words to others or a reader interpreting meaning for him or herself.

Here, the positions of these married characters represent this. As James Axton is the signifier, primarily, we get our viewpoint through his language about the relationship and its demise. In contrast, Kathryn is the signified, an object represented through James's words. She is lost, though, by the end in James's eyes. As he envisions her departure with Tap, James narrates a scene in which Tap and his mother see a red fishing boat on their way to sail out of his life, and the boat is named *Katerina* (134). Literally she is separated from the word that signifies her, her own name, as she is separated from James. Completing this symbolism associated with their family names, when Kathryn and James unite, Paul Maltby informs us that the product of their union's name, "Tap," is a pun on to "tap" into the power of the forms of language that "regenerate perception" (Maltby 502). His name also forms a pun on the tapping of the writer's keyboard, uniting signifier and signifier as both the product and process of writing. So overall, the work of language that is writing has yet to be done, and the question of whether we are saved in the end from terrorist disaster by language's power is open-ended, as is the question of whether James and Kathryn reunite at some future point after the narrative of this novel concludes.

Therefore, the ending of *The Names* is a beginning as well. It is the beginning of a multinovel investigation into mystery of the power of language as it expresses itself against the destructive flow of human history, of the nature and meaning of human life during the late 20th century, when as DeLillo indicates we live in extraordinarily dangerous times. Furthermore, returning to the symbolism of the roles people play in *The Names*, the work of language is not only writing but also reading and interpreting what

Maltby calls "the primal and pristine" (502) language of others. Thus, despite the fact that the novel ends with Tap's original rough draft inspired by Owen's powerful experience of the Kansas preacher, James's role as the narrator/signifier means that we depend upon his narration to understand Tap's rough fiction. Having learned about Owen's Kansas experiences, we can see that Tap has been inspired by the older man's past to write his own work. James is the reader or interlocutor of Tap's language, which itself is an interpretation or "reading" of Owen's words, and so forth. And of course, only such reading of experiences allows James to narrate them. So in order to narrate, one must be a reader or receptor of another's language, of stories. Reading, writing, and narrating are all work that is necessary to unlock language's power and use it as a moral force for good.

To conclude, *The Names* pits the power of language used creatively against certain destructive forces in history, like predatory capitalism and terrorist response. In a struggle to make a meaningful future that is both personal and political, DeLillo seems to stress that victory is not preordained. Possibly humans won't ever completely command or control language's mystery. Language is "our offering" (*The Names* 331), concludes Axton, but then that union is gone. If we can't read the names we write all over reality, though, disaster could be the result. Such is the situation of DeLillo's character Jack Gladney when a train accident toxically poisons him with a chronic and dangerous illness in *White Noise*.

Rightly, *White Noise* has been referred to as DeLillo's breakout book. Receiving the National Book Award in 1986, the novel propelled Don DeLillo to higher acclaim nationally and internationally as a major fiction writer. This unusual satire of American academic life thrust DeLillo into a brighter academic spotlight too. January 2006 saw the publication of the MLA guidebook *Approaches to Teaching* White Noise, indicating the book's wide circulation in college classrooms. Here, DeLillo continues using the technique of the first person narrator but creates a character more eccentric and unique perhaps than James Axton, with absurdly hilarious results. More importantly, though, DeLillo's follow-up to *The Names* connects logically in many ways with the themes introduced in the prior book. As we read over the plot and characters of this book, we will note how DeLillo portrays loyal family relationships as central to the resolution of conflict in *White Noise*. Furthermore, several thematic components add to the value of reading *White Noise*. Centering one's personal sense of self-worth on financial net worth is not a good thing for these characters. Secondly, a major concern in *White Noise* is the protection of the sanctity of the natural environment. As with *The Names*, DeLillo shows us that private corporate interests trump a sense of moral responsibility in the typical American simulated response to natural disaster in the novel. The power of the mass media to subvert our rational response to crisis is also presented through the perspectives of the main character and his four children in a blended family. Just as with *The Names*, DeLillo then returns to his more hopeful theme of the power of language as it sustains people during a crisis. Finally there is a twist, though, on the relationship between language and religion in *White Noise*. While critic Paul Maltby will help us see the transcendent power of language in *White Noise*, religion in this book is also a force for good. Specifically in the character of a Catholic nun who cares for the protagonist, religion takes the form of social responsibility, good language in action as opposed to an oppressive mask over the power of language as was the case in the analysis of *The Names* in the prior chapter. While people make mistakes or deliberately misuse language, the socially responsible exercise of religion as charity can create for people a morally correct perspective, becoming a vehicle for language's life-affirming power.

White Noise is the satirical story of Dr. Jack Gladney, a vacuous academic egotist who teaches a little-known field that he invented: Hitler studies. His place of employment is called the "College-on-the-Hill" and is located in the fictional town of Blacksmith. Four-times married, Jack has difficulty keeping track of his diverse children in the comically complex blended house of six: his wife Babette, and Heinrich (14), Denise (11), Stephanie (9), and Wilder (2 and a half). The Gladneys are a blended family, with each of the children having another natural parent living outside the home. Jack also has two other daughters who live outside the Gladney home, Bee (12) and Mary Alice (19). They watch television together every Friday night and are bombarded by a constant stream of advertisements and media messages. Even though by no means a stress-free life, Jack's existence is relatively uneventful until a train accident causes a lethally dangerous dispersal of the toxic chemical Nyodene D, a derivative of pesticide production. This poisonous cloud forces a nine-day evacuation, and the Gladneys begin to fear for their lives, with Babette nearly unable to wake up at one point (156). Upon examination by Dr. Sundar Chakravarty, Jack learns of the potentially fatal chronic tumor that he has as a result of contact with the Nyodene "D" gaseous cloud. He begins a desperate search for the meaning of his life, conversing frequently with his colleagues Murray J. Siskind, Alphonse Stomponato, and Winnie Richards about his condition, the fear of death, and other relevant issues. Upon learning of his wife's addiction to Dylar, a psychotropic drug that represses the fear of death, Jack becomes fascinated by the drug's impact on the mind. He also learns that his wife has been trading sex with a drug dealer named Willie Mink in exchange for her supply of Dylar. Given a Zumwalt automatic German pistol by Babette's visiting father, Vernon Dickey, Jack resolves to shoot the man who has ruined his marriage. Their gun battle leaves each man wounded and in the care of nuns at a Catholic hospital. Perhaps intellectually numbed by his experiences or perhaps simply accepting his illness, Jack finally spends more time with his stepson, Wilder, and Babette, gazing at the distant colorful cloud from the highway overpass overlooking their town, no longer anxious over the future to come.

Looking more closely at the characters that inhabit this town, some conflict emerges in the form of familial and collegial relationships. It stands to reason that resolution would involve these relationships also. Our main character, Dr. Jack Gladney, is greatly troubled by his complete ignorance of German, becoming reclusive and antisocial and finally "living on the edge of a landscape of vast shame" (31). To compensate for his ethnic and professional inadequacy, Gladney's chancellor advises Jack to change his name to "J.A.K." Gladney, a wealthier-sounding moniker that "intimated dignity, significance and prestige" (16). When the college town of Blacksmith suffers the toxic waste accident, Jack contracts a fatal tumor when poisoned by the insoluble toxin Nyodene D. This situation forces him to reevaluate his lifestyle and priorities and explore a number of means of coping with his fear of death. Above all, throughout his search, Jack remains "the man who wants genuinely to understand some timeless human riddle" (194)—the unspeakable mystery of innocent human suffering, death, or evil.

So he does not go it alone. Joining him in coping with the reality of human suffering is Jack's fourth wife, Babette. Unfortunately, Babette becomes preoccupied with caring for him and their children and doing other selfless tasks such as reading aloud to an old man or volunteering to teach living skills to senior citizens. It is not until after the toxic accident poisons him that Jack receives some shocking revelations. Babette's depressed and has become addicted to the psychiatric drug Dylar, which represses the fear of death. As the codependent facilitator of everyone else's needful behaviors, Babette's decline has a dramatic impact on the family, especially Jack, Steffie, and Denise. Her reaction to a surprise visit from her father shows that she is in many ways still immaturely attached to his approval. Yet Babette grieves mightily at the revelation of Jack's fatal illness, coupled with guilt at her own betrayal of him. But as they endure through the end of the novel, Babette seems to kick Dylar. One can examine the degree of her recovery.

With two self-absorbed parents, their relationship to the children of the household becomes an issue. Both Babette and Jack share a concern for Jack's 14-year-old son Heinrich. He has a precociously receding hairline, as if he has already begun to physically resemble Heinrich Himmler, which is perhaps to be expected for a boy whose father teaches "Hitler studies." Heinrich is alternately described as "evasive and moody" and even as "disturbingly compliant" (22). That his emotional state may be a symptom of repressed violence is his mother Babette's worry. Intelligent to the point of boredom, the young man is the kind of adolescent who needs a challenging project to channel his mental energy. Yet he appears to come of age in terms of self-assertion in Jack's eyes when giving a speech about the toxic effects of Nyodene D, the poisonous gas that is dispersed during the accident forming the main event of the novel. By the end of *White Noise*, Heinrich has maintained his philosophical skepticism. His skeptical outlook turns out to be strength of this character as he turns it toward his daredevil friend Orest Mercador, agreeing with his Dad that Orest is on a fool's quest. Another factor that potentially is strength for Heinrich is his mother Janet Savory, who has taken the Hindu name "Mother Devi." Heinreich's mother is kind and polite to Jack when she calls and offers to take Heinrich to her ashram for the summer. Though Jack is cold, she remains compassionate, and Heinrich might benefit from her gentleness during the proposed summer visit (272).

Weaker is the next in line in the Gladneys' blended family: Denise, the daughter of Babette and pathetic Bob Pardee. At the tender age of 11, this poor girl's face is already an "expert mask" restraining her emotions of "exasperation" (41). Her constant criticism of her mother can be seen as a response to Bob Pardee's demise, a projection of this repressed grief and anger. One of DeLillo's more tragic characters, she suffers from the toxic effects of the accident but does not trust her parents enough to share them. The only way in which Denise shows compassion is to her younger stepsister, assuming a motherly role since Babette is often preoccupied. Denise exhibits symptoms of toxic waste poisoning pretty frequently after the accident yet survives with her mother and stepfather. We last see her involved with her younger sibling Stephanie's efforts to keep Jack clean of Dylar.

In contrast to Denise, Stephanie Rose is dependent and suffers somewhat more from neglect than the older siblings. She's the child of Jack and the well-read Dana Breedlove, who reviews books for the CIA. The fact that Jack and Dana tried repeatedly to work out their relationship may have led to her daughter's heightened emotional sensitivity (213).

Stephanie is compassionate and perceptive enough to notice Babette's drug addiction and throws away the Dylar to keep Jack from indulging his addiction to the fear-reducing narcotic. Stephanie cares more about things than her older half-sister does, so she is the last to remove her gas mask during the accident. Fortunately, Stephanie gets to leave Blacksmith to spend some time with her mother. Stephanie is the younger sister of Jack and Dana's grown daughter Mary Alice (236), an environmentalist and potential hero of this story. She has some options that Denise unfortunately does not have.

Finally is Jack and Babette's two-year-old son Wilder. This boy is in fact neglected by his narcissistic and pleasure-seeking parents, as is indicated by their perennial question to each other, "Where's Wilder?" and by his unexplained crying for seven hours before the toxic accident. Jack does feel strongly about this baby of the family, but that may be because he "sense[s]" the toddler's "total ego, his freedom from limits" (289). Yet the parents must compensate for his inability to care for himself, and for most of the novel Jack and Babette do not do so. Like Denise, Wilder does not have the option of turning to an alternate mother figure like Heinrich and Stephanie have.

Instead of focusing on correcting his relationships to Babette, the children, and stepchildren when his quest for life's meaning overwhelms him, Jack turns to his colleagues. One is Murray Siskind, Professor of Elvis Studies, Murray's philosophical debates and inquiries with Gladney echo the cultural insights of postmodernists, willing to dismiss any search for truth for the sake of the pure pleasure of the chase. Jealous of Jack at the outset of the novel, Murray lusts after Babette, taking her hand in the grocery store (29) and also after the power and prestige Jack enjoys as his academic program of Hitler studies has been so successful (11). Though Murray claims to be happy, he pursues women pretty relentlessly, not getting married many times like Jack but rather falling "apart at the sight of long legs" (11). He is seen chatting with some prostitutes at the scene of the toxic waste event. Murray's conversations with Jack are relevant to important themes in *White Noise*, such as the power of the media to alter reality via the production of images. What Murray attempts to do with Elvis studies is an example of that power to reproduce "a structure with countless substructures" (12). Also, his reaction to Jack's struggle with death after the toxic spill is peculiarly detached: "Better you than me" (293). He goads Jack on like Heinrich does, with skeptical, Socratic questions, but seems not to really accept any answers. Perhaps his questions and challenges to Jack are naught but "hollow sounds," like those he makes drawing air on his pretentious pipe (291). If so, then Murray's friend's search for the purpose of his truncated life is pointless. It does not seem that this relationship can resolve conflict for Jack satisfactorily.

Jack's internist's hopeful, cheerful outlook is contrastive to Jack's bleak outlook on his own terminal condition. At the end of the novel, Jack refuses Dr. Chakravarty's calls (325). The data regarding his condition only reminds him of the urgent need to find life's purpose. Rather than focus on the facts of his disease, Jack turns to his supervisor, Dr. Alphonse "Fast Food" Stompanato. Assertive to a fault, his "bearish" reaction to Jack's possibly fatal tumor is yet another diatribe about Jack's need for greater social power, which to him is reflected in choosing a better known internist than Chakravarty. But more power is not an option for the dying Jack, nor is another internist. Like Siskind, Stompanato does not offer a successful suggestion to help Jack straighten out his relationships.

Ex-girlfriends only seem to complicate Jack's empty and materialistic life sometimes. For example there is Tweedy Browner, one of Jack's ex-wives and mother of his daughter Bee. Tweedy attempts to reactivate her romance with Jack, arriving on DeLillo's stage in the de rigueur schoolgirl ensemble of "Shetland sweater and penny loafers." Meeting Jack in an airport to hand over custody of their daughter for his turn (named "Bee" like the flying creature), she says: "Barring mechanical failures, turbulent weather and terrorist acts, an aircraft travelling at the speed of sound may be the last refuge of gracious living and civilized manners known to man" (93). In a pre-9/11 novel centered on a disastrous technical accident (the toxic waste spill or "airborne toxic event"), Tweedy's naïve infatuation with Jack's power and that of the doomed aircraft is an uproarious satire of the values and upper-class sensibilities of "gracious living." As DeLillo scholar Arthur Saltzman might put it, her sensibilities are simply "consumption brought to a higher altitude" (303). In the wake of their separation Tweedy has taken up with Malcolm, an intelligence agent whom she never sees. She suffers from the same elitism plaguing the other characters like Bob Pardee, numbing her fear of death through embracing a materialistic, upper-class "jet set" lifestyle.

Lastly, a final attempt to resolve relationship conflicts emerge in the thoughtless alternative answer to Jack's question provided by Vernon Dickey. Babette's natural father, Vernon is a transient and rugged guy who would feel perfectly at home in a country line dance or a mechanic's shop. He makes an already troubled Jack feel even less adequate with his workman's hands, "scarred, notched...permanently seamed with grease and mud" (244). Refreshingly pragmatic in a world full of impractical people,

Vernon at least raises the question that is perhaps on readers' minds: "Were people this dumb before television?" (249). Yet, his faith in macho vanity gets the best of him, Jack, and Babette. For as he sees Jack's weakened ego, he offers him a German handgun, a Zumwalt automatic (254) with which Jack hopes to recover some of his hurt pride by shooting the man with whom Babette betrayed him late in the novel, Willie Mink. Mink, the pusher of Dylar, is vaguely described by Jack as having a "spoon-shaped face" (307) as though consumption of narcotics has completely possessed and distorted his personal identity. He speaks in absurd non sequiturs, frequently interspersing some TV commercial slogans into his attempts at normal conversation with Jack. Out of touch with reality, Mink yet survives Jack's attempt on his life. Vernon's attempt to help Jack has a disastrous outcome nonetheless. So unless Jack can right the wrongs in his relationships, he is out of luck.

Instead of a violent political struggle over the resources of developing countries overseas as in *The Names*, here in *White Noise* we are in America competing over the "invisible turf" of ideas, besieged not so much by the imported violence of colonialism but rather by the familiar panic of bureaucratic response to preventable environmental disasters. There are many themes evoked and treated by Don DeLillo in *White Noise*. First, the idea that basing your self-worth on wealth has disastrous consequences for several characters. Another theme related to the search for personal value is how the sanctity of the natural environment has been damaged by human irresponsibility and its resultant damage. Third, DeLillo displays how Americans shamefully react to such damaging consequences of irresponsibility through creating simulations. But lest we abandon hope due to our misinformed social priorities, the final theme of the power of religion as an important aspect of the power of language returns even more prominently than in *The Names*. DeLillo will show us a more positive image of institutional religious faith. This dynamic image in turn reflects the power of language to resolve the sense of life's meaninglessness that subsumes the too-comfortable life of Jack Gladney in *White Noise*.

Let's examine the theme of basing your personal sense of self-worth on money, class status, or power. Before the toxic waste accident wreaks utter havoc in their lives, it seems that for Jack and the people in his life, loss of money and economic class status is the worst thing that can happen to a person. Babette's ex-husband Bob Pardee (53–56) is such a tragic figure, with his "hangdog look" implying a physical illness, though the cause of his death is not actually specified. Bob suffers a financial decline and overreacts by constantly stressing recreation to cover his loss, practicing golf swings constantly and taking the children out for donuts (58).

While Bob Pardee's retreat into hedonism to numb the loss of economic power kills him, in the case of Tweedy Browner, the "ex" is locked into immature role of "schoolgirl," arriving on DeLillo's stage in the de rigueur ensemble of "Shetland sweater and penny loafers" (84–85). Her new husband is not available to her, being constantly away on business. So like Bob Pardee she carries an aura of physical sickness and economic deprivation, her classy schoolgirl clothes being covered in "cigarette ash" (85). These characters live on the skids, desperately grasping at the straws of their once-privileged lives (Tweedy says, "God...we good together" to a bewildered Gladney) to form an ironic and sad foreshadowing of the more serious and steep decline Jack will soon endure. Losing money is the worst thing that can happen to a person in *White Noise*; that is, until the specter of other threats, like our damaging the environment, loom larger. Yet it seems that ignoring these larger dangers only takes the form of a reaction formation; the more one loses money and its power the more one seems to worship it. Tweedy also expresses this in her feelings about classy air travel, another symbol of the upper-class lifestyle. In a pre-9/11 insight centered on accidents, Tweedy's naïve infatuations with Jack and with air power form an uproarious satire of class-based sensibilities of "gracious living." In all, these white characters center their personal identity and sense of self-worth on their net financial worth and prospects.

Here in *White Noise* we can't ignore the vital theme of the sanctity of the natural environment. J.A.K. and friends give nary a thought to Mother Earth prior to the train wreck. The toxic cloud is frighteningly described as a "dark and bulky menace...a national promotion for death" (158). But the level of denial that the Gladneys display represents how ignorant we are of the ecological damage we can cause. Jack, Babette, and the kids dally for several minutes over canned peaches and sponge cake while the fire department urges immediately evacuation from the "cloud of deadly chemicals" (119). Relevant and topical as always, DeLillo is portraying in novel form an experience evocative of the chemical spill in Bhopal India, the fault of Union Carbide. In the early hours of December 3, 1984, methyl isocyanine (MIC) gas leaked from the Union Carbide India Limited (UCIL) plant in Bhopal, India. According to the state government of Madhya Pradesh, "approximately 3,800 people died and several thousand other individuals experienced permanent or partial disabilities" (Union Carbide 1).

Unlike that situation, no one attempts to offer a settlement or take responsibility for what has happened in Blacksmith. Instead, SIMUVAC contractors descend on the town to take data to simulate more fake accidents before the next one occurs. DeLillo is making a political statement here; the American social priority is to capitalize on tragedies almost as a reaction formation. The simulations prepare us for the next occurrence, but they make such occurrences more likely as we do not address the causes of the event. Rather than raise questions about the need for pesticides or the safety of railroad transportation of toxins, we hasten to the next tragedy. SIMUVAC is a private corporation working for profit much like Blackwater, the paramilitary contractors sent into New Orleans after the flooding caused by Hurricane Katrina. The SIMUVAC men are quite a mercenary band, with one contractor examining Jack's Nyodene tumor and disclosing no information to him at all. This one is described as having "the innocent prewar look of a rural murderer" (140) evoking again the historical image of Blackwater as in the paramilitary mercenaries that populate *Running Dog*. Jack recognizes that "terrifying data is now an industry in itself" (175). Jack is displeased with SIMUVAC's taking data on his fatal condition. In a surreal scene, a representative of "Advanced Disaster Management, a private consulting firm that conceives and operates simulated evacuations" (205) appears to conduct simulated drills in the middle of this actual toxic waste disaster! All in a day's work, as the matter of environmental damage is simply a "business" to capitalize on rather than a chance to improve American society. *White Noise* shows how our poor priorities cause failure to address such damage appropriately.

The power of the media to create fake events also is an important issue in *White Noise*. To capture the point about how extensive TV saturation (the Gladneys' set blares constantly in the background) manifests TV's "diseased brain-sucking power" (16), DeLillo makes use of an entirely original technique to convey a narrative point of view. Interruptive TV and radio voices blare through Jack's reflections, Steffie's words, and the plot action as a whole. Though looking on the surface like absurd non sequiturs, these "literary sound bites" actually elaborate on the plot and conditions of the characters. To give an example, in chapter 14, Jack is anxious about his ignorance of German once again. This time he is insecure about whether his knowledge of the language will be enough to demonstrate "uniqueness in world scholarship" (61), certainly hard to do if one cannot communicate with a group of international Hitler scholars conveys on his campus. The TV set blares in with, "And other trends which could dramatically impact your portfolio" (61). The commentary on Jack's condition is that his lack of a truly sophisticated fluency in German above and beyond mere conversational skills in the language could create a "trend" that could cause him to lose his job and thereby dramatically impact his financial portfolio. Furthermore, Jack's false mastery of German is only one among more destructive "other trends" about to cast a toxic shadow over his same campus.

Other blaring media sound bites punctuate the novel. Such a unique narrative invention of DeLillo's brilliantly conveys the heart of the problem illustrated in *White Noise*. In the post-crisis environment of the novel, Jack can't distinguish any rational causes of his condition, or as he states, "Remarks existed in a state of permanent fluctuation. No one thing was either more or less plausible than any other thing" (129). This inability to make sense of crisis is imitative of the nonsensical flow of televised sounds constantly and intrusively floating through TV: from sports to commercials and back to the QVC shopping network. The point of view in *White Noise* is that television, simulated reality, creates crisis by interrupting our natural mental process of recognizing the real cause of things, until we accidently create situations too complex to analyze. Then all one can do is react incoherently, as Jack does, and leave thinking behind in favor of more television. Nine days after the explosion, with toxic fumes still in their lungs, citizens of Blacksmith funnel from the shelter to home and then to the supermarket, where they hear the commercial voices still blaring: "Dristan Ultra, Dristan Ultra" (167).

With so many harmful factors found in *White Noise*, such as economic discrimination, environmental destruction, and the dumbing-down power of mass media, in what can the Gladneys, and we the readers, take hope? We found in *The Names* that the ultimate life-affirming power is language, the ability to name things and thus give us a handle on the world. But in *White Noise*, DeLillo delves into more detail about this transcendent power of words. Speaking about this, fellow DeLillo reader Paul Maltby discusses Stephanie's murmuring in her sleep and how Jack reacts in his essay, "The Romantic Metaphysics of Don DeLillo" (498–518). Here, Maltby turns to Stephanie's murmuring, "Toyota Celica, Toyota Celica" in her sleep and Jack's reaction that Stephanie's talking in her sleep is "a profound, revelatory utterance" (501), and takes Jack's reaction to her as DeLillo's viewpoint that Steffie's words show "a moment of splendid transcendence" (*White Noise* 155). Maltby may be partly right when he claims that DeLillo "wants to remind us that names are often invested with a significance that exceeds their immediate, practical function" (Maltby 501).

However, if he is right, one needs to trace this very important transcending significance through DeLillo's text, since one moment alone does not show the power of language. Maltby is not interested in Toyota product names per se, as he states, "The point of the passage is not that 'Toyota Celica' is the signifier of a commodity (and as such has only illusory significance as a visionary utterance) but that *as a name* it has a mystical significance and power" (501). Yet if we look at the writings of traditional mystics like Christians who believe that God is at least in the power of language, the significance of visionary words is never completely an illusion. As when Jesus Christ tells the parable of the Prodigal Son, the "immediate practical function" of the simple naming words, their everyday imperfection, is indispensible to their conveying of a transcending significance.

Therefore, DeLillo frequently adds significance to Toyota names referred to in *White Noise*. If the name of the old ultra-reliable Toyota Celica has become a name symbolic of language's transcendent power, Steffie's conversation with her family later takes on greater significance:

[Jack says:] Hot and cold are words. Think of them as words. We have to use words. We can't just grunt..."
"It's called the sun's corolla," Denise said to Steffie in a separate discussion. "We saw it the other night on the weather network."
"I thought Corolla was a car," Steffie said.
"Everything's a car," Heinrich said. (233)

This exchange among the Gladney kids ties into the references in Steffie's dream talk. Steffie is both correct and incorrect in her interpretation of the word "corolla" as referring to a Toyota, and her older stepsister is closer to the truth with her own interpretation, her own important mistake. Denise is pointing out to Steffie the very polyvalence of words, the fact that a word like "corolla "can mean two different things. Corolla means not only the still reliable Toyota car but also signifies flower petals and in the case of the children's mispronunciation, here evokes the sun's corona, or upper part of the atmosphere surrounding the sun. Even Denise's mistake becomes important: the sun's *corona as a "corolla"* evokes the petal-like superheated flares that constant burst out over the spherical surface of the sun, fires that the ever-skeptical Heinrich (note his dismissive tone used toward his sister) goes on to compare to the explosions of Russian nuclear missiles. These everyday imperfections, this series of children's mistakes, leads us to an important symbolic association in *White Noise*. Because they are polyvalent, words can have multiple meanings; for example, an "airborne toxic event" can be a toxic waste accident or the mushroom clouds of a nuclear holocaust. And the missiles, like Toyotas, were and are a product people put their faith in to prevent the very conflict they may precipitate. Certainly, language has a transcendent power, but the power seems contingent upon the facts of daily life, even of our mistakes. If we have any hope of surviving our current potential for the dangerous mistakes of toxic warfare and toxic accidents, then as the Gladneys' father figure Jack says, "We have to use words," and do so with care. Even if they are partly mistaken or illusory, they are vehicles, pun intended, of greater significance.

However, we have no guarantees of a future without gaffes or the misuse of language to help us transcend some negative conditions. In my analysis of *The Names*, I have suggested that DeLillo's vision of religion therein was a poor substitute for the power of language, a form of group hypnosis in which our impulse to identify life's ineffable mystery renders us into an easily corruptible "delirium" (as in *The Names* 276) and leaves us ready to follow demagogues into self-destructive battles. In *White Noise*, however, this vision of the relationship between transcendent language and mainstream religion is different. In Blacksmith, identifying or naming the ineffable mystery is still a concern to Jack and his friends. His terminal condition of having a tumor from the Nyodene D has made the issue of finding life's meaning all the more critical. His own life may come to an abrupt and unplanned end. Discussing the matter with another eternal skeptic, Murray Siskind, Jack is needled as usual by this colleague's line of questioning. They identify the religious impulse, the need to name or put into perspective the "whole huge nameless thing" (288) as being driven by the fear of death. Death is Jack's fear, of course, but in many ways shared by all, because as Murray accurately notes, "We're all aware there's no escape from death" (288). Because Jack and Murray are American academics, though, using religion to resolve their need to identify in words the meaning of life's ineffable mystery is not an option, completely "off the table." So here in *White Noise* religion could be more than simply mass group hysteria, but not from the point of view of most professors at the "College-on-the-Hill."

Yet here is where DeLillo puts institutional religion right back on the literary table. Manifesting itself as a form of faith in the power of language, the Catholic religion becomes not just a social grouping but a form of inspired moral action for good. For the first time in these major novels, DeLillo presents readers with a highly recognizable representative of a major religion: Sr. Hermann Marie. She is a hospital nurse at the ward where Jack and Mink are taken after the gun battle and reprimands him for his insincerity in questioning her faith. Offering no emotional panacea to Jack's philosophic quest, she is a stronger character than Winnie and will not be embarrassed at her inability or failure to address his neediness. Both he and Mink are taken to "Mother of Mercy, Commiseration and Rapport" Hospital. Her charitable action stands in stark contrast to her refusal to brook Jack's philosophical interrogation of her faith. Experiencing her care helps Jack along in terms of conversion, as after this event and the toxic waste accident, the image-conscious professor becomes more unselfish as he stops spending so much time watching television with his family (16) and more time outdoors watching the sunset pensively (324).

But to contrast this, *White Noise* is not exactly resolved in terms of whether this language or faith in it guarantees the desired transcendence. Even though the nun in this chapter of *White Noise* primarily forms a good image of the power of language in charitable action, she is a bit brusque with Jack, calling him "dumb head," so one can read her character negatively as well, a skeptical sister who does not really believe in the good work she does. Whether she knows it or not, her acts of responsible charity are the most effective in the novel in terms of changing Jack's priorities and outlook on life. We will look at her character again in chapter 6 on DeLillo's treatment of Roman Catholicism as an example of the contemporary crisis of subjectivity.

Religion gets a more favorable treatment here in *White Noise* than it did in *The Names*. Language's great power to affirm life and give it meaning is seen in terms of inspired action, a correction of human mistakes in the signifying events we make of such language. Reading Tolstoy and receiving charity, Jack moves beyond egocentric ambition. As we see in the treatment of Sr. Hermann Marie and in DeLillo's reference to Tolstoy's Ivan Ilyich, moral action and correct priorities like protecting our natural environment are vital. They displace bad values and actions such as greed, creating simulations, and basing one's worth on economic status or other superficial condition. Language's power properly used thus offers us a way out of the harmful impacts of mass media and environmental crisis in *White Noise*.

Unresolved is whether we will take that way out, climb that moral overpass and pass over our emotional messes, like Jack and Babette attempt to do. Beyond the laughter, tears, and hope of *White Noise* we still can't with surety know that the Gladneys live happily ever after. The power of language is clearly introduced in both *The Names* and *White Noise*, but we are still left with the mystery of "the whole huge nameless thing" (288) in both novels—the unresolved horror of unknown languages in *The Names*, the dark though fading cloud in *White Noise*. But if we fail in our quest for knowing or in our charitable action, this nameless thing beyond words may not be good for us at all. It may be an unspeakable evil instead. As we continue our study of DeLillo's novels, a truly historically real "toxic event," the shooting of beloved President John F. Kennedy, becomes the starting point for examining the unspeakable as evil in three later DeLillo novels. Here, media's power to encompass our attempts to identify ourselves in language will triumph in *Cosmopolis*, *Mao II*, and *Libra*.

_____ *Chapter 4* _____

Unspeakable Evil in *Libra*, *Mao II*, and *Cosmopolis*

DeLillo's *Libra*, a fictionalizing of the assassination of President John F. Kennedy, can properly be referred to as a dystopia. As far as its major theme goes, *Libra* provides us with an example of the theme of unspeakable evil. A definition of the concept "the Unspeakable" that can readily guide us comes from James W. Douglass's 2008 nonfiction treatment of exactly the same event DeLillo portrays in his novel *Libra*. *JFK and the Unspeakable: Why He Died and Why It Matters* is a book about the assassination of President John F. Kennedy on November 22, 1963, written as a direct and data-supported history of that killing, positing as objective truth what Don DeLillo's *Libra* is limited to suggesting: that the death of Kennedy was the result of a conspiracy and that the "lone gunman theory," posited by the Warren Commission Report, which DeLillo apparently had access to during the composition of *Libra*, is not accurate. Yet historical accuracy is not necessarily a priority in studying historically inspired novels. What's important here is that Wallace gives us the useful definition of "the Unspeakable" of Thomas Merton, a well-known Trappist monk and 1960s intellectual who communicated with the former president's sister-in-law, Ethel Kennedy, over his concerns about foreign policy events that emerged during Kennedy's administration. To quote Douglass, "'The Unspeakable' is a term [Merton] coined at the heart of the sixties after JFK's assassination—in the midst of the escalating Vietnam War, the nuclear arms race, and the further assassinations of Malcolm X, Martin Luther King Jr., and Robert Kennedy. In each of these... Merton sensed an evil whose depth and deceit seemed to go beyond the capacity of words to describe" (Douglass xv). Perceptive thinkers like Merton realized that the destruction threatening our planet and the horrible will manifesting itself in the killing of a man who helped prevent that destruction at one point (John F. Kennedy) needed to be written about. Merton added that our culture at his time "was stricken to the very core of its being by the presence of the Unspeakable" but that courage and compassion of heart could lead us to challenge and confront such evil (Douglass xv). Beginning with the very same event that led Merton and Douglass to contemplate these matters of unspeakable evil and compassionate response—Kennedy's assassination—DeLillo's *Libra* signals such a challenge, concerned not so much with a factual investigation of the conspiracy or precise record but with chasing down an understanding of unspeakable evil. Thus, to a degree, DeLillo's work challenges us to attain a better understanding of how and why such things happen.

Furthermore, *Libra* itself is but a beginning point for DeLillo's work on the unspeakable. Paralleling the subject-destroying action of *Libra*, we will see in this chapter how *Mao II* and *Cosmopolis* posit a similar total eclipse of the subject's power to process his own identity by virtue of media's all-encompassing influence. These three novels are powerfully juxtaposed, even though *Cosmopolis* is a later work. The attitudes of each protagonist in his narcissistic embrace of a media construct to replace personal identity produce the same disastrous result in each novel.

One of the most frequently quoted lines in Don DeLillo's oeuvre of work is "There is a tendency of plots to move toward death," which is one of Win Everett's reflections in *Libra* (221). Reading this historical novel based roughly on the plot to kill John Kennedy, we are committed to agree. *Libra* is the story of the assassination from primarily the point of view of Lee Harvey Oswald but is interspersed with other viewpoints as well, including that of Oswald's mother Marguerite. *Libra* begins with Lee Harvey Oswald's troubled youth in the Bronx and ends with the assassination of the man.

DeLillo does a brilliant job of not revising history as we know it. First we see the shots fired from Oswald's point of view in the book depository, and then coconspirator Raymo charges in from the grassy embankment, driven into position by partner Frank Vasquéz to complete the diabolical assassination (*Libra* 397). In this scene at no point does DeLillo attempt to finalize an answer to the question of the shots still being debated by historians today. Raymo leaves the scene with Frank in a surreal sequence interspersed with passages imitating the flow of speech on walkie-talkies and shouts of the police and Secret Service (403). The man who will be charged with shooting Kennedy shoots the police officer, stopping him with his .38, firing four shots. Coconspirator Wayne Elko sits prepared to kill Oswald in the

Texas Theater. As Elko looks on in this movie house, police finally tackle and apprehend Lee Harvey Oswald where ironically the upcoming feature is called *War Is Hell* (413). Captured and taken to jail, Oswald feels that he will be released if he can come up with a convincing enough story for the police. Realizing he has been made into "the dupe of history" by the conspirators, he stands ready to betray them and "name every name" (418). The second key historic episode of the novel, the killing of Oswald, occurs in the following section, titled "In Dallas." Here, Jack Ruby's mob superior Jack Karlinsky persuades him that the man who "gets Oswald" will become a great American hero. Jack Ruby is another Oswald in terms of his possession by the unspeakable evil of a complete media-eclipsing of his ability to self-define. A Jew himself, Ruby fears that the assassination was an attempt to incriminate American Jews for political reasons. Karlinsky says that in exchange for Ruby's "getting" of the incarcerated killer, mob boss Latta will forgive Ruby's "vig loan" (433). Ruby's shooting Oswald is presented in the form of the radio broadcast of the event as it was heard (438). On the November 25, the funeral of Lee Harvey Oswald is recounted. The service had been cancelled unbeknownst to the only mourners: his brother Robert, mother Marguerite, and their two baby girls. Marguerite is convinced in her paranoia that no Lutheran minister could be found to pray over her son's body. She also reflects that "it is the murderers who need a church. Isn't this what Jesus teaches?" (449).

Libra's treatment of the Cold War raises the very significant question of Oswald as representative of the individual in history, the measure of the contemporary person as the impact of media technologies affects his journey toward self-definition. Critic Jeremy Green calls attention to DeLillo's characterizing of Lee Harvey Oswald not so much as the prototypical American as the ultimate individualist, trying very consciously to write his life into history. To this, Green adds his opinion that DeLillo also lends credence to the possibility of the "official lone gunman story" (Green qtd. in Duvall 7) by presenting DeLillo's stylized representation of DeLillo's character of Lee Harvey Oswald as a cultural prototype of the "the violent loner" (Green 97) like the troubled gunmen who caused tragedies on the campuses of Virginia Tech and Northern Illinois University. Green picks up on the description DeLillo provides of Oswald where DeLillo states that after Oswald, cheap and easy access to credit cards, handguns, and open public spaces like the campus or small town mall combine to create a perfect storm of expression of violent rage and instant notoriety for expressing such rage (*Libra* 181). While it may be true that it was this perfect combination of factors that tempted or deluded the mad killer Oswald into thinking he could attain such heroic status by performing such a despicable act, I doubt that this is DeLillo's main point. Green along with fellow Cambridge scholar John Duvall puts forth the idea that Oswald's instant celebrity status as a "violent loner" gives credence to the theory that the gunman acted alone on that fateful Dallas day. However, to see DeLillo's *Libra* as only a defense of the lone gunman theory is a complete misreading. For one reason, DeLillo himself introduces the idea of the second gunman in the new introduction to the 2006 edition of this great novel: "In *Libra* there he is, the second shooter, a man with a name, a face and a nationality" (*Libra* ix). In contrast, DeLillo's intense focus on the individual mind of Oswald is part of the dystopia the author creates. Lee Harvey Oswald's semi-Oedipal obsession with making his own permanent mark on history forms a worst-case scenario intersection of the individual psyche and the social force of history. No freedom from its unspeakable power is possible in this novel's terms, and certainly this leaves open the possibility of conspiracy.

In the same introduction, DeLillo reflects on "the tremendous bruising force of history" (*Libra* x) as yielding to us a world where the image has become more important than "the blood," which is "thick and real," and the precision of the Zapruder film in its digitally remastered form becomes the standard by which we judge the importance of an event like John F. Kennedy's assassination. If we search merely for the precise explanation of the conspiracy, we tend to forget that "we are also dealing with human beings here" (xi). The "war of images" so to speak, takes on human casualties in the novel, and the bruises are felt by those living the event.

As mentioned above, Lee Harvey's mother Marguerite Oswald emerges in very important ways in the backdrop of the novel. Her presence adds emotional depth and realism to DeLillo's account of this tragedy. Much of Oswald's actions in the novel are a reaction formation against her overbearing presence. He thinks of her as "his mother never-ending" (107) and by this he means that she is unwavering in her obsession with Lee. We get a picture of a dysfunctional close mother/son relationship in which the son has replaced the absent husband (10–11). So repulsed is Oswald by his mother's issues that he uses his lifestyle transitions like joining the marines and even defecting to the Soviet Union as a means to flee from her. When he leaves for Russia, he does not tell his mother, making his wife Marina believe that his mother is dead. Marguerite contacts the State Department to learn of her son's whereabouts (200). However, the mother is not to blame for Oswald's criminality; apart from Marguerite he vents his frustration on his young Russian bride simply because she tries to conform to the standards of an American postwar life by shopping at the local Safeway

(*Libra* 226). The emotional depth Marguerite's presence adds to the treatment of history or historiography by DeLillo allows us to see lesser-known aspects of Oswald's motivation, abusive behavior, and psychological dysfunctions.

Furthermore, Oswald projects his emotional conflicts onto the Cold War, and so as he reads Marx and Lenin he begins to imagine himself as part of a "vast and sweeping" history. Just as DeLillo presents him, Oswald is attempting to assert his identity by losing it in "the struggle" (*Libra* 2) as he puts in, a grand and absolutely determining force of history that he imagines will give him an identity. Of course, this is an extremely faulted premise on which to base one's whole outlook on life and lifestyle choices. What follows is one of three dystopic narratives (*Libra, Mao II,* and *Cosmopolis*) in which the main character, despite living an experience that demonstrates the life-affirming power of language, fails to believe in or act on the belief in this power but rather puts his faith in another force of one sort or another. In the case of *Libra*, Oswald puts his faith in an absolutely powerful history as opposed to language. He attempts to make himself one with this allegedly all-powerful history embraced by Marx and philosophers who follow him. As we have seen in *The Names*, the power of language is involved with the power to represent or name reality. For Oswald, his imagining of himself into this concept of history will prove to be fatal as is indicated first by his failure to actually know himself by any one name. Throughout the text, a virtual catalogue of names that Oswald internalizes emerges; it seems that every different social group Oswald associates with renames and rebrands him in a constant figuration of revolving identities. During his wild youth, the other misfits from his boyhood times in the Bronx call him "Ozzie the Rabbit," as his quirky maneuvering inspires them to. To David Ferrie, the troubled homosexual coconspirator who develops an infatuation for Oswald, the infamous convict is "Leon." When he becomes a Soviet citizen or "true-blue Oswaldovich" (167), the sad, unfortunate Marina and the Russian public at large call him "Alek." Most significantly, Oswald secretly calls himself "Hidell" (90, 101) at his worst moments such as when he is held in the brig for a botched shooting during his otherwise nondescript military career. This last and evocative moniker seems to be a quasi-schizophrenic permutation of "Fidel [Castro]" and "hiding the Id" and "hell" (101). What has happened is that Oswald has developed a shadow-self on which to project socially unacceptable impulses since his mother never taught him how to accept his own imperfections. All these incongruent names add up to a failure to unify his identity. How can Oswald truly make history if he himself is nothing but a mess of contradicting selves?

His bizarre life of revolving names is almost a direct reflection of Stalinist Marxism's view of life as a conflict of forces or "class struggle," with the needs and desires of "Leon" diametrically opposed to those of "Alek," and so on. Oswald is literally multiplied into many fractious and destructive selves. Thus when his own shooting by Jack Ruby is commanded by Ruby's own underworld superior, Ruby is told to "turn him into a crowd" (432), a fatal process begun from deep inside Oswald's psyche.

So the process of losing one's self-identity to a mediated group or collective force is not limited to Oswald alone. Green correctly identifies some of the "truly paranoid" (101) as the ultra-rightists who wind up cherry-picking Oswald to be the fall guy for their scheme. Like the Soviet Aleksei Kirilenko, historically based characters like ex-FBI agent Guy Banister is one of the masterminds behind the group scheme. Selling his plot to Bay of Pigs veteran T. J. Mackey, menacingly referring to "things (Kennedy) has to answer for" (61), he refers to himself and his comurderers of John F. Kennedy as special men: "People like us... we have this dilemma we have to face. Serious men deprived of an outlet. Once we're pushed out, how do we retire to a chair on the lawn? Everyday lawful pursuits don't meet our special requirements." He laughed happily (63).

At least in DeLillo's stylized account of what happened, Guy Banister defines himself as part of an elite group of perpetrators of violence exempt from the standards of morals and legitimacy applicable to most people. Yet Banister is a man among the group who presumes to be fighting for that very decency and morality Americans associate with the capitalist system. Like Oswald, Banister believes in "forces in the air that compel men to act" (68), and though he does not die as notorious a death as Lee Harvey Oswald does, his legacy still is destroyed and fractured through his implication in the death of Kennedy. Therefore like Oswald he has lost self-identity to some of the destructive and impersonal forces he sought to bring to bear on enemies as part of his "special requirements" (63).

As with the case of Guy Banister, multiple profiles of each conspirator demonstrate this similarity between the rightist radical Cold War hawks and Lee Harvey Oswald; each man defines himself in light of a group or collective point of view. Larry Parmenter, the CIA operative who mostly provides cover and had invested money in Cuban businesses when Cuba was a capitalist country under Battista, defines himself basically in terms of the "Groton-Yale-OSS network of so-called gentleman spies... a member, ready to accede to the will of the leadership" (*Libra* 30). Again and again, the point is driven home that these conspirators have "turned themselves into a crowd" with all the destructive meanings that entails for self and others. Even the most experienced combat veteran among them, T. J. Mackey, sees life in terms of his own personal history, a series of past "evasions and betrayals" by the CIA, also a collective "set up to obscure the deeper responsibilities" (69) to self and others. In sum, Oswald and the others all fall prey to a collectivist belief in the absolute power of history, a death-grip of the past.

This collective viewpoint, which subscribes to such pervasive faith in the absolute power of these forces of history, is frequently faulty. This viewpoint is produced by a paranoid imagination. In the troubled paranoiac, we see a subjectivity or individual point of view deeply distorted by both personal and global histories, which seem to offset each other like the balancing of a scale ("Libra" being of course both the astrological sign of the scales and Oswald's personal zodiac sign). Simply to assert the fact of his own inner life Lee Harvey Oswald says to himself, "There is a world within the world" (47), and this refers to subjectivity.

He fails to recognize that we can only create this viewpoint and use this inner mental world to master the world outside through language. His process of self-definition has been terminally subverted by the mediated technologies surrounding him, the desire for 15 minutes of fame. Yet we see very clearly Oswald's failure of language in response to this media subjection, careless yet deliberate: he delays telling Marina that he wants to return to the United States and misspells his deception: *"I still hadn't told my wife"* (205). Doomed to fail, the famed shooter will wind up like most of T. J. Mackey's Bay of Pigs crew, "stranded in the smoke of remote meditations" (*Libra* 71) when Ruby materializes on the scene to play his own short but fatal role in DeLillo's historiographic narrative. To base one's self-identity on the perception of the public group who consumes the record of history is to fall into the unspeakable, since the group can never be relied upon to know the truth of one. He becomes, as is later stated in another DeLillo novel "The Lost Man of History."

As with all the novels we have read in Don DeLillo's body of work, there is a tendency to look for a note of hope, although taking on the Kennedy assassination certain precludes a very positive ending. With the idea of the "Lost Man of History," the female is not necessarily represented, so one can ask about the women who survive. The conclusion of *Libra* picks up on this with references to Lee Harvey Oswald's funeral to Marina and Marguerite. As said above, the novel does end with Marguerite's viewpoint, and by this point readers can see how imbalanced her views are, even comparing herself to the mother of Jesus in that "the mother is neglected" by history and both mothers disappear "from the record once he [the son] is crucified" (453).

It is true that Marguerite and Marina survive these unspeakable acts and horrible set of events, for even the killing of Oswald is presented in tragic terms with Ruby's insanity and cancer subsequent to the second shooting. DeLillo closes with the idea that the power of the name of the real main character belongs to "her and to history" (456).

Without wanting to fall into an accusatory posture about these women or necessarily to glorify them, we can ask whether for example Marina's fate as a character, under Secret Service protection as we last see her, is meant to say something positive about the power of American individualism in the international game of ideological or media-based perceptions. After all, she remains true to her own sense of the good and does not abandon the girls, at least as DeLillo presents her to us in *Libra*. Is her departure from Russia then "all for the best" in some imaginable way?

If so, then this American game not mostly about history but of the world of media images is in play. For her part, Marina has the idea of "a contract and a ghostwriter" (455) as a hope for herself to make something of the tragedy and create a life for herself and the two little girls, June and Rachel. Though Marguerite has much less, complaining at the end of this very fact, she still tasks herself to rewrite history, to move visual images around in the American mind, at the conclusion of *Libra*. If we leave DeLillo's race with the unspeakable here at this novel, it seems that for a change, media can play a positive role. On this note, even DeLillo praises the high-tech methods of investigation now applied to the Zapruder film: "It is possible to image a clear answer" (xi). And for Marguerite, one hopes so.

Finally, for Marina, setting the actual historical record aside, some American "advantage" in the interplay of media images that would result in a freedom-loving, creative individual lifestyle is also imaginable. But it does not always come to pass that a visual image will unite the individual and the redeemed community (such as America). Faith in history yields to faith in the media. In this ongoing chase, even the freedom of the American media does not provide an antidote to the mediated forces subjecting the contemporary individual. In *Mao II*, DeLillo confronts the unspeakable for a second time, no less hopefully. Even an American author the likes of J. D. Salinger cannot seem to wield his pen against it.

In the 2005 book, *Conversations with Don DeLillo*, DeLillo told Vince Pesaro that he had once seen two photographs, one of a mass wedding of 13,000 people in the Unification Church and another photo of J. D. Salinger stalked by paparazzi and finally caught to become the image on the front page of the *New York Post*. Don referred to these two photos, the attack on the great writer's privacy and the hypnotized crowd as "the polar extremes of *Mao II*, the arch individualist and the mass mind" (81). In this clash of opposites, the relative freedom of the American media does not provide an antidote to the unspeakable problems of modern life. Rather, in *Mao II*, DeLillo confronts the unspeakable for a second time and tilts the balance against a hopeful reading of the power of international media as an individual like J. D. Salinger could attempt to wield it. Once again, we will be hit with a dystopic vision in the next novel. Before its inexplicable omission from *The Cambridge Companion*'s list of major novels as those that contributed most to Don DeLillo's reputation, many other major publications gave *Mao II* excellent reviews, noting that DeLillo's gifts had never been put to better use than in this critically and commercially successful PEN/Faulkner Award winning novel. The novel begins from the point of view of Karen, a cult follower of a branch of the Unification Church at a mass wedding that is both her own and that of 13,000 devotees. Her parents, Roger and Maureen, look on helplessly, trying to spot her in the crowd, separated by gender from the future son-in-law they've never met. Karen reflects on how difficult it has been to sell flowers in airports, in "lost landscapes," "Nights downtown" and in "rows of neat homes in crashing rain" (12). The followers of the Master chant in unison, and "the future belongs to crowds" (16). Next, we meet reclusive American novelist Bill Gray: "Bookstores made him slightly sick at times. He looked at the gleaming best-sellers.... He could hear them shrieking *Buy me*" (19). Gray wisely avoids the glare of publicity and is very eager to get his autographing done and leave. He will soon be taken in to a political plot and tempted to use his fame and influence to free a kidnapped French poet. The writer is taken in by his devotee Karen, and ironically like her is defined by a mediated image of what an American writer ought to be. After some drunken carousing, he awakens in his hotel room undressed and remembers his quest to see Jean-Claude (*Mao II* 212). Bill Gray will never make it; he dies of his internal injuries probably combined with alcohol damage, and an old man takes his passport, identification, and all to sell to militia in Beirut. Bereft of his life and identity, Bill has failed on his quest.

Mao II's plot ends literally without a single note of hope: "Isn't there supposed to be an irony...some sense of peculiar human insistence on seeing past the larger madness into small and skewed practicalities, into off-shaded moments that help us consider a narrow hope?" (227) reflects the photographer Brita Nilsson as she tries to find the humor in the macabre stories of her driver as she attempts to photograph terrorist leader Abu Rashid (228). She has quit trying to photograph writers and instead has come full circle to being taken to meet an actual terrorist chief not in the mountains but rather in an epicenter of urban violence. Truly a dystopia, the world of *Mao II* ends in a time in which all writers, "came to a quiet end" (230). Facing direct censorship of her work as Rashid dictates what she can and can't record, there is no possibility for Brita to say or do anything in resistance to the absolute power of the dictator. He even runs schools in which for students "the image of Rashid is their identity" (233). When she raises a complaint, the tyrant's only response is "Don't bring your problems to Beirut" (232). The closing image of the novel, that of an outdoor wedding convoy being escorted by an armed tank, is the final dystopic snapshot we have of the normalizing of violence where terror has replaced art as the ultimate means of self-expression. As flashes of cameras become indistinguishable from phosphorescent bursts of gunfire in Beirut, we see "the dead city photographed one more time" (*Mao II* 241). Brita, Karen, and Bill are all three snuffed out by media reproductivity, the eclipse of the subject by a deluge of the technologized image.

The central metaphor of this novel is a silkscreen reproduction of a drawing of Chinese leader Mao Zedong that is also titled *Mao II*. When Karen and Bill's secretary, Scott Martineau, examine this picture (62), Scott's comment is that Mao does not seem dead because he never seemed real. Clearly, the theme being evoked here is once again, as in *White Noise* and *Libra*, the idea of the power of media simulations as a measure of what is real. But here what is focused on is the uniting of the media image of the individual as a focal point for the group as a cult. The fact that Karen has been deprogrammed from a cult serves as a measure of this power. Karen first appears while at her wedding ceremony with 6,500 other brides, and the content of her thinking reveals that, similar to the conspirators in *Libra*, her self-identity has been completely absorbed in the perceptions of the group or collective force as she "fades into the thousands, the columned mass... They're a world family now.... Master chooses every mate, seeing in a vision how backgrounds and characters match. It is a mandate from heaven, preordained" (10). Of course, this twisted post-hypnotic "vision" leads Karen only to poverty and many other problems. As we have seen in DeLillo's earlier novel, *The Names*, Karen has fallen victim to the same religious "delirium" (*The Names* 276) that in that novel made people more vulnerable to the influence of Emmerich.

However, it would appear to be consistent with other passages in DeLillo's work, like James Axton's successful escape from Iran in *The Names*, for example, or Jack Gladney's coming to some peace with his spouse and situation in *White Noise*, to find some hope in the power of language, especially since the character of Bill Gray clearly fits the mold of the American writer, a singularly powerful conduit of the force of language. Yet this is precisely where the contrast is most clear. Karen, like the grieving Madonna figures of Libra, survives the central tragedy but never really learns to think for herself.

Relying on the power of the juxtaposition of media images has not worked out for these characters. Unless the future of writing—that is, language—is put in the driver's seat, the future does not indeed belong "to her, and to history" (456) as the end of *Libra* implies. Staying with the resolutions of these two novels, Scott Martineau and Karen would be the worst possible "ghostwriters" for a figure like Marina Oswald as presented in *Libra*. In fact, here in *Mao II* the treatment of juxtaposition of media images seems to work against hope for the individual and for society. At many points in *Mao II*, DeLillo portrays the interplay of media images negatively. For example, when Brita visits an exhibit of Warhol-style images of Russian faces, including that of Mikhail Gorbachev, she notes that "it is possible to fuse images" through which the artist's life force is relayed to the viewer or to the reader in the case of literary art, as if "reprocessed through painted chains of being" (134–135). But this reproducibility of art images, a source of hope for Marina and for DeLillo's mother-figure Marguerite Oswald as she resolves at *Libra's* end to save the memory of her son from a vicious history, is in an era where the despot Abu Rashid can truthfully say, "We do history in the morning and change it after lunch" (235). For Brita, this line of reflection "wasn't funny": Warhol's "Dead-White Andy" is used to describe what happens to the individual artist in *Mao II's* simulated world of fused images. Part of this patch of tangled roots is the problem of the condition of the audience of the visual media best symbolized by Karen's mindless response to any kind of media pressure. Described as "thin-boundaried," she passively watches TV and believes it all (119). A crowd of such "Karens" becomes not even dead in the noble sense of passing on to blessed immortality but rather "dispersed": the crowd dispersed by jogging troops who move into the great space.... It is the preachment of history, whoever takes the great space and can hold it the longest (177).

History resolves itself only in sheer chaos; media displays of any sort, even those of "reprocessed" heroes like Bill, Hemingway, or Abraham Lincoln, do not in and of themselves grant hope. Despite DeLillo's hope noted in the *Libra* introduction for the reprocessing of the Zapruder film, it seems we cannot "image" or wordlessly, visually imagine a clear answer.

Even if written or visual images could provide hope, the celebrity American writer here fails to lead the way. Even if one can find redemption through written rather than painted chains of being, our Bill Gray makes a terribly bad moral choice not to go back to his own book (138). As stated above, he could have stopped attempting to make a moral stance for the freedom of the artist or author and been one in action. Instead of persisting in going to see Jean-Claude, the writer could have continued writing and finished the book. In a world without the books that help us make a moral stand, literature with moral force, the terrifying enemy is made more powerful. Like the unmarked weapons of the unidentified terrorist group (129) it cannot be spoken. Therefore as in *Libra* when Oswald's inner language fails ("*I still hadn't told my wife*"), language in a world external to the individual's psyche here fails. History and visual media aside, perhaps then the answer is a fully internalized language, extreme as that may sound. Such an extreme language, as fellow DeLillo reader Phillip Nel notes, would appear "both holy and primitive" (*Libra* 21). But if we choose as our defense against the unspeakable evil or evils a completely inner language, we may not yet be out of the murky dark waters. Joining Karen, Scott, and Brita in the losing game of "quoting Bill," I become a writer quoting a writer quoting himself as a system of private words: "The only private language I know is self-exaggeration" (37). Taking the chase further inside the self is a major theme of DeLillo's 2003 novel *Cosmopolis*.

To exchange contexts here from Marxist politics of *Libra* to the modern culture of reproduced art in *Mao II*, we wind up with the treatment of the new electronic world of finance in *Cosmopolis*. The story of the fall of young Wall Street billionaire Eric Packer, the novel opens up a third confrontation with the unspeakable in the reflections of a lonely man riding across New York City, committing wild acts of abandon on his way to get a haircut. Packer speaks to himself in a completely privatized inner language of self-exaggeration leading to destruction narcissistically based on the appreciation of art. Packer listened only to his own inner "mind in time...the noise in his head."

From October 2007 to November of 2008, the Dow Jones Industrial Average fell 6613 points and at the time of this writing has yet to regain even 500 of those consistently. Ahead of his time again, DeLillo in 2003 published this surreal novel of the collapse of Wall Street and the fall and death of corrupt billionaire capitalist Eric Packer. Packer loses his tens of billions in a default scheme betting against the clock on the fall of the yen. Juxtaposed with images of the fall of American capitalism, Eric Packer's fall is an extremely timely metaphor for the immorality of investor greed, the consequences of which are reverberating around the globe as I write. Here DeLillo explores and we read of the inner private language of a wealthy man, whose decline reveals problems with the narcissistic nature of the inner life and language in our capitalist system. The battle again with the unspeakable appears for a third time not to go well as this close look at Packer reveals.

Eric Packer is riding from one end of New York City to the other on one day in April 2000 to get a haircut at the particular barbershop where his father got his own hair cut. We ride along with him in his white stretch limousine, a fairly common sight in New York City during the stock boom times of the late 1990s to the beginning of the 21st century. Eric Packer and his motley crew of assistants: bald bodyguard Torval, driver Ibrahim Hamadou, who is a Sikh who has lost a finger, mathematician Michael Chin, and techno-geek Shiner plot the rise and fall of national currencies using cyber-technology in the limo. This glamorous vehicle is fully equipped with exterior security cameras, dashboard computers, laptops, cell phones, and even a micro spycam on Eric's wristwatch. We learn that Eric has a taste for complex and abstract art that "his guests did not know how to look at" (8). In other words, Packer uses art as a means both of displaying his own wealth and sophistication and of acquiring power over others by exercising his intellectual superiority over them, explaining the paintings. On route he spots his new wife of 22 days, Elise Shifrin, European banking fortune heiress and poet (15). The newlyweds divert from their parallel journeys to have breakfast together, as we learn that the couple has not spent enough time together as of late. Back in the limo, when Packer advises Chin to pursue more ardently the mysterious "interaction between technology and capital," the youth's only response is to say, "High school was the last true challenge" (23). These young masters of the world are not morally or socially committed to much of anything. Eric pulls over for an erotic tryst. We meet the first of many of his illicit sexual partners outside of his marriage, Didi Fancher, an art dealer critic who feels that learning about money has "helped her be a person" (29). She has encouraged Packer in his acquisitive ways. He sends her out with unlimited funds to buy all the art in a chapel, walls and all (30). As he ditches Didi and returns to his limo, Eric sees his professional enemy Arthur Rapp stabbed to death live right in the middle of a television interview (33).

Before he has too much time to revel in violent feelings of triumph at Rapp's death, he stops to intercept Jane Melman, his chief of finance, on her way jogging down the street to catch up to the limo. The rise of the Japanese yen could destroy Packer's fortune in hours, and Jane, who is also a single mother enjoying her only day off, has been called in at the last minute to help (40). However, what transpires between them is anything but a business meeting, with Eric getting a cardiac and prostrate exam by his substitute physician, Dr Ingram, the whole time. Eric seems to really want to share his physical emotional and philosophical pain, but their strange sexual encounter is completely without contact, and Jane is dropped off as unceremoniously as Didi was abandoned. Dr Ingram disturbs Eric with his report that Eric's prostate is "asymmetrical." Eric, Jane, and his crew have faith that the dynamics of the free market will begin to draw the yen back down and all will be well (54).

At this point, *Cosmopolis* cuts to the reflections of another character in a section titled "The Confessions of Benno Levin." Benno was a former employee of Packer's who suffers from bouts of "cultural panic." Taking his termination rather hard, Levin goes mad, writing 10,000 pages and making endless mental speeches to himself in an abandoned building he has set up as a derelict home/office. Reflecting on having shot someone, Benno is tensely found hovering around ATM machines, the only reliable register of his self-worth being the real cash he has on hand (61). Packer has noticed a mysterious-looking character hovering at an ATM near the limousine.

Accidently meeting his wife again at a bookstore, Eric Packer finds some troubles. They go to lunch, and Elise perceives that he's been sleeping around (68); he fails to impress her with his sophisticated way of expressing his need. Eric loses sight of her when he begins hallucinating that two giant rats are being flung about the luncheonette; his vision speaks to the immortality dominating his life. Eric is "rapt" (74) with amazement at this situation.

At the Church of St. Mary the Virgin, Packer picks up his chief of postmodern cultural theory, Vija Kinski. It is her job to theorize. The two justify Eric's wild and irresolute speculation with the idea that it is "cyber-capital that creates the future" (79). From the point of view of extreme relativism, these two can see no wrong in what he does, but of course to Vija, money has replaced all moral values of right and wrong: "[The] only thing that matters is the price you pay" (78). Time, too, has been displaced by the idea of cyber-money, as they reflect that people no longer think about eternity but rather about such absurd measurements as "nanoseconds...One billionth of a second" (79) and so forth. Even time itself has become a tool of the financial system, a "corporate asset" (79), and has been reduced to a measurement of monetary value. Kinski has no sense of good and evil in her theoretical analysis of Eric Packer's actions: for example, she finds no problem with his thriving on "ill will" toward his rivals. Another rival, Nikolai Kaganovich, has been found violently killed (82), but this causes Packer only joy.

Despite the fact that both Packer and Kinski realize that they are dealing with "a system that's out of control" and that Packer soon will borrow far more against the value of the yen than he can afford to pay back, he will not stop. Kinski's rationalizations passively encourage him, until the limo itself is stopped by a riot of anticapitalist protesters rocking the car, spraying it and smashing things all around them (91). His theorist interprets this anger and destruction as the end of capitalism but also as a product of the system. Even though Kinski is insightful enough to note that the system pretends not to see the horror and death that are the natural results of its actions, nothing bothers her about all this: "The urge to destroy is a creative urge" (92). Eric Packer looks upon his own image in the spycam, and a bomb destroys a nearby investment bank. The only thing that disturbs Vija Kinski is the spectacle of a man immolating himself in protest; his personal freedom to do this seems to contradict her theory about the "total" power of the market to create and destroy everything (100). Packer's limousine is by now spray-painted red and black and significantly dented; despite Torval's dire warnings of a "credible red" threat to Eric's life, he presses on in his quest for a haircut (101). Telling Kinski that he has purchased an old Soviet nuclear bomber, he only wants to look at it: "It's mine" (104). Sensing the imminent threat both of his own death and of the end of Wall Street only quickens Eric Packer's lust to live, although self-destructively.

Having broken boundaries with Jane Melman, Packer moves on to his ace bodyguard, brown-skinned Kendra Hays, requiring her to keep her body armor on while they have sex (111). Knowing that this will cause a lot of tension between the people he has hired to protect his life only quickens Packer more on his journey to his own unique self-immolation. He asks Kendra to Taser him, and she capitulates. Eric Packer is losing the ability to "maintain independent principles and convictions"—in short he has turned his own moral force against himself (115). Meanwhile, all of Wall Street begins to collapse, with banks failing and currencies tumbling at an incomprehensible rate.

Sadly, Eric runs into Elise one more time. She is visibly upset and has taken up smoking again and walked out of a new play, alone. She cannot deal with his infidelity and simply be "indifferent" or willing to put up with it and pretend all is well (122). He tells her his entire fortune is being lost, and she offers sympathy as a friend. She wants out of the marriage, and after she leaves he proceeds to use her personal online information to drain her bank accounts as well (124).

Eric proceeds to a rave nightclub with Danko, another bodyguard who is Kendra's partner. He can relate to the vacant stares of the clubbers, though he feels old. He leaves Danko behind and exits the club to meet Torval, still forecasting imminent death threats to Packer (129). They encounter rap manager Kozmo Thomas and the funeral of his client Brutha Fez, Eric's favorite rapper and inspiration. The spectacle of this funeral, with 36 white stretch limousines, break dancers, and Sufi whirling dervishes, impresses Eric Packer to the point where he wants his own funeral to be like this one (139). But his sorrow is for himself as well.

Suddenly, an attacker strikes Eric by surprise. It is "Andre Petrescu, the pastry assassin" (142), who hits the rich, powerful, and famous dictators, billionaires, and celebrities with pies. His acts of comical humiliation have a political impact as he has targeted the likes of Fidel Castro and Michael Jordan. Eric and Torval beat back Petrescu, his photographer, and the video cameraman savagely and purposelessly. Eric has no sense of humor (145). Torval continues his warnings, feeling "bonded now by violence" to the boss he trusts. They flee to an urban playground. Eric asks to examine Torval's gun and shoots the faithful man down in cold blood; the trusting bodyguard appears "confused" in his death (146). Nearby kids playing basketball on the same playground where Torval gets shot stop in amazement. Eric waves them off and throws Torval's gun into the bushes. After the loss of his personal fortune, Eric Packer felt that having Torval around would be a threat (148). For his part, Levin builds his resolve to kill Packer (155).

Eric and his driver finally arrive at their destination, Anthony Adubato's barbershop, where Eric's father took him frequently when he was a boy. Adubato offers Packer compassion in many forms, feeding him and his driver Ibrahim eggplant and rice for dinner. Relaxed by the familiar sounds of Adubato's voice and familiar details of his stories, Eric is finally able to fall asleep after this lengthy and destructive bout of insomnia. We learn that the driver was formerly "Acting Secretary of External Affairs" in his unspecified home country. After waking and overhearing the men discuss Eric's foolishness in disposing of his only means of protection, Eric discerns that Ibrahim's collapsed eye has been caused by his surviving some serious political turmoil, perhaps even the violence of torture (168). Rather than indulge Eric's curiosity about the past, Adubato and Ibrahim insist that Packer take the barber's pockmarked old revolver for self-protection. Eric gets up to leave with only half a haircut, refusing to allow the Italian American barber a chance to finish serving him compassionately. Adubato wants to make both sides even, but the billionaire refuses. Ibrahim grabs the gun and hands it to Eric. Packer takes it out of respect for his driver's secret past (170).

Driving along in the battered stretch limo, Eric and Ibrahim come across a surreal movie scene of 300 nude extras, lying on the street. They are pretending to be dead or senseless (173). Eric strips down to join them, wrapping the gun in his discarded clothing. In the amassed heap of bodies, he recognizes Elise, who only laughs when Eric discloses the fact that he has lost all her money. They make love, finally, but as soon as he realizes that he loves her, she is gone (178). As the trailers full of dressing extras finish leaving the scene, Eric abandons the forlorn white stretch limo and bids farewell to Ibrahim with a final embrace. A shot rings out and some-one howls, "ERIC MICHAEL PACKER," in a tone "more chilling than gunfire" (181). Eric fires shots in the direction of the sound. He enters the building and kicks open the door to Benno Levin's derelict apartment (186). Eric asks Levin why he wants to kill him. The two sit down to talk and Eric Packer knows immediately that "Benno Levin" is a false name. The novel concludes with the fatal confrontation between Eric Packer and his former employee Benno Levin, whose real name is revealed to be "Richard Sheets" (192). The two discuss issues of poverty and class struggle as Packer tries to talk the killer down from his act of violence. Ineffectually Eric tries to shoot his attacker, but the barber's gun misfires and blows a hole in the middle of the billionaire's hand. When Richard pleads, "I wanted you to save me" (204), Eric turns away to look at his own image on the micro-spycam wrist-watch he wears. As the novel draws to a close, we hear the final thoughts of Eric in death, identified only by the ambulance crew as "Male Z," as he plunges three and half feet to his death.

The turbulent events of this novel begin with an epigraph from Zbigniew Herbert, "A rat became the unit of currency." It is a line from Herbert's poem "Report from the Besieged City," an apocalyptic vision of an inva-sion written from the point of view of one of the victims of the invasion around the time that Poland was under Communist martial law. By thus beginning the tale, DeLillo seems to imply that New York City is under the siege of the Wall Street wildcat deregulated capitalism of the late 1990s and early 21st century. Eric Packer's viewpoint is just as much that of a victim as of a perpetrator. Ironically, Herbert was a great capitalist reformer and hero. Packer's situation only reveals the way in which Herbert's dream of a well-run and morally sound capitalism has gone awry, particularly in the sense of an individual's creative journey to freedom. Several symbols and references to myth are brought in by Don DeLillo to complete this portrayal of Eric Packer's failed journey, comparable in some ways to the plight of figures from *Mao II* and *Libra*.

That Eric Packer's pains are self-inflicted is fairly inarguable. He relates to his killer, Benno Levin or Richard Sheets, on the level of a mutually shared pain, which they call a "sickness…a crucial self-realization" (189). From his multiple betrayals of his beloved Elise to his squandering billions and himself and the limousine on a path toward the inevitable confrontation with Sheets, Packer's is partial self-immolation, unlike the Wall Street protestor who seeks to know and therefore ameliorate others' pain through self-inflicted wounds. Like his half-a-haircut, Packer's attempt to pierce his own shell of obscene wealth by hurting himself is finally incomplete, and like Lee Harvey Oswald and Bill Gray, he fails even to come to a new awareness of himself, let alone one of others.

But Packer honestly attempts to know him and others, even referring to Sheets as "the subject" in his final reflections (197). Eric's wounded hand is like a partial stigma, the hand wound as one of the five the wounds of Christ that appear on some devotees according to religious literature. But even though Richard Sheets appears to feel some sympathetic pain, the moment is incomplete because Eric cannot return the sympathy. The two seek something of a mutual transcendence, as Sheets advises his victim that he should have accepted his own imperfection as nature's own balance, his "asymmetrical prostrate" (200) as a sign of human "lopsidedness." Perhaps Packer then would not have fired the assassin and created this situation. Given the billionaire's fall from grace, we might be tempted to look at his opponent Sheets as the hero in this situation.

But this would be to disregard the fact that Sheets does not achieve anything of note by killing Eric. As a character, he is comparable to DeLillo's portrait of Oswald in *Libra*. Like the notorious figure, the shooter in *Cosmopolis* claims to have the force of history on his side (202). He is obsessive, drawn even more consciously than Oswald was toward the unspeakable evil of murder. Like Oswald too, he has constructed a false name for himself, "Benno," like "Hidell" created to put distance between himself and his act of murder. This "lost man of history" seeks to vindicate himself by killing the person he feels is most responsible for his woe; however, his resolution falters at the climactic point, and he struggles to respond to Eric when the troubled lover of art asks him the cause of his violence, the "truth" propelling the action (*Cosmopolis* 194–195). So Sheets is no hero put into DeLillo's story to rid the world of the villainous capitalist. He suffers the same imbalances as Eric Packer does and does not offer a real way out of them. Thus we really cannot say that Richard Sheets has attained a certain freedom to express his full potential any more than Packer has.

Responding to the novel, critics have neglected to note that the problem of the unspeakability of the deepest evil is noted in the mysterious recesses of the individual consciousness in *Cosmopolis*. For example, Joseph Conte in "Writing amid the ruins: 9/11 and *Cosmopolis*" claims that Packer's demise represents a kind of "transcendence of the disembodied mind" (Conte 186) through "sublime" technology, made possible by the power of the cyber-capital in which Packer invested not only his entire fortune but his moral worth and search for individual fulfillment in the shell of cyber-capital he'd constructed. Packer's final tormented thought—"Oh shit I'm dead" (206)—does not grant the power and freedom Conte implies by "transcendence." And as we will see, neither is the man's desire to encounter his childhood barber Anthony Rebate a "destination appearing dangerously nostalgic" (Conte 189). It is only Rubato's kind regard and familiar stories, evocative of the care of Packer's own father, that Eric will accept and allow to ease his own mind into sleep, temporarily curing the insomnia that is one of the reasons for Eric's wildly erroneous judgment propelling the suicidal journey of the man in his white limo. Again, as with *Mao II*'s Bill Gray and *Libra*'s Oswald, Eric is caught up in his own mediated image as ultimate art-collector and billionaire, who, like Narcissus, must destroy that self that is impossible for him to truly possess. Without a sense of self, he externalized the destruction into the heartless betrayal of his fiancée, his finances, his stretch limo, and even his loyal bodyguard.

Another reason for the mad trip, as we've noted above, is Eric's subscription to the "sublime" theories of Vija Kinski, postmodernist. As Kinski herself might do, Marc Schuster treats every significant moment of *Cosmopolis* (and all the other points in DeLillo he refers to) as an affirmative illustration of the correctness of the postmodern theories of Jean Baudrillard. Schuster disregards the fact that postmodernism is not favorably presented in Packer's trip as he can begin to "really live" only after absorbing Kinski's rambling and letting her out of the limousine. Yet she is the only woman who Packer does not imagine at his ultimate postmodern spectacle, his own funeral procession, inspired by that of his fellow master of culture rapper Brutha Fez. Though postmodernism reaffirms Packer's dangerous belief in his own invulnerability to complete self-destruction as it blinds him to the real *moral* consequences of what he is doing to himself and others, Packer is as surprised by the pain in his own hand when his gun misfires. Finally, relevant also is Conte's claim that *Cosmopolis* is a response in part to the terrorist attacks of September 11, 2001. But while Conte sees this response as a transformation of material Cold War evil into the 21st-century cyber-threat of terrorism, I might counter-argue that the scene of Eric and his lost-and-found love Elise Shifrin lying naked with the virtual 300 dead bodies, dead extras in the theatrical movie representing a deadly tragedy of the fall of New York, is Don DeLillo's expression of profound grief, an unspeakable sadness foreshadowing the 9/11 disaster. None of these astute critics, however, have noted the concept of the unspeakable that we have traced from Thomas Merton through *Libra* and *Mao II* and that we now will find in *Cosmopolis*.

Returning to *Cosmopolis*, if "Richard Sheets" is comparable in some ways to Lee Harvey Oswald, Eric is comparable with Bill Gray of *Mao II*. Injured and staggering with a wound to the hand or partial stigmata at the conclusion of each of their stories, both Bill and Eric cannot make good judgments near to the moment of death. The writer and the billionaire are also frustrated artists: Gray has been diverted from writing his long-awaited book to help in the cause of individual freedom for the French poet while Eric channels his own love of art into the need to acquire greedily all the beautiful things and the beautiful people that surround him. Both wind up destroying themselves by being too involved in their own self-image, or "hype." When the lost man of history meets the lost man of art, nothing is left save the inner "language of self-exaggeration" (*Mao II* 37), which Bill Gray knows so well and which Eric Packer lives out at the end of his life. For Packer, whose death is far more ignoble than Gray's, this self-exaggeration is the vanity of Narcissus, as his last living moments with Richard Sheets illustrates. Packer glances at his watch, and "the watch wasn't showing the time. There was an image, a face on the crystal, and it was his. This meant he'd activated the electron camera unintentionally, maybe when he'd shot himself. The camera was a device so microscopically refined it was almost pure information. It was almost metaphysics" (204).

The language used to describe the picture of Eric Packer is quite impor-tant. As with Narcissus, he is captivated with his own image and sees himself as perfect beauty, as "pure information" reflected through his technology, the picture on the spycam. Like Narcissus too, he is thwarted when his reflection is erased from the watch. Finally, in the earlier Greek myth, Narcissus ultimately committed acts of self-destruction, frustrated by his inability to capture the image of himself on the water; he literally beats himself up but at least becomes a flower. Packer loses his image in the camera as well after having spent most of the narrative ruining him-self and is not transformed. In this light, we can see a suicidal pun in Eric's reference that the image on the lens was taken "maybe when he'd shot himself" (204), with the pun on the accidental shot to his hand and shooting or taking the digital image of himself on the electron spycam in the watch. By trying to turn himself into the pure digital image or "pure technology," Eric Packer destroys his life. Unlike Conte, I do not see Eric's termination as a passage to a pure cyber-immortality but that "almost" metaphysics or being "almost" a pure spirit is worse than not being at all. Packer's opponent in this, Richard Sheets, quotes another Greek myth to shed light on the billionaire's death. Sheets says, "You have your complex. Icarus falling" (202) and ironically notes that Packer's fall will not be a flight to the sun as it was with the heroic Icarus legend. This failure in *Cosmopolis* of Packer to enact either the Icarus or Narcissus myths represents the failure of capitalism to mythologize itself, to be enough to serve as a vehicle (like the limo) for complete artistic, individual self-transcendence. Packer listened only to his own inner "mind in time...the noise in his head" (207), and who better qualified to test the theory that free-market capitalism gives the full opportunity for art to free the inner self, beyond the media (as in *Mao II*) and even history (as in *Libra*)? This is the theory that made Zbigniew Herbert's work so important. But lest the power of history exercised here by Sheets the gunman have the final say, we must note that our martyr for the cause of pure individuality in art made some fatal mistakes. His incomplete haircut serves as a rejection of the physical, material compassion the barber offers in memory of Packer's father. Further, he dismisses Rubato from his duty, as well as his driver, his bodyguard, and his wife from their physical, active relationship. At the end, he uses others as pure information to consume, but in the consumption does not become that outer beauty he sees. Rather, that half-haircut is simply an outer projection of the inner lack of symmetry ("the asymmetrical prostate") he so fears but should accept as simply the human condition, our imperfection as anything but "pure information." So what is left at the end of Packer's deregulated self-immolation, the failure of the completely inner language or "pure information" as a defense after history and media fail? Once again, the unspeakable emerges as a dominant force. Spectator at the rave club, watching the anorexic and "ovoid" dancers, Eric hears the dark and harmful music that is all that is left for the selfish billionaire in his final fall:

> There was a remote track under the music. . . . It spoke and it moaned. It said things that seemed to make sense but didn't. He listened to it speak outside the range of any language ever humanly employed . . . (126) . . . The things that made him who he was could hardly be identified much less converted to data. . . . He'd come to know himself, untranslatably, through his pain. (207)

Clearly, the dark music and intranslatable language into which the selfhood or subjectivity of Packer is submerged is the evil treated in the three novels featured herein. Highlighted here is Packer's lack of ability to identify himself or translate into language his radical pain. As with Gray and Oswald, another protagonist is tragically swallowed up in this unspeakable reality of things gone wrong. Taken together for perhaps the first time in this chapter, these three novels' references to the unspeakability of the worst things do not appear to offer us grounds for hope. It would seem that the unspeakable trumps or overpowers individual efforts at moral transcendence, and whether we seek to master over evil through history, art, or some more sophisticated media technology we are fairly doomed. Clearly, this dystopic vision though does not encompass an entire reading of all of Don DeLillo's work. Between the triumphant reception of *Mao II* and the later appreciation of *Cosmopolis*, we cannot ignore the epic masterpiece *Underworld*, an examination of good and evil on a grand scale, dealing with the realities of the Cold War.

Lest we leave our sense of the unspeakable behind hopelessly in these works, we note that one more character will face the idea rather unflinchingly in his excluded novel, and that is the Italian American heroic high school teacher Albert Bronzini. He too, as with the other characters in the trilogy under examination, reflects on things unspeakable. In *Underworld*, Bronzini walks by a group of city children playing a simple game of tag, not the kind of playful chase you'd think of as chasing the unspeakable. Yet:

> He was wondering about being *it*. This was one of those questions that he tortured himself deliciously with. Another player tags you and you're *it*. What exactly does this mean? The evil one whose name is too potent to be spoken. Or is the term just a cockney pronunciation of hit? When you tag someone, you hit her. You're *it*, missy. (677)

Unlike the other protagonists, Bronzini seems light and easy, almost frivolous in the face of such fearsome and awe-inspiring reality, treating human evil as the children do their game. Will Bronzini's jocular attitude place him in the same horrible position as the protagonists in these other novels? A simple high school teacher, his part in the massive scheme of things in *Underworld* may seem minor or unimportant at first. Here he appears, though, evoking the problems that bedeviled important figures in the works we have examined here. Similarly, he does play an important role in the *Underworld* as he ministers to some of the main characters as his students in science. And unlike some of the other figures who tragically fall in DeLillo's works, Bronzini evokes a moral force in language through his compassionate actions, an example of moral goodness in a world dominated by the historical reality of the nuclear arms race. DeLillo will refer to art, history, and the media in *Underworld*, and we will see Bronzini in a highly different sort of engagement with the realities of ultimate good and evil. Even the way Bronzini gets around is different—he walks as opposed to buzzing through New York City in a white stretch limo as Packer does. He does not "chase" the unspeakable as Oswald does to make history or Gray does to make art or distract himself from making art. In our next two chapters, we will see how the ultimate impact of Bronzini's moral choices is distinguishable from the failures of Packer or Oswald. This reference to the unspeakable as an evil thing does not always trump the sense of the moral triumph of good over evil, an indispensible part of the moral force of Don DeLillo's work. We begin our study by looking at the cultural context of this work and examining how our author not only makes general statements about the media's power but also by very specifically approaching the media's particular stereotype of Italian Americans, a cultural group very directly involved with the language of DeLillo's work.

_____ *Chapter 5* _____

Confronting Unspeakable Evil: DeLillo's "Filming" Italian Americans

As we have seen in the prior chapter, DeLillo's fictions are definitely concerned with the diabolical power of 20th/21st-century mass media to manipulate the self-perception of contemporary subjects. In the last chapter this pattern of manipulation, which is represented in my analysis here as "unspeakable evil," was seen in three novels but can be traced in others as well. From *White Noise*'s Dr. Jack Gladney, whose blended family's dialogue is constantly littered with the interruptions of reality-defining television and radio broadcasts, to *The Body Artist*'s Lauren Hartke's attempt to come to grips with the voices in her memory by using a tape recorder, to *Cosmopolis*'s billionaire Eric Packer, whose personal and financial self-worth are inseparable from his cell phone and other electronic interactions with the currency exchange market, these novels reflect relentlessly the media's encroachment on the contemporary individual's attempt to perceive and define his or her own personal identity as a subject. This encroachment does not, however, always reign supreme.

Once again, the issue of proper attention to surface patterns in the writing comes up, as the individual's power in the face of the pattern is neither a given nor absolutely denied in DeLillo's fictions. The first crucial cultural surface neglected by mainstream critics (see chapter 1) but important nevertheless is the representation of Italian American culture in DeLillo's work. This representation responds directly to mass-media stereotyping of the Italian American male as primarily a Mafia criminal. With the popularity of the well-crafted *Godfather* film series and that of the far less impressive and derivative HBO series *The Sopranos* as well as *Jersey Shore,* this mass-media attack on the subjective self-definition of Italian Americans is commonly seen, but never quite as nativized as Cecil B. DeMille or Harriet Beecher Stowe. Don DeLillo serves in a unique position to respond to this stereotype as an Italian American verbal artist, "fighting fire with fire," as the saying goes, by fictionalizing the individual's point of view to demonstrate the ways in which the individual can creatively transcend the determining forces of media with his or her own response, much as the director of a film controls that film's content. Tracing this evolution through his novels *Americana*, *Players*, *The Names*, *Libra*, and finally *Underworld*, the trope of Italian American novelist as filmmaker emerges. An evolving representation of the Italian American male is seen in the juxtapositioning of these five novels, from the stock gangster (*Americana*, *Players*) through the trickster figure (in *The Names* and *Libra*) and finally in *Underworld* to the amorally complex and creative individual capable of fully independent and creative self-definition. This evolution is in turn highlighted by the narrative trope of filmmaking. Whether directly stated with film as creative stock or portrayed in the exercise of its full potential, filmmaking becomes the metaphoric means by which DeLillo addresses one of the crucial surfaces of culture implicated both in text and context. The Italian American subject is thus utilized by the author to demonstrate the ways in which the individual can creatively transcend the determining forces of media with his or her own response.

Sequencing more specifically the evolution in the novels as they appear in this chapter, *Americana* simply and directly places the gangster figure as such into the mainstream American path of non-Italian filmmaker David Bell, who attempts through his self-produced film to respond creatively and cinematically to his sister's running off with a mobster. Never quite finding the balance between Italian master of film Fellini's "left eye of fantasy and right eye of reality" (*Americana* 293), Bell completes his film but does not resolve the issue of subjective transcendence. In *Running Dog*, the stock mob figure moves from being the object of the filmmaker's lens to film collector, with the film itself a morally repulsive fantasy, an allegedly pornographic record of Hitler's last days alive in his underground bunker. Here film and mafia stereotype are equated as corrupt cultural objects, pure fantasies as it were, with Vinnie the Eye's partial visual paralysis as representative of this condition (*Running Dog* 175). Moving on to *The Names*, Frank Volterra, the Italian American filmmaker, literalizes the metaphor, stating directly through his monologues and actions the notion of the Italian American male not as mobster but rather as trickster figure. Expanding on this is the character of Carmine Latta in *Libra*, again a fictionalized mobster but one who is utilized by DeLillo to draw political parallels between Mafia violence and legitimatized American covert actions. Like the Zapruder film, the mob figure in *Libra* stands as a metric against which the machinations of history in terms of the Kennedy assassination can be evaluated. Thus, *Libra* traces both the motif of the gangster stereotype in relation to the American mainstream and that of the truth-seeking power of filmmaking with greater precision than in *Americana* or *Running Dog*. Finally, in *Underworld*, through the Italian American male characters Nick and Matt Costanza Shay, their heroic teacher Albert Bronzini, and the narrative motif of the Eisenstein film, DeLillo captures how the subject can channel and thus transcend the media's encroachment upon self-definition.

A defense of the use of film as metaphor is wholly unnecessary; critics are pretty much in universal agreement that the impact of visual and mass communication media forms is well treated in DeLillo's work. But such a defense for treatment of Italian American themes in the work may be necessary. As stated in my brief profile of DeLillo for the 2005 *Greenwood Encyclopedia of Multiethnic American Literature*, DeLillo, having been compared favorably to William Faulkner, James Joyce, and Herman Melville, has been established as the premiere author of the Italian American milieu as well as one of the most important authors living today. Furthermore, the claim that DeLillo himself would share the critics' avoidance of Italian American culture would form an absurd proposition. On the contrary, DeLillo has publicized his treatment of this culture particularly in the case of 1997's epic novel *Underworld*, arguably his most ambitious work. In a 2005 interview with David Remnick published in the book *Conversation with Don DeLillo*, DeLillo recounted a childhood in a house he shared with his first generation Italian immigrant parents, grandparents, and other family. DeLillo told Remnick how both games of boccie ball and stickball, Italian American traditions, were part of his life. Responding to further questions by Remnick, DeLillo's stated that he waited until very late in his authorial career (*Underworld* was published in 1997, after the writer had been published and recognized to varying degrees for over 30 years) to treat the Italian American Bronx thoroughly and completely in a major novel. DeLillo told Remnick that he did this in order to "do it justice." I argue that this latter statement announces the writer's intent to address popular Italian American stereotypes in the novel. However, given the fact that *Underworld* was released when DeLillo's authorial reputation was completely established by the time of *Underworld*'s release in 1997 (in 1991 *Mao II* had won the PEN/Faulkner Award and 1985 saw *White Noise* win the National Book Award), he may have attempted to address negative stereotypes in earlier works but waited until such time as his audience was large enough and his credibility consolidated with readers. Yet *Underworld* is not the only novel to refer to Italian American culture in DeLillo's oeuvre. Albeit inconsistently and sometimes just in passing, *Americana*, *Running Dog*, *The Names*, *Libra*, and *Underworld* each refer to images or aspects of this culture in a pattern accumulating in the very extensive treatment of issues and characters infused with significant Italian American referentiality. Finally, to borrow an image from an iconic work of art, in Edvard Munch's *The Scream*, the volcanic red color of the sky adds to the tension one feels when viewing the work; it would not be the same painting without said background, nor would DeLillo's work be same without this Italian American background color.

From the same 2005 *Conversations*, in referring to his highly regarded and sensitive characterization of women, DeLillo remarked to Maria Nadottie that all people are "all of us made up not only of muscle, brains and blood, but also of the things which others tell us and of the things others see in us...it must be very disturbing to become suddenly invisible" (112). He was referring to the status of women who suffer a loss of respect in society for various reasons, but he could just as well have been discussing those Italian Americans who are invisible to a society that sees them only through the distorted lens of the outlaw stereotype. Clearly, also, DeLillo appears here to be sensitive enough to seek to change that lens. If his numerous achievements as a world-renowned author are not enough to do so, perhaps it is because of the approach of his academic critics.

Despite the fact that it seems reasonable to think that DeLillo would have addressed some anti-Italian American bias in his fiction, many readers who've published other books and articles about these works of DeLillo haven't addressed issues of Italian American characters or culture. Only a few critics do attempt to deal with Italian American themes and culture very specifically and how these traces of Italian or "italianita" are imbued into DeLillo's writing as transcendent "language webbed in the senses" (*Underworld* 683). One of the articles that does so successfully is John Paul Russo's article in his 2005 book *The Future without a Past* titled "Don DeLillo: Ethnicity, Religion and the Critique of Technology," in which Russo considers for the first time the epic novel *Underworld* in light of Italian and Catholic cultural references. The essay cites several examples of DeLillo's use of such cultural references in characterization and in theme. Professor Russo focuses on the character of Nick Costanza Shay, the Italian/Irish American central character of this epic novel. Nick is a product of New York street gangs who is reformed and becomes one of the owners of the game-winning baseball hit by Ralph Branca in the 1951 pennant game between the New York Giants and the Brooklyn Dodgers (*Underworld* 11–60). Nick becomes fully assimilated as a white American, becoming the executive head of a waste management company with a luxurious suburban home, fully grown children, and a successful education and marriage. Though Nick is not the sole narrator of *Underworld* in the manner in which Huckleberry Finn is the sole storyteller in the Twain novel that bears his name, he does relate much of the action to us, and a great deal of the novel concerns his life and the lives of those characters who are major players in his ethnic world. Russo asserts that the move out of the old Little Italy neighborhood is not necessarily all good for Nick. It seems to separate the man from a vital life force, as his priest and guide Father Andrew Paulus will later warn him of the dangers of being weak willed (539). Russo describes the Phoenix, Arizona, of Nick's Americanized, de-Italianated adulthood as "antiseptic" (Russo 236), a sort of "death-in-life" (235) that Nick does not really enjoy (237). Indeed, Nick emerges as a figure that misses the passionate oppositional tendencies of his youth. As an adult, he still longs for "the days when I was alive on the earth, rippling in the quick of my skin…the days of disarray when I walked real streets and did things slap-bang" (810). It is this passion that Russo associates masterfully with the sacred yet common everyday aspects of Nick's Italian world, the deep meaning of what Father Paulus calls "Quotidian things" (DeLillo 542 as qtd. in Russo 238). But which aspects of Nick's Italian American environment are to be treated as the sacred? Professor Russo realizes that these things Nick should consider sacred are *not* of the violent criminal lifestyle of the Mafiosi, or pure unreformed trickster, because Russo tells us how DeLillo's Catholic priest, Father Andrew Paulus, "by no means justifies" (Russo 237) Nick's past criminal act, an apparently accidental killing of a friend with a shotgun.

To answer the winnowing question of "what's good here," other DeLillo readers must explore more deeply aspects of the commonplace cultures one finds especially in *Underworld*. What John Paul Russo is saying about Nick's relationship to all aspects of being of Italian descent is that the central character simply "loses it in becoming the [non-Italian or de-ethnicized] Organizational Man" (238), not just the rage but all the subjective and passionate contact with his people of origin and their culture. Nick's lack of touch with this people and their culture is ascribed very astutely by John Paul Russo as symptomatic of the problem of "the general loss of social memory" (231). This loss is actually shown in one of the other characters, Marvin Lundy, who loses the Branca baseball that drives the action of the novel. This loss of personal and social history is addressed by Russo's thesis; hence his title *The Future without a Past.*

Yet as we read DeLillo, the question remains: How does one deal with the reality of being Italian American, representing the same, or in DeLillo's case doing both at the same time? I here echo the question John Paul Russo raises in regards to a character most other critics have largely ignored: "What could Bronzini be thinking now?" (Russo 235), referring to Albert Bronzini's reaction to Father Paulus's dismissive remarks about the future careers of both the young Matt and the young Nick. This Albert Bronzini is the Italian American heroic and saintly high school teacher of science who exercises a profound influence over Nick's younger brother, Matt Costanza Shay, and to a lesser degree over the scientist Nick himself. Thus Bronzini represents both the very antidote to the Mafia stereotype existent in the media and the answer to the question of the morally good or sacred aspect of this quotidian Italian American world DeLillo evokes consistently in *Underworld.*

Not only is *Underworld* the primary use of this background in DeLillo's work, but moreover a series of Italianate cultural characters and references in earlier groundbreaking and award-winning novels accumulate in the representation of culture in that epic novel. *Americana, Running Dog, The Names,* and *Libra* build up a forecasting series of brief cultural references to Italian America and its variegated symbols and characters and an anticipation of the portrait of Bronzini as the Italian American hero with whom the reader can break through stereotypical media images of Italian American people. Highlighting this portrayal is the vital metaphor of filmmaking in all five novels analyzed here.

In the first DeLillo novel, *Americana,* the Italian America mob/gangster stereotype simply appears as such without a direct challenge, but in fruitful juxtaposition to the metaphor of filmmaking as self-definition. The main character/narrator David Bell hopes to win his artistic freedom from the advertising-dominated world of network television by completing his first full-length documentary film, capturing American life in its subjective and diversified glory by assembling a series of soliloquies by various people he films along the way. He succeeds, highlighting among others the soliloquy of World War II veteran Glen Yost's soliloquy of the Bataan Death March in the Philippines in 1942, in which he reveals his memory of a live Filipino boy flung into a mass grave Yost was forced to dig, cavalierly tossed away as Yost calls him "the little wog" (298). In the context of this ethnic slur, the Mafia perspective gets a soliloquy and some flat characterization in *Americana.* Bell memorializes his best friend from high school, Tommy

Valerio, who conforms to the youthful gangster stereotype of the 1950's era greaser, stashing a bayonet under the seat of his '46 Chevy. An even more direct characterization of the mob occurs when David's sister Mary runs off with a character named Arondella, who is said to be "in the rackets." Mary tells David that it is Arondella's professional job to go up to Boston and kill a narcotics felon, but she adds that she prefers Arondella's "kind of death" to "the kind I have been fighting my whole life" (163). That Mafia violence might be morally equivalent to the kind of state-sanctioned violence that Glen Yost had participated in is hinted at here and by the pun on "rackets" that is formed when David and his father later defeat Arondella in a punishing game of tennis, pointless in terms of ending the relationship between Mary and her mob lover. But any inherent suggestion that the Mafia stereotype is brought up critically to suggest a moral equivalence between Mafia lifestyles and mainstream violent American culture is not pursued in *Americana*. To put the spiritual loss of his sister in perspective, David hires an actress, Carol Deming, to read the soliloquy of a woman married or erotically involved with a Mafiosi:

> He (her lover) was prepared to kill, quite literally to kill, in order to avenge the honor of someone he loved.... We have learned not to be afraid of the dark but we've forgotten that darkness means death. They haven't forgotten this. They are still in the hills of Sicily or Corsica.... I didn't want him to get out of the business...an atmosphere of death more real and personal than anything the newspapers can offer. (279)

In the form of Carol Deming's soliloquy, David's creative response to his sister Mary's situation and in the form of the characters of Arondella and Tommy Valerio, the Mafia stereotype appears. But it is not directly criticized or utilized. Is Bell's film an expose of Mafia violence to help his sister or a stylized reenactment? The conflict between fantasy and reality lives unresolved.

However, in *Americana* DeLillo does allude to the Italian filmmaker Federico Fellini when American David Bell extracts Glen Yost's non-Mafia-related soliloquy in *Americana*. As Yost haltingly relates the terrible scene of the boy in the trench, his long-term post-traumatic stress reveals itself in the injury to his left eye, which jumps around uncontrollably even as he calmly states that being forced to bury the boy alive "really wasn't too bad" (298). Bell reflects in response that "Fellini says the right eye is for reality and the left eye is the fantasy eye" (293). Both Glen Yost on film and American media culture in general are participating here in a fantasy of repression, in projection of normality in Yost's case on a moment of brutal violence. And in the case of the media culture, there is a projection of the idea of brutal violence on all Italian Americans as an ethnic group. But the fantasy cannot contain the reality, and the left eye jumps around with the difficulty of containing the emotional response to the real-life historical violence in history's right eye. Similarly, as the narrative of *Americana* keeps jumping back to the Mafia stereotype without deeper exploration of the parallel between mob violence and mainstream American violence, both Yost's soliloquy of the Bataan Death March and the filmed image of Carol Deming's Mafia lover offer "an atmosphere of death more real and personal than anything the newspapers can offer" (279), and both are fantasies of repression. To a degree, the novel does not challenge the stereotype as the protagonist is a white American, though clearly one who emulates the Italian filmmaker. This non-Italian filmmaker David Bell escapes the narrative with "film in the can" or creative project intact, but the author DeLillo's evocation of the Mafia as a filmed image raises more questions than it ultimately resolves.

Continuing, in *Running Dog* the stock mob figure is Vinnie "the Eye" Talerico, whose partial visual paralysis symbolizes an interpretation in perfect accord with the earlier Fellini metaphor used in *Americana*. The right side of his face is paralyzed, leaving the right eye dead, signifying that only the "left eye of fantasy" is functional (175). This novel concerns a cut-throat competition for a film believed to be a pornographic movie made by the Nazi inner circle during Hitler's last days in his bunker beneath the Reich Chancellery in falling Berlin. This stock mob figure Talerico moves from being the object of the filmmaker's lens to film collector, with the film itself a morally repulsive fantasy. Here film and mafia stereotype are equated as corrupt cultural objects, pure fantasies as it were, with Vinnie the Eye's partial visual paralysis as representative of this condition. He lives in a world of fantasy, justifying to himself the death of one of his underlings, Kidder, in a gun battle over the film with an American art collector, Ritchie Armbrister (206), reflecting that sooner or later such shootings are simply of a piece with the typically predictable "stress situation," justifying his own actions in terms of legitimate business dealings "in this line of work, in acquisitions" (206). He also alludes to the mainstream American fantasy of life "in the US where everybody owns a gun of one kind or another, for one purpose or other...Cowboys" (207). Yet as in *Americana*, his image is not probed more deeply for how it might inform DeLillo's audience about Italian American or American mainstream culture. For his part, Talerico, like

Glen Yost, suffers from a divided vision, living a fantasy of repression. He is the left eye jumping around, leaving the action virtually as soon as he arrives.

In terms of film, the Hitler film is equally fantastical. Not turning out to be pornographic at all, its content is an imaginative reversing of the trope of Charlie Chaplin clowning around in *The Great Dictator* (1940). The film shows Hitler dressed as a clown in an attempt to comfort the children and other survivors in the Reich bunker. It is only obscene in terms of its banal attempt at a self-justification both pathetic and pathological. Like Vinnie, the clown Hitler signifies a fantasy of repression, and all these collectors are running dogs. Once again, both the metaphor of film and the representation of Italian Americans run along parallel lines in *Running Dog* as corrupt fantastical cultural products.

DeLillo's next work makes explicit the metaphor of the Italian American as filmmaker in the character of Frank Volterra of *The Names*. Here the Italian American figure moves from filmed object to the maker of film. Frank Volterra accompanies the narrator/protagonist James Axton on his trip to find the Ta Onomata cult, a killing group of religious fanatics that chooses its victims based on the bizarre scheme of matching the victim's initials to the initials of the geographic location of the killing. Volterra attempts to balance the eyes of fantasy and reality by capturing a completely objective perspective on the group, claiming he wants to "just probe" the group's "homicidal calculations" (198–199). For this film he states, "There won't be a murder. Nobody gets hurt. At the end they raise their arms, holding the weapons.... That are all we see. We don't know what it means" (*The Names* 199). Fred Gardaphé in *Italian Signs/American Streets* comments that this character represents the protagonist's alter ego (190). Such an alter ego takes the form of the well-known Jungian figure of the trickster, leaving his film project behind to blaze the trail for commercial risk assessor James Axton to escape the assassination attempt by the cult. The protagonist had been in danger because his name matches the initials of Amman, Jordan. Yet he follows the path laid out by Volterra and escapes with a full "risk assessment," escaping the decaying cult and other Mideast terrorists, providing an exit for his ex-wife Katherine and their son "Tap" as well. Though Volterra and his film are not necessarily valorized as central figures in the novel, he is the first non-Mafia Italian American and is thus significant. His own name (in a novel called *The Names*) implies this significance suggestively. Frank Volterra is named after the important Florentine city Volterra once held by the Medicis, a city that contains in the Cathedral of Santa Maria Assunta dedicated to the Very Holy Name of Jesus a monogram of Christ attributed to St. Bernadine of Siena. This image cuts close to the heart of the pattern of imagery driving the novel and suggests the potential for great goodness associated with Italian culture or from those cultures derived from it such as Italian American culture. But the film is unfinished, and so is the implication of Volterra's name. In exploring *The Names* more deeply, one finds the focus of the novel to encompass other issues, such as the Iran Hostage crisis as it relates to the risk-assessing mission of James Axton. However, the pattern of characterizing Italian Americans as mobsters is definitively broken, and the accompanying imagery of filmmaking in DeLillo's major novels continues along through later works.

From the left eye of fantasy highlighted in *The Names, Running Dog,* and *Americana*, the motif shifts back to the right eye of history in DeLillo's novel *Libra*. Rather than the imaginary films of David Bell, the Hitler Reichstag cameraman, or Frank Volterra, we are given a reference to the real Zapruder film of the Kennedy assassination. DeLillo reflects upon the improved precision of the Zapruder document in its digitally remastered form in his "waveform analysis, confocal microscopes, digital replicas... Recovered, copied, deciphered" (*Libra* xi). Given these better methods, claims the author, we might someday "imagine a clear answer followed by a passionate set of informed objections" (xi). Ironically, DeLillo taunts us to "see the truth and know it if you can" (xi). However impossible it might be for us to discern the right-eye's historical or empirical truth in the case of the Kennedy assassination, the point of the filmed or fictional narrative is not to recount right-eye history only but to historicize, to balance the art of representation in terms of both the imagined (or fantasy) and reality. And this DeLillo does in *Libra*, not only in terms of a balanced analysis of the Oswald/Kennedy moment leaving open the question of whether the crazed assassin acted alone, but also in the case of a far greater improvement in the kind of Mafia characterization attempted in *Americana* and *The Names*. In *Libra,* DeLillo begins the use of the mob image to deconstruct American power politics and international CIA skullduggery. The notion of legitimacy of state violence in a false opposition to illegitimate mob violence is brought in and explicitly challenged when merely implied in the former two novels. With greater precision, DeLillo creates the mobster Carmine Latta, a fictional mob lieutenant of Sam Giancana, whom some historians believe resented Attorney General Robert Kennedy's crackdown on his own syndicate. Latta gives money to David Ferrie, a disgraced pilot believed to have plotted with Kennedy's enemies as well, to be used for arms and ammunition for regrouping anti-Castro forces. These forces hated the Kennedys as well due to the lack of support for the Bay of Pigs invasion. Going from the pre-Castro Cuba of "a billion dollars a year in total business" to the "systematic humiliation" of the ongoing investigation has driven Latta to "put out a contract" on Castro and JFK. Here DeLillo explicitly connects Mafia violence to CIA official-state sanctioned violence in Latta's observation that "we [the Mob] are realistic people. We don't do tricks with smoke and mirrors. The styles [of the Bay of Pigs forces and the Mafia respectively] don't match" (171). Latta significantly sees the only difference between Mafia violence and state-sanctioned black ops like the Bay of Pigs as one only of "style." He has a point—the "smoke and mirrors" refers to the elaborate cover-ups needed to keep "legitimate" operations secret, while most mob hits are done with less concern for consequents, even out in public. Whereas the Americans involved in this conspiratorial plot stretching from Havana to the grassy knoll in Dallas, Texas, are hiding the corrupt nature of their actions behind the mask of legitimacy, promoting democracy, if Latta and his cronies are exposed, they might kill each other or be passed over as just more dead Italian gangsters. The irony of the moral equivalency of covert operations and Mafia activities is heightened by the characterization of Larry Parmenter, a CIA operative who does not land in the Bay of Pigs but rather monitors the invasion from headquarters and dislikes dealing with Latta and other "roly-poly wops" (162). This comparison of mainstream American culture and Mafia culture hits with greater accuracy in the case of anti-Italian bigotry, of Mafia representation, and above all the assassination, the object of the Zapruder film. So once again in DeLillo's fiction, the evolution of Italian American characters and the use of film imagery move along parallel lines. The direction of *Libra* the novel is not an attempt at any justification but a search for historical truth, Fellini's right-eye reality, and it is not the finding of the absolute secret of JFK's killing (as one example) that is important but rather the search itself. Thus far, though, all we have seen would seem to point to the media's seemingly absolute subjectifying powers. *Americana*'s David Bell and *Libra*'s Lee Harvey Oswald are completely determined by unspeakable media force, Bell by his need to make film and the assassin by the famous photo of himself with the shotgun he attempts to flesh out. We do not see fully how the subject can creatively transcend the determining forces of stereotyping media.

Though some more Italian American characters can be found in other DeLillo fictions, such as Carmine Latta, the Mafioso who represents a gangland complicity in the assassination of John F. Kennedy in the novel *Libra*, it is only in DeLillo's magnum opus *Underworld* that we see fully explored this parallel motif that defines the use of Italian American culture in his fiction. The novel concerns American society from the first successful test detonation of a Soviet atomic bomb to 1992 and the end of the Cold War. It is centered on the various owners of a baseball hit by Ralph Branca in the 1951 pennant game between the New York Giants and the Brooklyn Dodgers, the "shot heard round the world" as juxtaposed with this Soviet shot. Thematically, this epic work takes on the enormous danger of nuclear holocaust and much of the Cold War ideology that propelled the arms race. Because a large part of the action takes place in the Little Italy of New York during this long stretch of the 20th century, Italian American characters and culture take a far more prominent role than they had in previous Don DeLillo novels. Here, the range of characters expands beyond gangster figures to include a wider range of men and women of Italian descent. Rather than simply play upon perceptions of mob stereotypes, in *Underworld* DeLillo explicitly challenges them by providing a revealing look at the maturation of two Italian American men. Nick Costanza Shay and his brother Matty are featured as they react to the disappearance of their father and become part of mainstream American society. DeLillo also features other notable characters of Italian American descent, most especially Nick and Matt's high school science teacher Albert Bronzini, to round out his portrayal of Italian Americans, their occasionally heroic moral stature, and the issue of their professional identities. Reinforcing his characterization with aspects of the setting and other references to Italian language and culture, DeLillo creates a most extensive and thorough parallel thematic structure to reinforce his theme of a retrospective look at the bipolar nuclear crisis that once divided the world. Further, his use of the Italian American culture as background also reinforces the theme of how we survived this particularly dangerous period of history.

To begin, Italian American culture in *Underworld* exists in a diverse template that DeLillo portrays in the urban New York of its time period: "The Italians. They sat on the stoop with paper fans and orangeades. They made their world. They said who's better than me? She could never say that. They knew how to sit there and be happy" (207). Despite this ethnic pride, Jimmy Costanza's disappearance has a huge impact on his sons. Matty cannot stop hoping for his return, and the older brother, Nick, maintains his hope that his father may have either died innocently or at least not violently (208). Looking again at Rosemary's reflections, we see Jimmy as immature and boyish, a kid down on his luck more than a man. With the abandonment of the father, Don DeLillo is unflinching in his portrayal of Italian American culture, not denying the worst aspects yet also reaffirming the best. Rather than simply dismissing or judging the image of the mob Italian, DeLillo uses this figure to set up other characters' emotional struggles. Characters like

Matt, Nick, and their teacher Albert Bronzini actually recognize the limits that the trickster's misbehavior points out and learn by their attempts to transcend them.

Not all Italian Americans are outlaws, and so too not all the Italian Americans in *Underworld* are mobsters. Nick successfully completes his Italian American journey of self-fulfillment by utilizing the resources his cultural background affords him. As with the prior novels *The Names* and *White Noise*, the main motif formed by his journey is reinforced by a structure of symbolic action in the journey of his younger brother Matt Costanza Shay. Nick takes the road from an outlaw life as a juvenile delinquent through his training by an intelligent Jesuit priest to become a leader in the field of waste management. Matt, in contrast, never lives outside the confines of the law. A precocious and neglected boy, it is through the combined attention of the aforementioned priest, but more importantly through the experiences of his bond with his former teacher Albert Bronzini, that Matt is able to complete his own journey. Finally, both boys show the influence of their science teacher because both pursue science-related occupations as their careers of choice. Nick becomes an environmental waste manager and Matt a nuclear physicist, involved in the making of bombs. Matt's choice might be seen as morally inferior, because he actually is making weapons. Later, Matt will change jobs, and we must consider this a very important plot detail because DeLillo's epic is particularly concerned with how fin-de-siècle American society survived the Cold War nuclear arms race. So the role of Bronzini becomes very important to trace as a counterbalancing influence in their lives to that of Jimmy Costanza. Further, this influence is used to represent a contrasting aspect of Italian American society, going beyond the outlaw image.

In tracing the development of these characters, one must take into account the fact that DeLillo's chronology works backward, showing the present situation of each character and then going back to the past, so that as one puts together Nick's story or Matty's one must tackle the later scenes in reverse order to the earlier ones. *Underworld* closes in the present, though, so it is easy to resolve the conclusion of each character's tale. With Nick, if we begin at the end, young Nick kills George Manza with a shotgun (780–781). The two had been involved with small-time crimes, such as gambling, but George hadn't told his friend that the sawed-off shotgun he gave him was loaded. This killing could be considered an accidental homicide, even though in terms of the consequences, it does not matter. Like the killing of George Manza, the reality of the nuclear arms race especially during the Cold War years was fraught with terrifying tales of accidents like nuclear "near misses" such as armed B-52s crashing and bombs lost at sea. So an analogy is formed between these two cultures of fatal accident: the world of gang warfare and that of nuclear warfare. Emphasized here is a kind of amoral avoidance of responsibility and an expansion of the symbolic parallel between state-sanctioned violence and Mafia violence.

Rather than stay stilted in this amoral world, though, Nick will benefit from his contact in reform school with the Jesuit priest Andrew Paulus. As will be demonstrated in my discussion of the Roman Catholic Church in *Underworld*, Father Paulus's influence is the most constructive in Nick's case and helps to transform him from young criminal to productive member of mainstream society. The priest is young and inspired when he begins his work with Nick, although he seems to be doing so reluctantly, repulsed by Nick Costanza Shay's origins among the working Italian poor of the Bronx. Father Andrew's college, Fordham University, has begun an outreach program to the community that involves taking on impoverished youth like Nick. This same program is not available to the same degree later to Nick's younger brother Matt as the priest has already committed himself to too many others. In all, Nick's interactions with Father Paulus do not center on Nick's Italian American background, which the priest sees as something to transcend. For his part, the Italian American high school science teacher Albert Bronzini also wants to transcend the poverty-laden world he inhabits, wanting better things for himself and his wife Klara than the pinochle-playing crowd he encounters in the early scenes of Little Italy in *Underworld* (768). He will find his transcendence through helping others like Matt primarily, and Nick. As the older boy goes out to make trouble with his gang, "Mr. Bronzini" has dinner with Matt and his family, discussing the fact that "a deep truth is what you want" (698). Unfortunately, though, Nick grows beyond the reach of Bronzini's positive moral influence, dropping out of school and walking the halls with his outlaw posse instead (701).

Yet Nick's experience of poverty and ethnic alienation sensitizes us to the fact that such legitimacy is frequently relative to one's wealth and social status. This is revealed as the narrative focus shifts; Nick is not the narrator of every scene, and we get a more generalized viewpoint to encompass both magnetic poles of the Italian American moral compass. As DeLillo describes a scene of an eviction from the neighborhood in Little Italy that Nick, Albert, and Matt share, the Italians reflect on how their socially marginalized condition renders them a spectacle to mainstream Americans, as if they live in a "museum of poverty" (768). Because hard work by the standards of Horatio Algers's America is always rewarded by wealth,

wealth is therefore the sure sign of moral virtue, poverty is evil, and to be alien is to be a demon or miscreant, or in the Italianate dialect of DeLillo's Italian American New York, a "Tizzoon" (768). Both mystified by the moral contradictions of the system and tantalized by their exclusion from its material "wonders," DeLillo's Italian Americans search for a proper target for their skepticism, a way to understand the American world they are excluded from.

Since inclusion or legitimacy is so vital and yet so elusive in this Italian American context, the role of the trickster becomes important in the narrative of *Underworld* as well as other DeLillo fictions. Such a one is the character of Nick Costanza Shay, especially in his irresolute youth. Neither completely evil as the "Tizzoon" nor morally good as Italian characters we'll meet later, Nick is best described by another Italian American dialect term his knockaround pal Vito calls him: "scucciamente" (695). A dialectical rough blend of two actual Italian words, "scoccia" meaning irritating and "mestatore" signifying "make mischief," it is a terrific term to describe a trickster, who deliberately breaks social barriers to establish his relevance. Here, Nick raucously relieves himself against a hospital wall, delaying a caper he is to pull off with Vito. This act is a quintessential trickster move, its inappropriateness signifying the social boundaries of health and sickness that George, Nick, and Vito seek to break.

But the role of Nick as the trickster is a bit more complicated than that. Nick functions as a narrator or storyteller of *Underworld*. His is not the only point of view through which we glean the events of the plot, but one of the central ones. Here DeLillo takes the model of the Italian American trickster beyond the role of the gangster. Trickster figures can also tell stories, as with Mark Twain's comic narrator Huck Finn. In *Underworld*, Nick's role as storyteller as he reads comic books to his younger brother Matt and friends emerges. Socially speaking, both the reader and his audience are marginalized by their lack of wealth and primarily Italian American ethnicity, for as the text explains, "Who else would read to them?" (210). As with Frank Volterra, Nick incorporates aspects of the trickster into his personality. Carl Jung talked about how civilized people tend to project forbidden desires and activities onto the trickster. Thus, in native American narratives like the Winnebago trickster cycle, the trickster actually teaches the recipient of the stories important lessons about life through his errors—what plants not to consume, and the like (Radin 3–55). This teaching capacity can be noted in Nick's reading to his younger and friends. Furthermore Nick is able to actively assimilate the mob trickster stereotype into his total personality, imitating a mob character he names "Mario Badalato" for the amusement and professional edification of his colleagues. So Nick begins to grow beyond the stereotypical role of the trickster/gangster and into a more legitimate and enlightened point of view.

As *Underworld* moves on, Nick's character continues to evolve to bring together an outsider perspective with the critical intelligence to pass moral judgment on the practices of society. Unlike some of the Italian Americans who do not leave the ghetto, Nick leaves to transcend his sordid and troubled past. He finds the proper object for his skepticism as he describes in another scene with his colleague Sims; the concept of *dietrologia* reflects this development or personal evolution: "There is a word in Italian. Dietrologia. It means the science of what is behind something. A suspicious event" (281). Nick will become the kind of skeptical thinker who can ultimately see beyond the ideological and cultural veneer that made nuclear mass destruction a thinkable alternative. He goes from Mafia underling to waste manager, finally confronting the consequences of the Cold War nuclear arms race.

With his Russian colleague Viktor he goes overseas to observe the sinister and destructive realities of nuclear weapons testing and nuclear waste (794). He also tours a hospital full of victims of Soviet nuclear testing; Nick comes to the conscious realization that the victim's disfigurations, cancers, and other nearly unspeakable sufferings are "all part of the same surreal" landscape of nuclear violence (800). Nick's intuitive *dietrologia* is an aspect of his Italian American identity, evolving out of his trickster's outsider viewpoint, a skepticism finding its proper object. As a trickster, Nick has revealed in his path to maturation the boundaries of what is permissible, shocking us with how the margins of "legitimate" American social practices actually hide the least possibly permissible moral crimes. With the character of Nick, Don DeLillo transforms the figure of the Italian American trickster from the simple hoodlum to a far richer figure, one who by the conclusion of *Underworld* is capable of understanding finer moral distinctions and a wider moral viewpoint than that of the immature gangster and whose viewpoint renders to the reader "the thick lived tenor of things" (827).

One could argue that though the starting point of Nick's journey is necessarily Italian American, the means by which he arrives at its endpoint are not necessarily so. Indeed, Nick's moral and intellectual reform can be accredited to the influence of a Catholic Jesuit priest, Father Andrew Paulus, who is not necessarily Italian. However, what is arguably the central thematic concern of *Underworld*, the accounting of the turning of hearts and minds away from the violence of the arms race, finds a parallel structure in the conversion of Nick. What is more, Nick's character, though inarguably a very important one in *Underworld*, is far from the only variation from the typical Italian American mafia stereotypes; his character may have Mafia tendencies, but they are recessive. Nevertheless, one cannot fully cover DeLillo's representation of Italian America in *Underworld* without considering the journey of Nick's younger brother, ex-nuclear weapon designer Matt Costanza Shay. More intimately connected with the perpetuation of the arms race, Matt's struggle to find a meaningful path will also confront symbolic contradictions and also redemptive aspects of Italian American culture. Along this path also emerges Albert Bronzini, the character who shows the starkest contrast from the commonplace Mafiosi by virtue of his ethical brilliance in DeLillo's version of the Italian American world.

For Matt Costanza Shay, who never flaunts the rules as his big brother does, life is in many ways a lot more difficult than it is for Nick. Matt is younger when his father Jimmy disappears, never to return alive. Nick notes that Matt longs for the return of Jim and is never able to let go of his feelings of abandonment during his father's absence. To make things even worse, Father Andrew Paulus, the priest who is so helpful to Nick, does not appear to provide that same fatherly care to Matty. When Albert Bronzini, the high school history teacher who has generously given of his own time to teach 12-year-old Matt to play chess, asks the priest to help Matt, Paulus emphatically refuses, revealing absolutely no compassion for Matt at all (674). He may be too caught up in Nick's case to be of help. But in the very same scene he volunteers, "I don't know what to tell you about the older brother" (675). He does not appear to be very interested in either Nick's or Matt's case even though Bronzini finally prevails upon him to attend a few matches. Matt does become a chess champion eventually, but not a particularly happy one or a particularly well-balanced person. It seems somehow that Matt does not fit the mold of what Paulus is looking for the special "Collegium" program Fordham is offering in the 1950s: "We have an idea, some of us, that's taking shape. A new sort of collegium.... We will teach subjects that people don't realize they need to know.... We'll want a special kind of boy. Special circumstances. Something he is. Something he's done. But something" (675).

Designing this pedagogy along these lines is a cruel gesture, setting up an expectation Matt cannot conform to. It is impossible for Matt to gain the experience he would require to be accepted into this "Collegium" and impossible for him to be accepted without the unquantifiable "special" experience the institution seeks. Andrew Paulus's cold and cruel rationale fails Matt utterly in the moral sense; the boy at first evolves into precisely the opposite of what a Jesuit Catholic education ought to produce.

The youthful chess champ internalizes what Father Paulus referred to as the "killer instinct" of chess too well; he grows up to become a "consequence analyst...figuring out the lurid mathematics of a nuclear accident or limited exchange" (402). As in his chess training, Matt must squelch all human feeling to project these consequences, excusing the accidental release of nuclear bombs with the rejoinder "Nobody's perfect, OK?" We can see this in his job conditions. Matty cannot remove the safety gloves nuclear technicians like himself are required to wear. They protect themselves from radioactive materials via a "sealed glove box" (403). To contemplate Armageddon requires a complete emotional suppression of all feelings of compassion. So Matt will suffer in relationships as a result of said emotional constipation. His love interest is Janet Urbaniak, an ER nurse, and they have a very bland and passionless-sounding relationship: "They were on-again, off-again, mostly on, often impatient with each other but always strongly joined, the kind of star-matched couple born to meet and disagree" (412). The spectacle of the nurse dating the young architect of the nuclear holocaust is grotesquely humorous; the natural fruition of his work would render hers impossible. They appear to delay having a family because of the "complexity of the undertaking...how hard it is to do everything right." Janet shares Matt's complete emotional detachment from the human condition: "She was matter of fact about it, bodies flopping on the just-mopped floor of the corridor, relative dragging in a knife victim or OD" (414). When they are together, the sparks do not seem to fly. Janet is nervous and uncomfortable in the hotel, their lovemaking "melancholy and slightly odd, it was calm and sweet and loving but also odd and slightly resigned and they lay together without speaking for a long time afterward" (461). This is troublesome when Matt reflects on stopping to help out a female anti-nuclear protester but finally admits internally that he only wants "mutually tolerant sex" with her (412). As in *End Zone*, the juxtaposition of anti-nuclear themes and symbolic contradiction is important.

Moreover, not only does Matt lose out on loving relationships, but even in his primary relationship to himself, as DeLillo reveals that Matt wanted to enter the field of weapons design "for the self-knowledge he might find in a sterner life, in the fixing of willful limits" (422). Yet all he does on this quest is to get stoned "at parties, where he'd go through the sociable motions, taking a pull on the long-stemmed pipe with a clay bowl" (421). As with his relationships, this quest of a man abandoned by both his father and his would-be priest leads to a dead end, where consciousness becomes "a thing retained in the snake-brain of early experience." As this scene concludes, "Matt drove west, deeper into the white parts of the map, where he would try to find a clue to his future" (422). His literal and figurative retreat into oblivion signifies the failure of the journey to self-knowledge, a dual failure of his primary relationship with himself and others.

To heighten the tension in the case of this out-of-touch technician of mass destruction, Matt seems to be beyond the reach of the American Catholic Church, which was so helpful in his brother's case. The metaphor of film and filmmaking returns here. DeLillo paints him beautifully in this alienated state. Eight days after his father leaves the family for good

> the boy took all the change he could find in the apartment...going to the Grand Concourse, where the movie theater stood, the Loew's Paradise.... He sees himself from this distance in the white sands standing across the street looking at the great italianate façade of the Paradise.... He looked at the etched glass chandeliers...paintings hung in gilded frames. He thought this was a thousand times holier than church. (407)

The empty movie house embraces the significance of the filmmaking metaphor as well. If filmmaking is as an act of self-representation, Matt's truncated self-representation is well represented by the blank screen he watches, the emptiness of his self-esteem and deadened emotional state. Both the church and the Italian American neighborhood are to him at this point a mere façade, as unreal as the movies shown at the Paradise Theater. All Matt can do is wait "for his father, for the ghost or soul of his father to make a visitation" (408).

Enter Albert Bronzini, the Italian American science teacher who both provided Matt with an education and also gave of his free time to teach Matt chess. Bronzini's compassion, shown to almost everyone he encounters, renders him a redemptive figure within DeLillo's portrayal of Italian Americans in their New York setting. In his younger days, Bronzini takes his mother into his care, a woman dying of a neuromuscular condition. We also see him teaching his daughter to say the word "tangerine" (683). This image connects him all the way back to the orange-flavored sodas the Costanza family enjoys, an idea of earthly pleasure. As we see the happy little Bronzini family, the father taking a bath and the lovely artist-wife Klara Sax as mother, dipping baby Theresa's stocking feet into Daddy's tub, the scene is one of complete sensual bliss: "This was happiness as it was meant to evolve when first conceived in caves, in mud huts on the grassy plain. Mamalah and our beautiful bambina" (681). DeLillo's additional comment that nothing suits the body as well as water enriches the feeling of compassionate fulfillment. Even the image of the "tangerine" that Bronzini himself correctly associates with Tangiers, the port of origin for this citrus fruit, brings to mind exotic pleasures. These pleasures are short-lived: Klara and Albert divorce as she is unfaithful to him. We experience his pain as he passes his old schoolhouse and sees nothing but an "old squat pile of limestone and brick" (235). Out of his suffering, Bronzini finds more people to help, taking care of his ailing sister Laura when his mother dies and Clara has left. This spirit of compassion is later shared by his daughter Theresa when she grows up, marries, has two children of her own, and starts a child-care center (231). In fact, when we see Albert later in time as a much older man, he is helping his friend Eddie Robles by cutting Eddie's hair. Robles was a subway token-taker crippled by an accident and later by age. Bronzini's barber tools become images symbols of this compassionate practice as something imbued in Italian American culture. He uses a "beautiful pair of scissors, made in Italy, a family possession for generations" (222).

However, it is more than just tender care and the chess lessons that enable Matt to get back in touch with his emotions and show some moral maturation. Remembering his kindly teacher, Matt returns to see Mr. Bronzini, and the mentor advises him to visit the sights of their Little Italy Bronx neighborhood of his youth to restore his spirits (214).

The Italian American mentor, a clear literary representation of great real Italian American educators such as New York's Angelo Patri and Leonard Covello, advises Matt further to open himself to a vision of Little Italy that can serve as a new film for Matt's mental blank screen: "And these were your streets. It's a curious rite of passage, isn't it? Visit the old places.... There are things here, people who show the highest human qualities, outside all notice" (214). Projecting this "notice" of the real moral quality of Italian American people into Matt's mind, Bronzini has been able to prompt the other man to show greater moral sensibility.

Matt begins by moving away from his government weapons research. More open to compassion because he has received it from his Italian American teacher, Matt's response at Jimmy's funeral shows greater emotional maturity. He leans on Nick, grieving, and the two brothers grow closer as they can release themselves from the pain of Jimmy's disappearance. For Matt, the emotional suppression of his career as a weapons research, his cold chess-like analysis of nuclear consequences, and his sense of internal disconnection from self and others all fade in light of this experience of some Italian American compassion. So in summary, Nick and Matt's journey, guided in part by Albert Bronzini, shows that their particular culture is much richer and more morally sophisticated that most of the media representations outside of DeLillo's original work might cause readers or viewers to believe. Bronzini, though he is weakened by age and his wife's betrayal, emerges finally as the alternative to gangsters and other less-than-savory characters, unlocking the divine and compassionate potential DeLillo perhaps alludes to in his earliest reference in *The Names* to the chapel in the real town of Volterra.

Finally, as is the case with all the prior novels examined in this chapter, the filmmaking motif parallels and reinforces precisely the evolution of the representation or literary "filming" of Italian American characters by the author DeLillo. Largely a novel about spiritual and moral conversions, such as Matt's and Nick's and that of the conservative Catholic nun Sister Alma Edgar, a conversion of another sort happens as a result of viewing a film. The idea in the filmmaker becomes a postmodern metaphor above and beyond the isolated right eye of factual history (as in *Libra*) and the indeterminate and imaginative eye of fantasy (as in *Americana* and other novels). Here DeLillo invents an imagined film of the historically real Russian filmmaker Sergei Eisenstein to illustrate the process of the author or story maker raising the reader's consciousness through the text or film. Albert Bronzini's ex-wife and former lover of Nick, Klara Sax, becomes the focus of *Underworld*. During the early years of her career as a single mom and artist, she attends a screening of a fictitious early Sergei Eisenstein science fiction film in Russian of a mad scientist keeping prisoners underground and mutating them with atomic rays (428). Titled as the novel is *Unterwelt*, it becomes an apt metaphor for the forced compliance of the Soviet people to the atomic testing and mutations Nick sees the consequences of in Kazakhstan with Viktor. Klara grows in moral sensitivity, an audience member open to film and filled with reverential awe as was Matt in New York. She ultimately begins to relate to the filmed prisoners, seeing in them the suffering of Eisenstein the artist/filmmaker: "the independent artist who is disciplined and Sovietized" (443). When Nick, who has viewed these mutations in the "right eye" of reality or historical fact, and Klara, who has seen these mutations through the "left eye" of fantasy film, reunite, we learn that she is creating an artistic project of repainting retired B-52 bombers in life-affirming colors and peace signs. Though she insists this effort is not a peace project, it would seem the film has inspired her with an antinuclear impulse. Like the mob stereotypes the author transforms via Nick's creativity and Bronzini's compassion, the repainted B-52s are an image of destruction transformed into something creative, a force for beauty and good like film or fiction itself. Moving from the fantasized stock mob figures of *Americana* and *Running Dog* through the historicized real connections between mob and mainstream government in *Libra* to the final wide-angle lens over Little Italy in all its moral and immoral glory in *Underworld*, film or text has finally become the site in which the subject can transcend the determining power of media representation.

Thus DeLillo's "filming" of Italian Americans in various degrees of filming or representing themselves closes on a hopeful note. Like Matt, Nick, and Albert, the contemporary subject moves through determining mediations of him or herself with a relative degree of autonomy. The author himself as an image stands as an excellent example of indetermination and freedom from the Italian American stereotype. There is, however, yet a wider screen on which to view morality and the issues of self-representation emerging from the fiction. The poignancy of Bronzini's character being left alone to root through the "squat pile of bricks" that had consumed his life is haunting enough. Though the parallel motifs of Italian American representation and film point to ways in which the individual *can* transcend sinister mediation, it is only a naïve appreciation of Don DeLillo's work that will assert that he or she always *will* be able to do so under any conditions. Rather, this complex epistemological explanation of the contemporary subject needs an ever-wider angle lens over crucial cultural surfaces. In the next chapter, I will examine the moral conflicts involved in DeLillo's representation of the Roman Catholic Church in its philosophical complexity during the late 20th century. So doing will unearth both more dietrologia and a clearer moral path for the individual living in our times.

Chapter 6

The Inner Divisions of People and Systems in *Underworld*'s Roman Catholic Church

DeLillo's treatment of the Italian American stereotype and his deconstruction of it in the last chapter is a sufficient example of resistance to the contemporary mediated attack on the subject, but there is more to some of the larger moral issues at stake than simply the phenomenon of ethnic identity. To evoke metaphysical ideas is a risky move, and discussion of an unspeakable evil tends to bring in the opposite pole of dialectic: what about a nameless, ineffable good? About this unattained good, John Paul Russo argues that *Underworld*'s final word, "Peace," is more of an "uttered prayer" than a "claim fulfilled" (Russo, "*Religion*" 123). Part of everyday material reality participates in a higher good as its crucial surface, materialized in the moral compassion displayed through the character of Bronzini. But since the evils presented in DeLillo's fictions can accurately be called socially, historically, and materially grounded as in the case of Oswald (see chapter 4), so too would be their opposite, a concretized material agenda traceable in the historicized fiction of *Underworld*. Final peace in the nuclear age is indeed but a future hope, as Russo posits. But certain trends within our very present and "quotidian" (Russo, "Religion") history would bring such peace closer and some push it further away; therefore, we would also need to read this good represented in a dialectical form, as a field interactive with some stultifying or "Sovietizing" forces in the worse sense meant in Klara Sax's reflections. So to broaden our view of the crucial cultural surfaces that bind up the patterns in DeLillo's fictions, his presentation of the Roman Catholic Church, with all of its internal moral contradictions intact though dialectically in tension with each other, will here be analyzed as it is introduced in *White Noise* and developed more fully in *Underworld*. The same crafty authorial stylization of history that gave us a scene of JFK's shooting both believable in terms of known fact and not finalizable in a way that would quench future investigations of the truth presents to us a historical speculation on the lifestyle of a group within the American Catholic Church whose role is to demonstrate a possible path to survival in the nuclear age. This is not to diminish the significance of the prior treatment of Italian Americans that we find in DeLillo; however, the societal nature of the surface texture of the writings takes us out of Little Italy and into the minds of Catholic clerics.

DeLillo was certainly not the only author assessing Catholic culture at the end of the 20th century, but he was perhaps the only good one. The flash-in-the-pan success of *The DaVinci Code* ironically demonstrates that Don DeLillo certainly was not the only popular writer thinking about moral questions of good and evil and Catholicism at the time *Underworld* was being written. But unlike the well-known treatments of disguised Jesuits, Masons, and lurid excitement, DeLillo's underground priests and nuns do not greet each other with secret handshakes and decoder rings. They are "under the radar" in a different sense, dealing with today's urban poor of New York City and poverty-stricken countries like Colombia, rather than medieval archeological digs and antiquated skullduggeries. They are unknown because they care about those people whom society avoids. So for Don to treat some Catholic reality in his fiction is certainly to open the door a bit more widely towards a more diverse and multicultural view of the problems of good and evil we are searching for in our own decoding of his work. In addition, Don's picture of the "underground" Catholic Church beat Dan Brown's to the presses by several years, as *Underworld* was a bestseller in 1999, some four years before *The DaVinci Code*. Furthermore and fortunately, unlike with the case of DeLillo's Italians, academic writers have been more willing to join me in opening up the idea of popular religion in DeLillo's work. Scholarship here has made some progress on the question of novelized Catholicism. Yale professor Amy Hungerford argues in "Don DeLillo's Latin Mass" that our Italian American master of fiction "ultimately transfers a version of mysticism from the Catholic context into the literary one . . . through the model of the Latin Mass" (343). To this Joseph Dewey adds in his 2006 book, "Catholicism gives DeLillo's work an essential vocabulary of spirituality . . . it endows his vision with a gravitas, a sense of complexity to existence" (11). But Hungerford says, "This transfer (of Catholic thinking) does not, moreover, mark him as either doctrinaire or conservative in the sense one might think" (343). She's arguing that just because the author talks about his religion in his work does not mean that any of his novels unabashedly support the Catholic Church in all its positions. In fact, my case here is that DeLillo's position on Church philosophy and practices is dialectical in nature. Operating from a viewpoint greatly informed by Catholic education, DeLillo deconstructs the conservative and dichotomized politics and theology of early 20th-century Catholicism while also exposing little-known trends in the Americanized ideology and politics of the more liberal and variegated Catholic paradigm that emerged after the detonation of the Soviet bomb around which *Underworld* revolves. Beginning with the enigmatic figure of Sister Hermann Marie in *White Noise*, this dialectical portrayal of contradictory American Catholicism(s) evolves into the more sophisticated and divided portrayals of the American Jesuit Father Andrew Paulus, Sister Alma Edgar, and Sister Grace Fahey of *Underworld*.

What follows here is a reading of DeLillo's priests and nuns as they appear in moral conflict, both with the forces of war and oppression in society and sometimes even within their own hearts. From *White Noise*, Sister Hermann Marie is a paradoxical and comically contradictory figure who, in the conflict between her words and actions, manages to embody both the pre–Vatican II and post–Vatican II theo-political tendencies of American Catholicism. In *Underworld*, the major figure of Andrew Paulus S.J. is deployed by DeLillo to expose the difficult position of the Roman Catholic Church in the modern American political landscape. Though his impact on Nick is quite clearly positive, the priest's ultimate status is indeterminate and inextricably interwoven with the more ethnically marked figure of Italian American teacher Albert Bronzini, complicating the issue of narrowing down the personal and political impact of the priest. However, both the oppressive and liberating tendencies of the postwar American Catholic church find their proper placement in DeLillo's ideological schema as each tendency is reflected in Sister Alma's and Sister Grace's characters respectively. Against the backdrop of the historical changes in American culture in the 1950s and beyond, elements of setting reinforce the inevitable theological conflict as well as its resolution. Never before in the history of American letters have the ideological and practical aspects of radical nonviolent Catholic clerics been thus valorized. Nor has the potential of their lifestyles both as a suggestion for contemporary action and retrospectively, from the point of view of the narrative as a product of the cantastoria or singer of history, been portrayed at all in American literature. However, rather than as a simple political direct statement, the presence of this dialectical perspective on Catholicism as a social force has wider implications for DeLillo's vision of literary art and the social responsibility of the artist. *Underworld*'s presentation of this dialectical tension and its resolution is finally, completely consistent with the portrayals of American society found in his other novels and with certain public actions the author himself has notably undertaken. Art in DeLillo is not reducible to its political implications, yet it is simultaneously inseparable from them. However, a sociological and historical approach to DeLillo's clerical figures may be far more important and less reductionist than many DeLillo critics might have us believe. DeLillo's work and its moral implications challenge us to open up our horizons in defining what fiction might be and could achieve.

To sum up the treatment of the priest, protagonist Nick Costanza Shay experiences a positive moral reform at the hands of Jesuit father Andrew Paulus. However, it took some time for Paulus to evolve into the more compassion man he is. But there is an inconsistency here, as a lengthy look at Matt Costanza Shay reveals that Father Paulus does not, and maybe cannot, exert the same influence on Matt as he did on Nick. A more positive portrait of Catholicism comes about when we consider the sisters Alma and Grace in *Underworld*. These sisters come to represent the actions of the antiwar Catholic left, a group that few know about but that exerted a powerful moral influence in Cold War American society anyway.

DeLillo's portrayal of Roman Catholicism is a mix of positive and negative images; thus the writer achieves a balanced representation of this institution in his fiction. Such a mixed representation of Catholicism, as a church with great potential to change the world for the better but also one with real moral problems, sustains via the figures in DeLillo's other major novel *Underworld*. In comparison to *White Noise*, *Underworld* offers a greater variety of characters to represent Catholicism in many aspects. One of the most important figures in *Underworld* is the Jesuit priest Father Andrew Paulus, who serves as mentor to the protagonist Nick Costanza Shay and is acquainted with his brother Matt Shay and the boys' science teacher Albert Bronzini. Two other Catholic clerics are the two nuns in *Underworld*, Sister Alma Edgar and Sister Grace Fahey, both of whom have been the subject of much DeLillo scholarship of late. Many of the other characters experience the Catholic faith as well from a layperson's point of view. By focusing on these clerics we gain a deep insight into DeLillo's perspective on Church practices in everyday operation.

To begin to see DeLillo's dialectical representation of Catholicism in action, we return to *White Noise*'s satirical handling of Sister Hermann Marie's treatment of the injured Jack Gladney as he is hospitalized for gunshot wounds. A positive representation of a socially responsible Catholicism is evoked by a picture "of Jack Kennedy holding hands with Pope John XXIII in Heaven" (316). In a novel dealing with issues of toxic waste and thus symbolically evoking the idea of nuclear waste and the arms race, this picturing hanging in Jack's hospital has significance. On the issue of nuclear arms, John XXIII's statement was that "nuclear weapons must be banned. A general agreement must be reached on a suitable disarmament program, with an effective system of mutual control" (John XXIII, "Need" 112). In accord with John XXIII, President John F. Kennedy was a Catholic who advocated these causes. Kennedy limited the seemingly endless expansion of the airborne toxic impact of nuclear weapon use during the Cold War by bringing about the limited atmospheric nuclear test-ban treaty of August 3, 1963.

Thematically, this emblematic picture of the two major Catholic public figures is relevant because Gladney is suffering the impact of a toxic waste accident and violence, the consequences of social irresponsibility as opposed to the appropriate social responsibility of liberal Catholicism here represented. So DeLillo represents Catholicism as having the potential to make a positive impact on society, easing social problems by exercising the Church's moralizing power. Jack feels a certain draw towards this faith as the scene progresses: "Why shouldn't it be true? Why shouldn't we all meet, as in some epic of protean gods and ordinary people, aloft, well-formed, shining?" (317). Despite the somewhat sarcastic reference to "protean gods," the protagonist Gladney is sincerely looking to religious faith for transcendence in his time of suffering as the repetition of his question indicates. Sister Hermann Marie is the Catholic nun who cares for Jack Gladney in his time of need. Yet she resists the conservative traditionalist rationalizations for the faith, defying Jack's inquiries for simple, pat formulaic answers to questions about her faith:

> I said to my nun, "What does the Church say about heaven today . . . if it isn't the abode of God and the angels and the souls of those who are saved?"
> "Saved? What is saved? This is a dumb head, who would come in here to talk about angels. Show me an angel. Please. I want to see." (317)

Jack does not know how to take the good sister's reaction. He is troubled that he cannot base his own personal faith on her certitude in action, becoming "frustrated and puzzled, close to shouting" (317). In his quest to find some meaning and solace, Gladney cannot rely upon the robotic pat answers of pre-Vatican II Catholicism. She is not a mindless automaton, mouthing formulaic answers to difficult personal questions. By refusing his requests for such easy answers, she is very cleverly forcing him to take responsibility for his own search for faith. If she had admitted to Catholic beliefs, Gladney may

have mocked her with skeptical questions, as he frequently does with Heinrich or his friend Murray Siskin (50–51). But instead, Sr. Marie forces him to
accept responsibility for his own actions, confronting the spectacle of angst
in the midst of faith. Speaking of her own community's faith, she states,

> It is for others. Not for us. . . . It is our task in the world to believe things
> no one else takes seriously. To abandon such beliefs completely, the human
> race would die. . . . We surrender our lives to make your nonbelief possible. . . .
> There is no truth without fools. We are your fools, your madwomen, rising
> at dawn to pray, lighting candles, asking statues for good health, a long
> life. (319)

Although the last phrase is a bit mocking, Sr. Marie's point is well taken.
In Jack Gladney's selfish and image-conscious world (seen in many places
throughout *White Noise* including his obsession with his academic robe and
dark glasses) her unselfish active faith, here found in her tending to Jack's
gunshot wounds (318), is the most necessary and proper expression of religious faith. This example stands in contrast to the world DeLillo portrays
in *White Noise*, where selfish and rampant capitalism causes the airborne
disaster, as the toxic waste is the by-product of insecticide manufacture.
This toxic waste is a metaphor for toxic nuclear waste as a by-product of
the Cold War arms race, with the enemy Soviet Union as the "pest" to be
exterminated.

In contrast to the messy and violent world DeLillo portrays in *White
Noise*, Sr. Marie's example is that of charity, evoking the idea of social
responsibility inherent in the Vatican II–era Catholic faith of John XXIII
and John F. Kennedy. The Second Vatican Council, or "Vatican II," was
an international gathering of church hierarchy to legislate on all matters
of theology and church operations, especially in terms of the development
of modern technologized society. Therefore, Vatican II is relevant to the
interaction taking place here in DeLillo's work, as certain reforms it caused
within the Catholic Church emphasized dealing with issues such as urban
violence, environmental protection, and the international violence of the
nuclear arms race (*Documents of the Second Vatican Council*).

Sister Marie is charitable and socially engaged in helping the sick without proselytizing; despite what her words imply, her actions signify a more
action-based Christian faith. However, there is another pole to the dialectical crisis of faith she represents. Her actions signify this magnificent trend
in contemporary Catholicism, but is her heart in her work? The harshness
of her response to Jack is taken to a satirical extreme; one would think

that with such serious issues at play a single word of comfort would be appropriate while she is also associated with the complex issue of media simulation in *White Noise*. She tells Jack very explicitly that the picture with all of its symbolic implications of socially responsible and morally positive Catholicism is simply there "for others. Not for us" (318). This oblique response, in context, denies the reader access to a determinant sense of which tendency within Catholicism reigns dominant in her system—its socially engaged and compassionate side or its cold denial of Jack's perhaps real need for affirmation in favor of a compartmentalized approach to faith; she tells him to "go elsewhere" to discuss the metaphysics of heaven.

With this dialectical portrayal of Catholicism thus outlined in a kind of brown study, we must turn to *Underworld* for an expansion and elaboration of the statement made about subjectivity and faith by the author. To begin, Father Andrew Paulus's role in the life of the protagonist Nick Costanza Shay is a morally positive presentation of Catholic clerics, but this portrayal is balanced with emotional realism and the other pole of the dialectic. Paulus is a Jesuit priest. His name is significant in its etymological implications—the name "Andrew" is of Greek origin and means "warrior," while "Paulus" is a Latin term meaning "little or short." So this priest is the "little warrior" who will perform an ethical/moral battle to save Nick Costanza Shay from the evil that threatens to take him down. Nick, a young man of strong will, endures the academic rigor and discipline the priest imposes and emerges from the process a changed man.

For background information, the Jesuit priesthood was founded by Catholic St. Ignatius of Loyola in 1534 and dedicated to the practice of Catholic higher education from its onset. They continue their good work worldwide, even receiving death threats from paramilitary groups in Colombia ("An Appeal for Reflection" 1). Father Paulus is the only person Nick can rely upon to help him when he is a juvenile delinquent, having shot a friend during his troubled youth. In the court system, Nick is classified as "an E-felony, criminally negligent homicide, reduced from a charge of manslaughter in the second degree" (502), and this violent youth is taken in by the priest and given a kind of "tough love" that ultimately will benefit him. To begin, a veteran Father Paulus is represented as a solid and respectable priest who offers young Nick a reliable form of guidance; he tells the juvenile, "Rage and violence can be elements of productive tension in a soul. They can serve the fullness of one's identity" (538). He is counseling the youth to channel his problematic anger into some useful action, and he does so with a sense of traditional ethics and an open-minded spirit for the youth to follow. His knowledge is of the writings of St. Thomas Aquinas, a Catholic theologian who practiced logical systems of analysis and classification to prove the existence of God via his "Five Ways." Aquinas thought God could be known through intelligence or "natural reason," which Father Paulus tries to get Nick to develop in this scene (Soccio 227–254). Paulus's awareness of Aquinas serves well to help enlighten Nick:

> Have you come across the word velleity? A nice Thomistic ring to it. Voli-
> tion at its lowest ebb. . . . If you're low-willed, you see, you end up living in
> the shallowest turns and bends of your own preoccupations. Are we getting
> anywhere? Aquinas said only intense actions will strengthen a habit. Not
> mere repetition. Intensity makes for moral accomplishment. An intense and
> persevering will. This is an element of seriousness. Constancy. This is an ele-
> ment. A sense of purpose. A self-chosen goal. Tell me I'm babbling. I'll respect
> you for it. (539)

He is encouraging a boy who has already shown criminal tendencies to value his own will and strong volitions yet transform them into moral ones. Here he also is open to criticism as he says he will "respect" Nick's disagreement and as he checks in to see if the delinquent youth is being attentive: "Are we getting anywhere?" He talks to Nick Costanza Shay in terms of "constancy" and "moral accomplishment" and may well be the first adult ever to do so in this boy's life. Furthermore, Fr. Andrew Paulus shows some compassion by teaching Nick Aristotelian classification; the young man cannot discern the difference between productive and destructive tension. Aristotle's system of classification, or identifying entities via sameness and difference to others, is of great use to Nick as Fr. Paulus here guides him to a better understanding of the purpose of life (Soccio 167–194).

Fr. Paulus teaches him to classify knowledge by getting him to identify the parts of a shoe (542). The lesson is harshly comic but is effective as Nick's rage begins to yield to a practical awareness of his own ignorance and subsequent humility. Finally, Fr. Andrew Paulus attempts to raise Nick Costanza Shay's political consciousness when the latter joins a pro-McCarthy group. Father Paulus asks if Nick comprehends why the Senate had condemned Joseph McCarthy (543) but cannot effectively convince Nick at this point of the error of his ways of supporting the 1950's rabid anti-Communist McCarthy. So Nick is very fortunate to receive three kinds of compassionate help from the Jesuit Paulus. He has a teacher well-versed in the kinds of moral teaching he needs, that teacher is very open to Nick's opinions about the material, and finally the priest is trying to open Nick's mind to alternative political points of view. A Roman Catholic like the characters in this scene, McCarthy became notorious for falsely accusing both colleagues and rivals of being Communist and thus exploiting concurrent American fears such as that Sr. Alma Edgar has. McCarthy was given information by J. Edgar Hoover's FBI (Simkin 1).

Not surprisingly, Nick's brother Matthew Costanza Shay and his mother teasingly refer to an older, morally reformed Nick as "the Jesuit," behind Nick's back (450). This comic nickname is both a tribute to and a sign of Father Andrew Paulus's influence.

With all the excellent support the reader finds in *Underworld* for the Jesuit's positive influence on Nick's life, one might feel that DeLillo overwhelming supports the Church's practices in everyday operation. But this good priest was not always so good, as we follow his character's development, or rather its unraveling, through DeLillo's reverse chronology. As mentioned above, DeLillo presents very positive and extremely negative aspects of the Catholic Church's social role in a balanced fashion. Therefore, the reader finds on the symbolic and thematic level severe issues in Father Paulus's character that evoke the deep problems of the Catholic Church at the end of the twentieth century. Because of the ethnic and class-based divisions of society, the Catholic Church also is hampered in its attempts to help its constituents morally and to change what DeLillo clearly sees as a troubled American society. Look at the physical description of Father Andrew: the priest is satirically described as "built low and cozy" (668), almost as if he has been mass-produced on a Ford or Chevy assembly line. On a similar note, despite Paulus's arguably successful handling of Nick's intellectual development, the priest earlier on in the chronology of the novel reveals again his class bias and his anti-Italian bias in the scene where kindly high school history teacher Albert Bronzini attempts to enlist his aid in training Matty Costanza Shay in competitive chess playing. Matt, "only 11" at the time of this scene, has shown some promise in chess as Bronzini has tutored him "three days a week, a couple of hours each visit" (671). Here, Father Andrew Paulus reveals in a powerful way his many evocative character flaws. Though Bronzini has taken Matt under his wing as a chess disciple, Fr. Paulus's attitude toward Bronzini's request for help is pretty deplorable, as he reminds the teacher of the emotional burden of working with Matty: "You've made your plea. Consider your duty effectively discharged, Albert" (671). By calling this request a "duty," Andrew Paulus removes the element of compassion so important in Bronzini's interaction with Matt Costanza Shay. Bronzini does not appear to be pleased with Andrew Paulus's response to his request; he must remember to laugh when the two share a joke about their students. Bronzini pleads here on behalf of

Matt's mother, "What a waste if a youngster like this were to end up in a stockroom or garage" (671). Yet the priest has absolutely no empathy for Matt and his situation, making callous comments about how Matt's father abandoned him without giving the boy many chess lessons (671).

When Bronzini begins to plead more earnestly, Andrew Paulus "sat upright in his chair, formally withdrawing, it seemed, to a more objective level of discourse" (674); he is of course showing through body language his lack of compassion and refusal to help. Finally he gives Bronzini some unpriestly advice for how to deal with Matt: "The psychology is in the player, not the game. He must enjoy the company of danger. He must have a killer instinct. He must be prideful, arrogant, contemptuous and dominating. Willful in the extreme. All the sins, Albert, of the noncarnal type" (674).

Clearly, the priest is correct in his description of the instinct Matt needs to master chess. But he's advising him to turn Matt into a moral Frankenstein monster, egocentric in the extreme just as the priest himself is when he confesses in the same scene to Bronzini his real regrets about the celibate lifestyle, "What, not marrying? . . . I don't want to marry. I would like to screw a movie star, Albert. I want to screw her in the worst way possible and I mean that in every sense" (672). So for Andrew Paulus, this repressed sex drive has become the egocentric killer instinct of the chess player. For Bronzini's part, he thinks Paulus is subtly upbraiding him for not being serious enough about helping Matt: "The man's remarks were directed at his own [Albert's] genial drift, of course, not the boy's" (674). Yet is Bronzini correct in his judgment of Paulus's remarks or just trying to reassure himself?

Matty does not have a "genial drift" in this scene; he's not even at the table with his teacher and this priest. As a further response to Albert's pleas on Matty's behalf, Fr. Paulus is quick to minimize the perception of a need for help, reflecting, "Children find a way. They sidestep time, as it were, and the ravages of progress" (671). After warning Bronzini that one would have to spend "hours and days. Whole days at chess. Days and weeks," an impossible task for the compassionate high school teacher who at this point in the narrative has a wife and two year-old daughter, and hearing Bronzini's fear that he himself would be "unequal to the job," Andrew Paulus issues a very telling response. Quoth the Jesuit, "Please. Do you think I'd even consider tutoring the boy? Albert, please, I have a life, such as it is" (674). This response tells us that the priest's bitterness and despair at his own unfulfilling life has choked off any compassion he might have had for Matty, even though he will come to Nick's aid later in time. Eventually,

Bronzini's persistence on Matt's behalf wears down his opponent's resistance to help Matt: "Look, I'm willing to attend a match or two. Give you some guidance if I can. But I don't want to be his teacher. No no no no" (674). These last four "Nos" slam the door on Matty's future development in more ways than one. Thus the Jesuit, the teaching-priest, denies Matt's desperate need for a teacher.

What's worse, especially for the Italian American reader of this scene, is Fr. Andrew Paulus's reaction to the visibly ethnic Italian American grandmother who serves Bronzini and Fr. Paulus their coffee at the restaurant where they are talking of Matty:

> [The Italian grandmother] poured an ashy dram [of white sambuca] into each demitasse and the priest colored slightly as he seemed to do in the close company of people who were markedly different. Their unknown lives disconcerted him, making his smile go stiff and bringing to his cheeks a formal blush of deference. (675)

Nona's "marked difference," her Italian American identity, troubles the priest. Perhaps Fr. Paulus fears the need her economic class status and Italian ethnic identity. All this could be forgiven in light of Paulus's generosity to Nick, but this same elitist fear, this being troubled by markers of difference, emerges even in Paulus's interactions with Nick Costanza Shay. It seems class-based prejudices against the poor blind even the Catholic Church's highly competent and educated representatives.

Ergo, the all-too-human power of Fr. Paulus as a priest is revealed in Nick's response to him in the scene where he visits the priest in his office. Nick reflects, "You were always afraid of disappointing Father, being unequal to the level of discourse. Being bland when he wanted a more spirited sort of traffic, even a bullshit act, wiseass and slouchy. Bland and plodding when he wanted independence and open argument" (538).

Second-guessing the priest's expectations is a survival skill for the reform school student. Yet despite this power, and the implicit trust Nick puts in Father Paulus, the priest does not consider the Italian American student to be an intelligent enough receptacle for the knowledge he imparts to his students at the reform school, or even at Fordham: "Sometimes I think the education we dispense is better suited to a fifty-year old who feels he missed the point the first time around. . . . You'd be better served looking at your shoe and naming the parts. *You in particular, Shay, coming from the place you come from*" (540; italics mine). As discussed earlier in this chapter, Paulus then proceeds to teach Nick the parts of the shoe, certainly a unique means of imparting to him the pedagogy of classification and division as the important intellectual training mentioned earlier. On the other hand, perhaps Paulus thinks Nick can only become a shoemaker since Nick comes from the Italian American section of the Bronx that surrounds the priest's wealthier place of employment, Fordham University. As Bronzini puts it, "Our two schools, Andy, directly across the road from each other and completely remote. My students, some of them don't know, they remain completely unaware of the fact that there's a university lurking in the trees" (671). Reminding the reader of his good sense of humor, though, the priest responds, "Some of my students have the same problem" (671). Economic conditions and social ethnic prejudices would appear to trump the morally redemptive power of the Catholic cleric in service to the poverty-stricken Italian American Nick Costanza Shay.

Though humorous in nature, Fr Andrew Paulus's jaded take on Fordham and his bitter belittling of the place Nick comes from disclose a troubling spiritual dysfunction. In the section labeled "January 11, 1955," Paulus dismisses a student's comment about rumors concerning "Pope Pius having mystical visions" with another defamatory statement, as follows: "If you'd been drinking dago red until three in the morning, you'd be having visions too" (536). Here the students in Paulus's class have misunderstood reports about Pope Pius XII, predecessor to John XXIII, who convened Vatican II. Being head of the church from 1939–1958, Pius XII authored a document called "Mystici Corpus" or "The Church as Mystical Body of Christ" and a worn-down Fr. Andrew misses a teaching moment (Pius XII 2). Fr. Paulus' discomfort with Nona at the cafe, his comment defaming the Italian American Bronx Nick hails from, and his reference to "dago red" when discussing the pope do not speak very well of his attitude towards italianita, or Italian American ethnicity in general, In fact, they rather evidence John Paul Russo's comment in *The Future without a Past* that the assimilation of Italian American Catholics by more mainstream Catholics like Fr. Paulus became the "'Italian Problem': how to make Italian immigrants into American Catholics. As it happened, becoming an American Catholic entailed becoming a modern American" (Russo 219). Unmodern in the sense of their search for a substitute patriarch, Nick and Matty represent to Andrew Paulus an ethnicity that burns him out even further. One could well ask each of these impoverished Italian American boys W.E.B. Du Bois's question, "How does it feel to be a problem?" (Du Bois 1996).

Therefore, DeLillo sums up this negative representation of Paulus. The priest is symbolically associated with "autumnal pink Parma ham" (672), which he consumes while touring Little Italy with Bronzini as guide.

DeLillo's choice of foods is quite deliberate, with the use of Parma ham being symbolic. The anointing that occurs during the rite of Holy Orders is here symbolized, even when DeLillo presents the physical description of Fr. Paulus as follows:

> You had to look hard at Andrew Paulus to find a trace of aging. Unfurrowed and oddly aglow, with a faint baked glaze keeping his skin pink and fresh . . . Bronzini wondered if this is what happens to men who forswear a woman's tangling touch and love. They stay a child, preserved in clean and chilly light. (669)

The anointing of this priest is a preservation of the flesh not the spirit like the curing of Parma ham. Despite DeLillo's treasuring of Catholicism alongside and intertwined with italianita as a meaningful source of insight, and his positive representation of other Catholic clerics in *Underworld* such as Sisters Edgar and Gracie, some negative portrayal of Catholic clerics happens as well.

To further evidence this portrayal, one need recognize the complex impact on Nick and Matty of their Jesuit training. Largely successful in terms of most of their intellectual and moral development, each seems to lack to one degree or another the moral courage required to act upon the powerful insight afforded them by their training. As shown in the prior chapter, Matty has a much more difficult time with his own moral development. Of the two brothers Shay, Matty most clearly shows this trend, as he becomes the cold-hearted moral Frankenstein as a result of developing the "killer instinct" of the chess master as Paulus had advised. Our youthful chess champ becomes a "consequence analyst" (402), "figuring out the lurid mathematics of a nuclear accident or limited exchange." As in training for chess, Matt must squelch all human feeling to project these consequences, excusing the accidental release of nuclear bombs with the rejoinder "Nobody's perfect, OK?" (402). This reminds the reader that if we deny the compassionate purpose of life, we risk the loss of all life.

Seeing this emotional monster as the result of his Catholic miseducation sets up a negative description of Father Paulus in terms of his stereotypical views as they emerge in thought and action, in the abovementioned symbolism of the "ham," and in the possible negative impact he may have had on Matt Costanza Shay. At this point, the reader may feel hard pressed to think in positive terms about DeLillo's representation of the Catholic Church at all; however, the reader should note that DeLillo's chronology is reversed throughout the narrative structure of *Underworld*. So for the characterization of Father Paulus, DeLillo portrays the man as starting off in a weaker position morally with Matt but later showing compassion for Nick as the narrative moves forward in time. Yet there is always this balance between the most noble and least honorable aspects of the Church as an institution, shown through these clerical figures.

But DeLillo has more to offer. As the reader also examines further the treatment of Sr. Alma Edgar and Sr. Grace Fahey in *Underworld*, this balanced representation of Roman Catholicism is sustained. As opposed to the above-mentioned sketch of Sister Hermann Marie, DeLillo goes into greater depth in his dual characterizations of these two charitable sisters who come to the aid of the urban poor in *Underworld*'s inner-city New York. Other than the fact that this poverty-stricken setting is very important to the novel, the reader should note that Don DeLillo's examination of the Catholic sisterhood is far more in depth than that in *White Noise* in terms of viewpoint, with focus on each character instead of the use of Jack Gladney's narrative viewpoint. The two sisters, by virtue of their contrasting characterizations, represent different social aspects of the Church: Sr. Alma stands as a symbol of the conservative, intellectually repressive, and polarized side, while Sr. Grace represents the more socially engaged and charitable liberal/progressive faction of Catholicism. In addition to this fruitful contrast, Sister Alma also undergoes dramatic and dynamic changes. However, to fully elaborate on all of these would run the risk of depriving the reader of full appreciation of a "prima vista" experience of reading Don DeLillo's *Underworld*.

Beginning with Sister Alma Edgar, DeLillo portrays again the negative side of the Catholic Church, as he did with Sister Hermann Marie's apparent skepticism and the bitterness and biases of Father Andrew Paulus. Like the other two complex Catholic clerics, Alma is described dolefully "feeling pain in every joint" (237). Also, she cannot see the beauty of the world outside of her window save in terms of moral decay: "That's creation out there, little green apples and infectious disease" (237). DeLillo's allusion to the Garden of Eden and to disease shows us how Sister Edgar tends to focus on the corrupt and painful aspects of human life, blinded as she is to life's more pleasurable aspects by the suffering she experiences. Further, in describing her DeLillo forms a significant pun on the words "verily" and "velleity" from Father Paulus's section. Here, Sister Alma Edgar's strong-willed nature, her velleity, is not based on truth. The narrative highlights the fact of Sister's frequently repeated "amen" at her morning prayers. Thus, "amen" is " an olden word [hearkening] back to Greek and Hebrew, verily" (237). Alma Edgar sees the world of the physical body and the world of the body politic in similarly bipolarized terms. For the physical body, she entertains an obsession with an unattainable state of ideal and absolutely pure health (the reader will note how she obsessively washes "with coarse brown soap" [237]). Thinking about the American body politic, she also fears the disease-like spread of communism. The fact that she believes capitalism is communism's diametrically opposed good is implied by her view of prayer as "a practical strategy, the gaining of temporal advantage in the capital markets of Sin and Remission" (237). If prayer is "capital," then capitalism must be the state of holy and pure goodness as opposed to its opposite. This bipolarized view, coupled with her fear of contagion by any of these "evils," renders her incapable in her attempts to exercise the compassionate social charity so important to DeLillo's Roman Catholic Church. As she and her partner Sister Grace pass out food and other essentials to the poorest of New York's inner-city poor, "babies born without immune systems" (246), Sister Edgar never displays any emotional involvement or compassion; she is "a presence only, a uniformed aura in regimented black-and-whites" (246). As with Sister Hermann Marie, and Andrew Paulus at his worst, she does not appear to be a figure DeLillo's readers would associate with a loving God. Certainly, her character carries other associations.

Rather than with Jesus or God, as DeLillo scholars Irving Malin and Joseph Dewey note in their 2002 study, *Underwords*, which they edited with Steven G. Kellman, Sister Alma Edgar is symbolically associated with J. Edgar Hoover, a historical figure appearing in the novel with whom she shares an obsession with contagious Communism. Further, as Dewey and Malin also note, she bears an explicit resemblance to the character of the Raven in Edgar Allan Poe's poem of the same title. These scholars inform the reader of three factors connecting the character to the poem: first, the fact that this sister frequently reads the poem, second, that DeLillo her as having a "raven's heart" (*Underworld* 249), which they refer to as "a metaphor for her lack of . . . compassion," and third, she happens to be obsessed with that Poe poem and assigns it to her students on an ongoing basis (Dewey, Kellman, and Malin 27). Obsessiveness and the melancholic tone of Edgar Allan Poe's poem certainly are qualities applicable to Sister Edgar's character as well. Yet the Raven itself as a character in the poem remains static and unchanging, never transcending the obsessive melancholia that imbues both the poem and the reader's experience of reading the poem. In contrast, Sister Alma Edgar is a very round character.

Stressing what they consider to be a lack of closure in DeLillo's work and an emphasis on indeterminacy, Malin and Dewey argue:

> Thus the third Edgar [here DeLillo's use of the Raven as an allusion with
> Sister Edgar] cautions one that DeLillo's novel, like Poe's poem, is ultimately

about that game itself-not its resolution . . . reading itself is a game that means
nothing—and yet, everything. What beauty! What power! (Dewey, Kellman,
and Malin 27)

Yet Poe and DeLillo are not playing the same game. Given the fact that
there is so much good in what Fr. Andrew Paulus does for Nick (and later
in another Catholic cleric the reader of *Underworld* will meet, Sister Grace
Fahey) the game in the sense of the lives that the novel characterizes as
touched by faith is resolved, and resolved in the form of very dynamic
moments of metanoia. Alma Edgar does not remain locked in her study as
the obsessive speaker who can't stop "reading" the symbol of his visitor the
Raven does. Furthermore, surely in this matter of representing the Catholic
Church, readers cannot interpret *Underworld* as simply being a book about
the indeterminate relativity of reading and interpretation.

Rather, in Andrew Paulus's character, the inner contradictions of being
emerge in the dialectical image of the Church on the one hand as a kind
and compassionate force and on the other as cold and uncompassionate.
In order to properly address these questions, we need to meet the morally
best representative of the Catholic clergy in *Underworld*: Sister Edgar's colleague Sister Grace Fahey. To whit: in contrast to the struggle her colleague
Sister Alma Edgar feels when attempting to merely experience compassion,
Sister Grace Fahey is an exemplary model of Catholic clerical action at its
best. She consistently says and does what is right on both the political and
personal levels. Her moral example rounds out DeLillo's representation of
Catholicism at its best and worst. Grace is completely "real" in the sense
of moral responsibility with her corrective viewpoint on the dominant cultural paradigm. Her work stands as a testimony against the social evils
DeLillo portrays in *Underworld*. She is not afraid to embrace the victims
of AIDS and gangbangers who inhabit this poverty-stricken world of the
South Bronx, which is a literal interpretation of the phrase "Underworld"
to which DeLillo's title may be said to refer. Sr. Fahey is even seen exchang-
ing groceries for heroin in order to feed New York's poorest; this qualifies
her as "a soldier, a fighter for human worth" (249). In comparison to the
emotionally bound-up Edgar, Gracie does not retreat but rather faces up
to the poverty resultant from the arms race that *Underworld* protagonist
Nick Costanza Shay perpetuates with his nuclear-waste disposal work. For
her part, Sister Grace, like Sr. Hermann Marie and unlike Sr. Alma Edgar,
will not simply defer to quietude and be a "good little nun." Rather, Gracie
expresses a just moral outrage at the conditions the poor must face, living
literally near a "crater filled with red-bag waste. Hospital waste, laboratory

waste" (249). She graphically recounts to the dismayed and disgusted Sister Alma the disposal of amputated limbs and other infectious material in terms evocative of both the grotesque paintings of medieval artist Hieronymus Bosch and of the 2007 documentary film by Michael Moore, *Sicko*, which exposed corruption and socioeconomic inequality in the healthcare system. Bosch's paintings, such as "The Death of a Miser," stressed plague and physical torments as the moral consequences of evil, while in contrast the author is demonstrating that the victims of the social evil of economic inequality already suffer such dire physical conditions (Jheronimus Bosch Art Center). These visuals evoke the scene also in *Sicko* with the images of landfills and garbage dumps where such medical wastes including severed limbs are disposed.

Returning to the plot, the anger of DeLillo's socially engaged nun escalates when a group of European cultural aficionados on a tourist bus labeled "South Bronx Surreal" exit their vehicle and take photos of the dire poverty and suffering pouring out of this "ailanthus jungle" and surrounding debris. Gracie shouts at the Europeans, "Brussels is surreal. Milan is surreal. This is real. The Bronx is real" (247). Why is this compassionate nun so angry, and what do her comments to these European voyeurs of poverty mean? What upsets Sister Gracie is the fact that the bus tourists treat the tragedy they see before them as a mere cultural spectacle, an example of "the surreal," viewing human misery as if it were a Salvador Dali exhibit. These tourists reflect the same lack of compassion in the face of human suffering as does Sister Alma Edgar. In the context of this juxtaposition of the two Catholic sisters, the word "real" takes on a significant connotation. When Grace accuse the tourists of being "unreal," she means this in terms of moral authenticity, a concept coming from German existentialist philosopher Martin Heidegger and meaning to live one's life in direct correspondence with the image one projects as self-identity to others in the world—to live out one's moral commitments as Sister Grace does.

She would rather they be "real" in the sense of being emotionally present and acting in accord with the best of Western values of compassion in response to the poverty of the South Bronx. Also, when Sr. Gracie Fahey accuses the tourist of being "unreal," she is creating an interesting connotation. Here, real means empirical fact rather than some bourgeois text for artistic appreciation.

Once again, responding in a more compassionate way would be a response to a real fact for the tourists. Symbolically speaking, Gracie's position behind the steering wheel of the nuns' van is quite significant. Don DeLillo is implying that the kind of empirically real, authentic compassion ought to be the driving force as we read our way through these descriptions of New York. This supplants the obsessive reader's position implied in "The Raven," which we would be led to in terms of Dewey and Malin's use of Poe as a model of postmodern indeterminacy. Representing such a driving force within the institutional Church, Grace Fahey certainly represents Catholicism at its best, a socially engaged cleric. She is the opposite pole in the dialectic whose negatives we see present in the characters of Alma Edgar and Paulus. Like Sister Hermann Marie, who substitutes compassion for the sick with playing the role of theologically correct nun when dealing with the philosophical challenges of Jack Gladney, Gracie has her priorities straight when it comes to moral action. Together, as argued above, Sister Alma Edgar and Sister Grace Fahey balance each other as representations of what is morally best and what is least desirable in today's Catholic Church.

Perhaps this comparison between Sr. Grace and Sister Edgar then contradicts the issue of reading of literature, Church, and American culture as a permanently indeterminate game that Dewey and Malin place on the reader's plate irrevocably when they bring up Edgar Allan Poe as an allusion in the complex web of allusions both within and outside of the text of *Underworld* relevant to the figure of Sister Edgar. If reading is not simply a game of indetermination, as DeLillo's explicit characterizations of Catholic clerics seem to suggest, then what is the point of all these Edgars? Perhaps even some multiple "Graces" might be revealed via extending the comparison.

My case is that one cannot properly read or interpret DeLillo's representation of the Catholic Church completely without understanding further symbolic historical allusions inherent in the character of Grace Fahey. In order to do so correctly, one must note the historical allusions to the social radicalism of 1960s American Catholic clerics that underscore Sr. Grace's presence in the novel just as cold warrior J. Edgar Hoover underscores Sr. Edgar's. Taking us aboard the mind of the copilot in the cockpit of a fully-armed B-52 bomber, here seen attacking Hanoi, her pilot a veteran of aboveground atomic testing, more Cold War bipolarized narrative drops the name of a significant moment in radical Catholic history: "the student protesters, the war resisters and flower people, the Chicago 7, the Chicago 8, the Catonsville 9—they were all, pretty much, the enemy" (612). This last group of protesters, the "Catonsville 9," was completely different from the violent protesters of Chicago 7 and Chicago 8 fame. They included Daniel and Philip Berrigan, Irish American priests. These first Americans to burn their draft cards during the Vietnam era embraced a nonviolent clerical lifestyle almost identical to that of fictional Grace Fahey, providing a specific ministry to urban American poor folk in New York and elsewhere. Furthermore, their nonviolent style of protest caught on among the antiwar activists of the 1960s, who successfully helped to stop the unpopular and unjust Vietnam conflict. Many Americans followed the Berrigans' example of burning draft cards, and thus their creative protesting style was a driving force as with Grace being the driving force in this important set of connections in DeLillo's work. Later we see specific reference to the Catonsville 9, an all-Catholic protest during which the Berrigans and seven other Catholics broke into the Selective Service offices at Catonsville, Maryland, to destroy hundreds of draft records and thus effectively disrupt the Vietnam War effort. Using homemade napalm, they yet refused to injure any fellow humans, apologizing for "the burning of paper instead of children" ("Catonsville 9 40th Anniversary" 1).

To add to this, Grace is symbolically associated with the gracefully Catholic pacifism of the Berrigans via her Irish American clerical identity. Yet what is important here is not a matter of a character's name or even ethnicity but rather an ethical or moral state generated by a lifestyle. Survival and peace in the nuclear age involves not simply the sometimes chancy act of making some symbolic connections as Dewey and Malin do, and as I do here, but rather following the moral example the Berrigans provided and that Sister Grace Fahey's character represents in DeLillo's work. Her lifestyle is that of the protestor Matt Shay sees at the gate of his workplace.

Moreover, the Berrigans' later antinuclear symbolic "Plowshares" protests involved sometimes painting designs on nuclear weapons and facilities, just as the artist-character Klara Sax does in this novel *Underworld* when we first meet her. So the many "graces" are the fruits of creative, nonviolent, and peace-inducing actions to cure the earth of the obsessive melancholia of nuclear arms so painfully present in *Underworld*. Years later, in September of 1980, Daniel and Philip Berrigan along with six other protesters committed another symbolic protest action, hammering small dents into nuclear warhead nose cones and pouring blood onto documents and files. Repeated 78 times in the United States through May 2003 and most recently in New Zealand, the Berrigans' style of artistic altering of weaponry, echoed in DeLillo's portrayal of Klara Sax, seems once again to have been influential (Laffin 1).

It can be argued that symbolism reinforces even further a rich treatment of the Catholic religion also when the events of July 2, 1959, are related. Protagonist Nick Costanza Shay returns to center stage to take his casual girlfriend ("we were a fling that had run intermittently for two years only

because we lived in different cities . . . she was the last thing I needed
in this world") to Mexico to receive an abortion from an American doctor (588–589). DeLillo does not paint this event in very happy tones. The
woman, Amy, "half hates" herself for what the couple has made happen.
Furthermore, the waiting room Nick is confined to while Dr. Swearingen
performs the abortion is disturbing to the young Catholic man, decorated
with "occult symbols" and "mucho mystical drivel." After her surgery,
poor Amy must deal with the pain of a bumpy cab ride back across the
border. Such is certainly the case for Amy and this young man, who in
retrospect considers their action "hopeless, worthless and weak" even
though he thought he was doing something "responsible," and "making
sacrifices" (588–589). Afterward, he describes their experience in terms of
a sad and "strange shaded grief" and refers to the aborted as a "child"
with an "unlived life" (589). This passage, the only account of abortion in
DeLillo's five major novels, is significant. For one thing, this is a negative
portrayal of abortion, very much in line with the life-conducing stance on
the topic Catholicism evokes. Secondly, the reversed chronological structure
of *Underworld* itself, the entire 827-page tome, is evoked as "we seemed
to be having a conversation that went backwards." Here, as with the most
violent acts referred to in the novel, a regressive evil is treated, and the narrative clock's running backward indicates that Nick and his friend are not
maturing via acting responsibly but instead doing something wrong via the
abortion, which, like the production and detonation of nuclear weapons,
unmakes rather than creates. Here is perhaps the most pro-Catholic statement in DeLillo's oeuvre.

To wrap up, both critics of the Catholic Church as an institution and
supporters of its most progressive and liberating trends will find evidence
to reaffirm their viewpoints in DeLillo's dialectical portrayal of the faith
found in the novels *White Noise* and *Underworld*. But readers must bear
in mind the complex strategies of allusion and balanced representation that
the author deploys to introduce the reader to an underground Catholic
social history and atypical clerics many may not have encountered unless in
DeLillo's work. Finally, when analyzing the changes that happen to important Catholic characters like Matt Shay, Sister Alma Edgar, or even the
protagonist Nick Costanza Shay by the time of the conclusion of the for-
midable *Underworld*, I would argue that the information we gather about
the Church must shape one's results. So how does the author want us to
view Roman Catholicism in its American manifestation? Perhaps the narrative comments made about the mythical Eisenstein film describe best the
author's crafty representation of Catholicism in its complexity: "All [he]

wants you to see, in the end, are the contradictions of being . . . the inner divisions of people and systems, and how forces will clash and fasten, compelling the swerve from evenness that marks a thing lastingly" (444).

Buried amid this contradictory mass of Catholic references, the nuclear clutter of the *Underworld*, may be the very moral key readers and authors seek, the clerical and creative means of surviving nuclear Armageddon and attaining the "word extending itself ever outward . . . Peace" (827) through DeLillo's literary valorization of the antinuclear heroic acts of protest of the Berrigans, "under the radar," which mainstream American history may yet record as the very means by which humanity survived the era of nuclear bipolarization. Prowar or antiwar, pro-Catholic or anti-Catholic, what "marks lastingly" DeLillo's dialectical portrait of the American Catholic church in the latter half of the twentieth century is its verisimilitude in our age of ongoing interactive conflict.

_____ *Chapter 7* _____

Artists, Writers, and Moral Accountability

This chapter will explore the notion of moral accountability as it applies to the portrayal of the individual artist emerging on several levels in DeLillo's novels being examined in this book. The idea that the artist struggles with the idea of morality is or should be familiar to readers of DeLillo's major fictions up to this point. *Mao II*'s tracing of the failure of writer Bill Gray to live up to his own ideal in the rescue of a fellow writer does not necessarily imply that the problem is with the ideal; it may rather be with Bill. In *Underworld* as well, the idea of the responsibility on the one hand to beauty and its production is difficult to reconcile with the notion on the other of a duty to society as typologized in Grace Fahey's supportive entry into the wildly creative world of Ismael Muñoz and Juano and her inspiration to the "Moonman" to add compassion to his approach to his work (see chapter 1 of this book). Failure is more common than success in many of the works; not only Bill Gray but also Klara Sax struggles even as she seems to come to a new moral vision as represented in her painting of the B-52 bombers. The collapse of her marriage to Albert Bronzini taints this ideal of the socially engaged artist, as do Bill Gray's bouts of alcoholism in *Mao II*. Many explanations could be offered to shed light on the American artist's struggle to reconcile personal and social spheres of morality. Perhaps one is found in the accumulation of the representation of the author's own reactions to the concept of unspeakable evil. Close study of *Underworld* has presented us with two notable examples: the carefully crafted internovel metaphor of the filmmaker as associated with response to Italian American stereotyping (chapter 5) and the dialectical presentation of Catholicism (chapter 6). Taking this close reading one step further, we could posit another tension between that of a unified or holistic representation of the moral ideal in DeLillo and the philosophical dialectic or self-opposed representation in the same writer's work. Audiences surely have some awareness of this dual phenomenon simply in how they read DeLillo; otherwise there would be no debate between postmodern or dialectical readers of the author and others, modernists or neorealists (see again chapter 1). To finalize then this appreciation of the novels, here follows an assessment of the statement we can find in the three remaining novels current to his 2010 oeuvre: *The Body Artist, Falling Man,* and *Point Omega.* To begin, *The Body Artist* conveys the fact that the artist is first and foremost accountable to preserve his or her integral self, predominantly made manifest in the ability to communicate in language and live in mortal time. Realizing that morality can't be limited to the personal sphere, *Falling Man* contributes marvelously to DeLillo's representation of social morality. The post-9/11 novel signifies DeLillo's return to the theme of terrorism also seen in *Players, The Names,* and *Mao II* and expands and clarifies his early vision of a significant condition of our times. Moreover, the novel's central thematic concern is an illustration of the notion of the social responsibility of the artist or writer in the face of post-9/11 terrorism. The artist or writer must enable a real bridging of the personal subjective distance between artist and audience through a creative counteraction opposed to the destructive power of the new symbolic terrorism 9/11 represents. The promise of this latest merging of the modes of unified historical representation and indeterminate dialectical signing though is hard to see in the enigmatic concluding piece to this trilogy, *Point Omega.*

Given the difficulty of the last text, I will augment an image of the artist in terms of moral accountability with some references to images of DeLillo's own career, suggesting a kind of coherence between ideas suggested in these late works and the lifestyle of limited personal and political engagement that career demonstrates.

Introducing the idea of the moral role of the artist we turn to DeLillo's first post-*Underworld* novel, *The Body Artist,* and its protagonist Lauren Hartke. An overview of this novel yields a look at the concept that an artist's first moral responsibility is to his or her integral self. As a tracing of Lauren's development as a character and the plot will be seen to reveal, this self is involved with the ability to communicate in the powerful medium of language and to imagine oneself as living in mortal time. Lauren Hartke is an avant-garde dance/body motion specialist who is mourning the self-induced death of her husband, Spanish-born film director Alejandro Alquezar, or Rey Robles, as he had renamed himself after a character he portrayed in a minor film (30). Though their relationship appears to be very one-sided (he is clearly completely depressed and somewhat abusive to her in the brief time we see them together), Lauren is devastated by the loss and cannot seem to live as we imagine her in real time following Rey's passing. Then she becomes aware of a mysterious and uncommunicative stranger living in an infrequently used part of the house. Lauren names this man "Mr. Tuttle" based on the fact that he resembles her old high school science teacher of the same name. His presence in the story is somewhat ghostly, and he suffers a strange sort of selective autism. He appears to be able to speak from memory words Lauren spoke to Rey, perhaps because he was listening to them while in hiding.

Lauren works hard to try to engage Tuttle in a normal dialogue, with little success (45). She is haunted by the fact that he seems to be able to imitate her voice with eerie similarity. But she cannot get him to mimic the sound or recall the words of Rey. Her attempt represents an effort on her part to anesthetize herself against her loss. Lauren finds she cannot recall or deal with her memories or grief about Rey Robles without thinking of this "Mr. Tuttle." Eventually, though, the man disappears, and Lauren Hartke hears of the arrival of a man matching his description at a local psychiatric hospital. To deal with the trauma Rey's disappearance and Mr. Tuttle's unexpected appearance in her life caused, Lauren performs a show that arguably could be said to have death as its theme. After thus being able to put the loss of Rey and subsequent separation from Tuttle into perspective, Lauren moves beyond her grief and is able finally to emerge from it with her integral self intact.

The relationship between Lauren and Rey is not presented by DeLillo as a mutually beneficial one, given Rey's condition. Life in language and in time is not something the couple appears to relish. For example, as Lauren sits reading the headlines early on in the novel she reflects that "there are people being tortured halfway around the world . . . you have conversations with them uncontrollably" (21). In DeLillo's omnibus, to be thus out of touch with the world, reliant upon the media for the simulacra of political reality, is to be out of touch with oneself, conducting imaginary conversations as she later will with Tuttle. When we first meet them, his depression leads him to take a sarcastic tone, calling her the young woman who lives forever (17). Living in a house full of old bent utensils, she has no spoon for the carefully prepared breakfast granola. Rey himself has not provided for her an effective example of how to live successfully and healthfully as an artist. The filmmaker's romantic view that "the answer to life is the movies" (30) does not match well with the imperative in the novel to "believe what you see and hear" (124) because of the oft-cited theme of the manipulative power of the media to distort reality in the perception of the viewer or reader, here made manifest also in Lauren's uncontrollable conversations with her newspaper. In contrast to Lauren, Rey has been horrendous in bodily self-care, smoking every day since he was 12. In fact, DeLillo's description of his death is very provocative: Rey becomes "the smoke . . . the thing in the air, vaporous, drifting into every space" (35). He literally becomes the poison he's consumed his whole adult life, suffering the fate Lauren's friend later warns, "You don't want to fold up into yourself" (41), and Rey has folded up into the smoke he has become. The toxic impact of Rey's persona and of this relationship on Lauren continues beyond the moment of the film-maker's death. Her need for Rey was so extreme that this death has severely unsettled even her capacity to grieve, an indication that her sense of integral self is not functioning either in time or in language. Despite the fact that she denies being "undone" (34), she is still overwhelmed at the daunting task of finishing "his bullshit autobiography" and cannot seem to focus on any one task at hand.

Into this breech in her consciousness steps the ghostly Mr. Tuttle, sleep-ing unbeknownst to her in the spare room upstairs (46). Further, the rela-tionship between Lauren Hartke and Mr. Tuttle does beg the question of whether or not his existence is primarily as a figment of her imagination. Given the narrated fact that Lauren hears about the commitment of a man matching Tuttle's description, one can assume his reality for the sake of coherence. Weak and limited to quasi-autistic responses to her promptings, the character is an interesting study in language unconfined by the conven-tional boundaries of rational linear time. He can only speak of himself in the neuter third person, as an object: "It is not able," he says in response to Lauren's questioning how long he had been staying in their house (45). As with Lauren, Tuttle cannot live as an integral self in temporal and linguistic context and seems indeed not to have a sense of an integral self—at least not one that he can functionally express. He is a self nearly disembodied from the material world, coming and going without warning and never really seeming to fit into place anywhere.

Significantly, the person whom Lauren names him after was a disheveled teacher "who scotch-taped a split-seam in his loafers once . . . and made the students feel embarrassed on his behalf" (49) Lauren Hartke was one of those students, and she sees the same self-disintegrating vulnerability in her charge. Tuttle's speech patterns, "shadow-inching" his way "through a sentence" (49), draw an important connection between faith in the power of language and the existence of an integral self. With the Catholic philoso-pher Descartes, an integral character must be able to consciously proclaim,

"I think, therefore I am," and know precisely the moment of which she is thinking. But this is not an option for Tuttle as his mind cannot live in rational time, as Lauren reflects: "There is nothing he can do to imagine time existing in reassuring sequence, passing, flowing, happening—the world happens" (79). Implicitly, Tuttle can of course be compared to Rey, existing in a fully disembodied state outside of time by virtue of his death as opposed to Mr. Tuttle's linguistic temporality and completely unselfconscious state caused by his mental condition. Overall, his importance in the narrative of Lauren's world stems from the fact that she is projecting her own pain and vulnerability onto Tuttle, as shown here: "How could such a surplus of vulnerability find itself alone in the world? Because it is made that way. Because it is vulnerable. Because it is alone" (98). Although Lauren is consciously reflecting on Tuttle here, she could just as well be discussing herself, very vulnerable as the surviving spouse.

Furthermore, her difficulties letting go of Rey are reproduced in her difficulties letting go of Tuttle. Lauren does debate whether or not she should take Mr. Tuttle to an institution right away (81), raising some questions about society's treatment of the mentally ill; however, this issue is not her focus in contemplating her situation with him. More likely, Lauren's care for and obsession with the homeless "Tuttle" is a means for her of insulating herself against a healthy grief over Rey. She finally realizes that "she could not miss Rey, could not consider his absence, the loss of Rey, without thinking along the margins of Mr. Tuttle" (84). To some readers this would raise the question of whether or not Tuttle actually existed or was simply Lauren's imaginative projection of what Rey had come to mean in her life. Two strikes against this theory would be the response she receives from the health care professional at the institution and the fact that she continues to perceive everything else fairly normally. No matter, whether physical or not, the obsessive need to nurture Tuttle distracts her from the important work of letting go.

Continued examination reveals that the danger of her losing her sanity due to this grief and subsequent obsession is extreme. She yearns, through her latter conversations with Tuttle, for the confessional conversations she had with Rey, which consisted of "confession as belief in each other, not unburdening of guilt but avowals of belief, mostly his and stricken by need" (63). This is what she has lost via Rey's passing—the capacity to believe in oneself as seen and heard. This danger of the loss of reason is represented symbolically by her birdfeeder: the "birds going crazy on the feeder" (69). When Rey was alive, Lauren tended to the birdfeeder; now things are slipping loose from control. Also, her attempt to follow the "discontinuity" of

Tuttle's language, which moves in "quantum hops," is disconcerting. Above all, the clearest measure of Lauren's precariousness in her new situation is her inappropriate response to Rey's lawyer calling in her late husband's massive debts. Lauren could get into serious trouble on this, as indicated by the lawyer's reference to "sinister transits of spousal responsibility" (96). But Lauren simply laughs this subtle warning off, disregarding the danger. DeLillo portrays a woman in need of a major shift in her perspective to cope successfully with the future.

However, in this short work by DeLillo the subjective transcendence of the artist is portrayed, and Lauren's show does allow her to let go of the obsession through self-expression. One central image that is presented in Lauren's show is the motif of a woman in work clothes checking her wrist-watch while hailing a taxi; this motif occurs repeatedly as one of a series of surreal motions composing the show (108). Enacting this slow-motion reproduction of a symbol of life in time, body motion becomes the language of Lauren's slow yet graceful transition out of her own noncommunica-tion with the deepest reaches of self. She is able to leave the house she shared with Rey and later with Tuttle, a personal break from the memories impeding her ability to maintain an integral self (126). Remaining to this portrayal of the artist's moral responsibility is a social dimension; one can-not limit the representation of ethics in the novels to the sphere of personal coping alone, though *The Body Artist* does remind us of the priority of the Kantian duty to self-care.

Moving on to wider spheres, 2007's *Falling Man* continues to elaborate on the theme of the moral responsibility of the artist that DeLillo brings forth to the reader in *Underworld* and to present a challenge to the amoral-ity of postmodern perspectives on subjectivity in the creative act of response to historical forces as they operate on people. As regards this, Randy Laist has addressed DeLillo's representation of technology as one such histori-cal force, yet his 2010 book *Technology and Postmodern Subjectivity in Don DeLillo's Novels* does not treat *Falling Man*, opting instead to choose 2003's *Cosmopolis* to represent DeLillo's production for the first decade of the 21st century. However, *Falling Man*'s thematic concern with the 2001 terrorist attack on the Twin Towers, a historical reference point that has been called the opening of the first world war of this century, qualifies it as at least an equally worthy representative of DeLillo's post-2000 fictions. DeLillo's return to the theme of terrorism also seen in *Players*, *The Names*, and *Mao II* expands and clarifies his early vision of a significant condition of our times. The social responsibility of the artist or writer in the face of post-9/11 realities is to enable a real bridging of the personal subjective distance between artist and audience through a creative counteraction opposed to the destructive power of the new symbolic terrorism 9/11 represents. Don DeLillo presents this bridging via the portrayal of the title character of *Falling Man*, a performance artist named David Janiak who reenacts the posture of one of the more famous jumpers from the Twin Towers, a man with his legs crossed. Relating this artistic venture to the field of writing is accomplished through the character most impacted by Janiak's art, an editor who teaches a writing class for Alzheimer's patients. Through her life and that of those around her, we see the metaphor of falling developed into a statement regarding the imperative facing post-9/11 America to find a rational and ethical way of coping with the act without degenerating into bellicose rage and wild paranoia. DeLillo's *Falling Man* also significantly revises the author's earlier approaches to terrorism, assimilating the new realities of the al-Qaeda event with the same astute and accurate ear for history that informed such earlier works as *Libra* and *Underworld*. Not only is *Falling Man* a crucial representative of DeLillo's 21st-century thinking, but it is a novel of vital importance to any American attempting to cope with what is arguably the greatest historical shock our generation has had to endure.

The novel is a jarring and interrupted journey into the times and spaces of several New York characters whose lives are altered by the 9/11 attacks. Lianne Glenn has been separated from her husband Keith, yet he shows up at her door with his face full of glass shrapnel and with other injuries as well. He had been working in one of the offices in the North Tower (4). Like many, Keith survived the initial impact of the first plane at 8:45 because he was working below the floors where American Airlines Flight 11 hit. As a result of their contact, the two experiment with a reunion. Lianne's mother, Nina, is a retired art history professor and art critic who frequently visits with her longtime lover Martin, who is an international art dealer and a German expatriate. Keith and Lianne have a son, Justin, who spends an inordinate amount of time scanning the skies for an imaginary villain he and his neighborhood friends call "Bill Lawton," a misnomer apparently based on the name "Osama Bin Laden" (17). Their obsession reflects the post-9/11 American phobia centered on the terrorist in the days following the attacks. Interspersed with the scenes of Lianne's family is an account of a mysterious artist called "Falling Man" who engages in random jumps off buildings at different locations throughout New York. Suspended from a harness, this radical artist displays a kind of suspended die-in similar to antiwar protests at the Pentagon, always attempting to wind up in the position pictured in one of the famous photographs of those who leapt from the burning towers: the portrait of the man falling head-first with one leg extended in a kind of swan-dive mudra. Seeing Janiak jump off an old railroad platform changes Lianne's perspective significantly. Also interspersed is DeLillo's speculative representation of Mohammed Atta and the lives of the hijackers as they prepared for the attacks. The plot does not stray far from the characters' struggles to carry on with their lives in the wake of the attacks and how such conflict is ultimately resolved.

Well known is the view DeLillo has articulated that the terrorist has replaced the novelist as the culturally acknowledged harbinger of the symbolic event. Associated with this claim is the idea of the novelist or terrorist as having the ultimate fate of the "man alone in a room," an alienated individual only able to communicate through the symbolic event, a fate Lauren Hartke manages to avoid. While these statements hold for figures in earlier novels such as Lyle or Jay Kinnear in *Players* or the shadowy crews who attack for religious or political ends in *The Names*, the context is vastly different in *Falling Man*. For one thing, the American landscape is irrevocably altered by the attacks of 9/11. The apartment building where young Justin's friends, the "siblings" Robert and Katie, live is jokingly referred to as "Godzilla apartments" or simply "The Godzilla" (71). A post-9/11 movie monster, this description of the building forms an image of the act of terrorism as a fatal piece of artwork, a negative simulation, the destructive impact of an artifice, with "strong currents of air . . . shearing down the face of the building and knocking old people to the pavement" (71). Such destructive impact is another image of the threat of ideological disorder facing post-9/11 America. Bush's (now Obama's) "War on Terrorism" can transform American thinking into a nationalist fantasy driven by a paranoia resembling the mentality of the game of Lianne's son Justin and his young friends, constantly scanning the skies and the neighborhood for any sign of terrorism. Though terrorism has not completely swallowed the American mind, the danger that it could do so is articulated both in terms of the simulated nightmarish outlook of the children and the haunting real destruction evoked by the wind shears. This is a major alteration of the earlier presentation of domestic terrorism found in *Players* and other novels.

Expanding this portrayal of terrorism is DeLillo's treatment of the inner lives of the plotting hijackers themselves and their associates (77). This treatment is probably based on the facts of the story originally published by John Tagliabue in the *New York Times* on November 18, 2001. According to this story, three of the ringleaders, including hijackers and those who were trained for the plot but never flew, met in Hamburg in an affluent area at the address "Marienstrasse 54." Hammad, one of the hijackers, reminisces about being in Saddam's army and watching wave after wave of young boys die "the martyrs of the Ayatollah" (77). This image will return time and again to the mind of the hijacker as an ideal of martyrdom he will draw on in preparing for the attack. We also learn that Mohammed Atta is known to the group as Amir (80). More significantly, DeLillo notes an ideological contradiction in the perspective of the al-Qaeda: the ideal of martyrdom is the technologically ill-equipped and backward force of the early 80s. To continue, as Hammad suffers in pain on his way to a final collision with the North Tower, this figure recalls "the Shia boys on the battlefield" and takes "strength from this" (238). He reflects that despite the state's technological power represented by "fiber optics," the state is inferior to the terrorist cell that communicates naturally "through eyes, through word and look" (81). However, despite this implicit critique of technology as unholy, the 9/11 al-Qaeda terrorists choose technology as the means of retribution against the United States. Thus, this hijacker does not die in the time-and-tradition honored way he worships; his last action before the moment of death is to fasten his seatbelt (239), a ritual homage not to the martyrdom dating back to pretechnological days but rather to the ethics of the in-flight safety card, a product of the technological society he is aligned against. So despite the incredible impact that the attacks have had, a final victory for terrorism is by no means a given, riddled as it is by this ideological contradiction. This innovation again must be counted if one surveys DeLillo's highly relevant treatment of terrorism through his novels in progression, following the zeitgeist of each decade.

Consequently, unlike the novel or works of legitimate art, terrorism emerges as a warped and perversely violent attempt to bridge the subjective limitations between symbolic actor and audience inherent in the symbolic event. This is seen also in the consequences of the attack as it affects Keith Neudecker in the hospital. His physician informs him of the reality of "organic shrapnel" . . . "tiny fragments of the suicide bomber's body," which implant themselves into the bodies of innocent bystanders during a terrorist attack (16). Fortunately Keith does not carry organic shrapnel, yet this image is one of a dysfunctional attempt to cross artistic boundaries, to transcend the subjective barrier between self and other through an act of violence. To follow the extremist edict to "become each other's running blood" (83) entails such macabre self-destruction to be taken to completion. If all this was not stunningly sinister enough, Hammad's ironic reference to corruption, to transgressions following other aspects of the extreme jihadist's ethics in the realms of food and sex (83), serve to doom the terrorist act to a representative failure in terms of the spiritual redemption promised as reward for their martyrdom. Outside of the predetermined spiritual failure of the symbolic attack, of further ironic import is the fact that Hammad never seems to find the answer to his own interior question of whether one has to kill himself to accomplish a goal in this world (175). So DeLillo's characterization of the more prominent and extreme terrorism of the 21st century elaborates his earlier portrayals of the "man alone" terrorist whose attack threatens to usurp the power of narrative art.

Beyond DeLillo's fictionalizing of the al-Qaeda hijackers, there is the characterization of Martin Ridnour, Nina's lover in *Falling Man*. The reader discovers that he is living under a pseudonym and that his actual name is Ernst Hechinger. His role in the lives of Nina and Lianne is unsettling on many levels. Even though they have been in a serious relationship for many years, Nina knows very little about him and his unusual habits in the art world, and this frustrates and frightens Lianne. She has seen, though, a poster that "Martin" or Ernst keeps of 19 member of the old East German terrorist group "Kommune 1," which stood against the traditional family structure and was at one time wanted for acts of violence (146). By reason of his false identity and known terrorist associations, Ernst becomes an object of Nina's and Lianne's suspicion. This "man alone" also displays sympathy for the 9/11 attackers. Debating with the two women, he proclaims, "Weren't the towers build as fantasies of wealth and power that would one day become fantasies of destruction . . . The provocation is obvious" (116). To Martin/ Ernst's credit he brings to the debates that expose the underlying ideological struggle of the novel an awareness and sensitivity regarding the perspective of relatively powerless people toward the United States. As the trio views a still life of Giorgio Morandi's, Ernst remarks that he sees the Twin Towers in a well-known image of two wine bottles in an architecturally evocative arrangement. But what Lianne, Nina, and all of America needs is a paradigm shift. The need is to focus on how to live on in the post-9/11 world without obsessing about the attacks, myopically seeing the towers in every work of art and articulating that monolithic vision as critique of the art. Ernst, the terrorist/aesthete, finally does stand as DeLillo's "man alone." He is not a foot-soldier terrorist but alone is the Euro-Marxist critic/theorist of terror, the publicist Samuel Johnson to al-Qaeda's Shakespeare if terrorism has replaced narrative art. Ernst's departure from the novel signifies both a relief and an ongoing need for that paradigm shift beyond obsession. Finally, it is clear that unlike this pseudonymous character, DeLillo's sympathies do not lie with 21st-century new terrorism.

If these several remarkable new angles on terrorism since *Mao II* do not yield any answers to the troubling questions New Yorkers and other Americans faced, then a study of the victim of the attacks may. Ostensibly a main character, Keith Neudecker does not fully participate in the central change of consciousness driving most of the important action in *Falling Man*. Obviously affected by the initial impact; he loses his drinking and poker buddy Rumsey in the attack. Rumsey dies as Neudecker attempts to carry him from the North Tower (242). Rumsey had given Keith a sense of direction in his life after his first separation from Lianne; their weekly poker game with some others became the focal point of Keith's life. As Keith attempts to hoist Rumsey over his shoulder he hears the man's death rattle, and the body is described as "fallen away" from Keith—an apparent pun on the novel's title (243). Death is another variety of falling, although not all ways of falling are quite as destructive as Rumsey's fall. Primarily, a "fall" in the novel signifies a kind of paradigm shift for an individual; obviously death can be thus characterized, though none can conclusively specify the result of this extreme change. Returning to Keith, he "falls away" in a completely different sense of the word than Rumsey does. Neudecker finds himself back at Lianne and Justin's place as he cannot return to his poker-headquarter digs following the attacks. His post-traumatic disorientation can really be seen as a kind of positive reorientation; the love that Keith and Lianne experience is rekindled, although this is a very fleeting reality.

Rather than pursue the renewal of this bond and also that with Justin, Keith drifts into the world of professional gambling and spends less and less time at home while increasing the commitment to the casino and professional poker. When we last see him, he admits to himself that he's "always lacked . . . that edge of unexpected learning" (231). That emotional void left by his friend is not creatively refilled by the love and fatherhood he is welcomed back to by Lianne and Justin. If the 9/11 moment is an opportunity for the transformation of national and personal consciousness, then Neudecker has missed his chance. Ironically, he feels that "fortune favors the brave" (231) yet lacks the courage to experience that "edge" his survival afforded him. On another level, his penchant for gambling represents an extreme form of the paradigm informing the free-market trade the Twin Towers were built to house. Neither Keith nor his society (which is our society) care to examine those factors that brought about the sentiments leading to the attacks. Thus, the unprocessed sentiments and memories he experienced on the day of the attacks remain lodged in his consciousness like the inorganic shrapnel the doctor removes from his face (16).

Furthermore, Keith is all too willing with Lianne to "sink into our little lives" (75) following the attack. Rather than follow organic lines of attachment back into improved relations with Lianne and Justin, Keith follows an inorganic remnant of the attacks, a lost briefcase containing identity tokens of its owner, Florence Givens. They have an affair born of the post-traumatic stress of surviving the attacks on the towers (88). Neither with Florence nor with Lianne can Keith sort through his post-9/11 feelings; when he learns that Florence "talks to God" (92) he can't be sure whether Lianne does so as well. Using Florence to numb himself against all his reactions to the event, even the potentially good ones, Keith has lost that aforementioned experiential "edge" he might have learned from.

Worse still, he sinks ultimately further downward into a lower consciousness. Keith lives out the life of hedonism Kierkegaard condemned as humanity's lowest rung of paradigm development. Later, we will find out that Kierkegaard is significant because of his being Lianne's ideal philosopher. As a professional gambler, Keith attempts to control that future Kierkegaard would have us resign ourselves to utterly. Keith's need to control the outcome of the endless poker hands he will forever play is almost diabolical as he wills the cards to make his opponents "spill their precious losers' blood" (230). He finally does not fall authentically as Lianne does back into love but rather is stuck in a gambler's "dream of paralysis" (230), never to transcend the impact of 9/11 by transforming it into something positive in his life. To highlight his decline, the disjointed structure of the novel *Falling Man* follows a pattern around Keith; we follow a loop back in time to his arrival at home after spending several chapters dealing with later events. And as with *Underworld*, the novel ends at its beginning with Keith attempting to save Rumsey. Arguably this disjointed structure reflects the disjointed consciousness of the typical American victimized by the attacks, as Keith most dramatically was.

On a far more hopeful note, Lianne is more open to the paradigm shifts that intrude into her life in the aftermath of the attacks. Surprised by Keith's sudden appearance after the attack, she nonetheless takes charge of him as he is hospitalized. Further, she does not allow any bitterness about their former relationship on her part to interfere as Keith gradually reintegrates himself into their lives. Lianne is a professional editor and writer who is considering editing a book on ancient alphabets; by professional and occupation she is thematically aligned with a long-standing issue in DeLillo's work going back to *The Names*—she is here concerned with rational signification in language. Such power to make sense of experience in words has taken on a new urgency in the distorted and disorienting landscape of New York City after the planes hit. Lianne runs feeling like "a skirt and blouse without a body" (23), symbolizing the loss of self-identity and rational signification that the inability to come to terms with the grief involved engenders.

She represents the role of the writer in the face of a history that threatens to unravel both a personal and collective sense of rational identity.

Then, Lianne takes another job leading a group of Alzheimer's patients in journalizing their experiences. This new position fits perfectly as a metaphor for the epistemological and moral imperative facing the post-9/11 New York community. DeLillo develops this metaphor through Lianne's recounting of a member of her writing group, Rosellen S., who gets lost trying to find her way home and winds up in a church. Rosellen's loss of reason to the disease is described as a kind of falling: "she was not lost so much as falling" (94). Lianne must use language in a losing battle to keep a rational grip on things for Rosellen's sake. On the other hand, Rosellen's loss of proper orientation relative to home elaborates the metaphor of America's post-9/11 mental trauma as Alzheimer's. There is a loss of reason or individual consciousness representing the parallel loss of national American identity in the wake of the attacks; our multiculturalist and compassionate sense of nationhood to be replaced by Bush-era paranoia like Justin and the siblings searching the sky. Like Rosellen, we are losing our domestic sense—a proper sense of the immigrant-welcoming America as homeland and ever drifting into an obsession with "Homeland Security." But this type of falling is not at all for which the individual is to be faulted. Endless though the struggle may be, of the many ways to fall, the right way is the one in which the individual takes responsibility to create meaning out of the fall like Lianne making sense of Alzheimer's—to fall well as Lianne will and later as the symbolic artist called Falling Man will.

However, Lianne has her own issues getting to a psychic resolution of post-9/11 traumas. Her neighbor Elena, who wears a headscarf and listens to unusually loud music at all hours of day and night, has begun to play her music even more loudly. Nowhere in *Falling Man* is it specified that Elena is a Muslim woman, but the conflict they have coupled with the fact that Elena wears a headscarf seems to indicate that the general anti-Muslim bias affecting the United States, particularly since the attacks, is involved in their conflict. The battle between neighbors degenerates into near fisticuffs (119), at which point Lianne feels she is beginning to go crazy. This conflict between Lianne and Elena remains unresolved as the two pass a tense moment in the laundry room (151). Though their conflict seems to be a diversion from the main plot, it represents the central drama of American culture continuing even at the time of this writing as anti-Muslim sentiment draws to a head over issues such as the construction of a new Islamic cultural center in New York City near the site of the attacks. In the world of the novel, the question is how the symbolic action of Falling Man could serve as a hopeful sign by which to establish inter-cultural dialogue.

Whatever the resolution, Lianne emerges from these testing fires to become an ideal Kierkegaardian in terms of moral authenticity. Watching televised poker with Keith, Lianne sees in the "deadpan, slouched" faces of the play-ers herself, struggling with reading Kierkegaard as a college student: "She read her Kierkegaard with a feverish expectancy, straight into the Protes-tant badlands of sickness unto death" (118). DeLillo turns a well-crafted phrase when he writes that Lianne's mind "made a leap to Kierkegaard." This passage is very significant both in Lianne's favorite philosopher and in the symbolic patterns being formed in the novel by consistent references to falling, leaping, and the like. In Kierkegaard's world, the leap of faith is an act of belief regardless of the consequences. Basing his theology on the story of Abraham's near-sacrifice of Isaac, the Danish absurdist argued that a faith beyond reason was superior to the precisely correct and all-encompassing rationalism of Plato. Lianne, in her embrace of Keith's return, makes precisely this leap of faith not realizing what the consequences will be. And unfortunately, as in the forlorn case of Søren Kierkegaard him-self. Kierkegaard "sacrificed" a fledging engagement in the name of duty to God, a choice he called a leap of faith from which there was no turning back. The consequences of her "fall" into a trusting and loving relation-ship with her ex is precisely the opposite of the optimal hoped-for outcome as Keith immediately commences cheating with Florence. Living out this paradigm, Lianne is an exemplary Kierkegaardian, living authentically her own commitments and maintaining her course even after Keith's second self-inflicted collapse.

As if by the pull of some moral gravity no less compelling than the physi-cal force of gravity pulling Falling Man into "the ideal falling motion of a body subject only to the earth's gravitational field" (228), Lianne's authentic path leads her into a very direct encounter with the symbolic protest action of Falling Man. As Falling Man, whose real name is David Janiak (181), prepares to jump off an old railway platform, Lianne has a very disturbing encounter with him (162). She draws close enough to one of his symbolic actions to see him prepare to jump off the railway platform and can't just write it off as "some kind of antic street theater" (163). Rather, it affects her as "too near and too deep, too personal" (163). Janiak's dramatic per-formance strikes a panic attack in the crowd, recreating the crisis mentality of the actual day of the attacks; one woman calls the emergency number 911 (163). Lianne's observation of this is first hand—no one is closer to Falling Man than she is, close enough to speak to the artist as he hangs in

position (168). His art has the intended impact, crossing subjective boundaries effectively as opposed to the hurtful means of the terrorist. Falling
Man's impact is particularly devastating to her because it reminds Lianne of
her own father's suicide. Watching him, she is haunted by the thought that
he "died by his own hand" (169). Yet this galvanizes her to take the pages
written by her Alzheimer's group home and bind them; inspired by this
brush with Janiak, she lives authentically, putting into language the perspectives of the victims (170). Thus, Janiak's symbolic reordering of the 9/11
incident, his casting of himself into the role of victim rather than the role
of aggressor (the terrorists), the unrepentant gambler/capitalist (Keith), or
the paranoid watcher-for-terrorists (Justin), has served in a healing capacity
quite accidently. It evokes the common empathic bond of human suffering
personified in Lianne's case by her father's suicide. In turn, both Lianne
and David enact the power of art as text to heal. This power is present in
her work with language, in Janiak's symbolic reenactments, and in the idea
of writing and the novel itself. The novelist also becomes a kind of Falling
Man, putting into language the perspectives of the set of those impacted
by the disaster, making a leap of faith for the reader to enact the paradigm
change needed.

Finally, the artist is presented as a symbolic character, the Falling Man
himself or David Janiak being another pseudonym to counterbalance that
of Ernst Hechinger, the apologist for terror. This symbol provides a catalyst for an important and sustainable post-attack paradigm shift. The shift
is made manifest as we return to Lianne's story in 2003 as she and Justin
attend a peace march. Though it is 500,000 strong, the march is compartmentalized by the police, portrayed with a certain liberal irony as DeLillo
comments on "detaining the overcommitted and uncontrollable" (181) in a
culture that is on the dangerous verge of chaos. At the march, Lianne is not
completely impressed with the peace movement or the crowd but actually
is "there for the kid" (182), meaning Justin, and simply wants to raise his
consciousness to "allow him to feel the argument against war and misrule"
(182). But the protest itself is no more the point than the fact that it is Charlie Parker's birthday or that Justin opens up his mind to read a pamphlet
on Islam. The protest is simply the outer manifestation of the change in
Lianne that has taken place after her encounter with David Janiak and the
capacity that encounter has given her to place into her perspective her past
relationship with her father. She's arrived at a place "Cut free from rage and
foreboding" (182). Again, I see this change of consciousness as relevant to
the post-9/11 cultural environ DeLillo is sketching in *Falling Man*. Such
freedom from rage is cast as an alternative to the jingoism stemming from

the attacks and a return to rationality and empathy. Her fate to live "in the spirit of what is ever impending" (212) is a healthier outcome than that of Keith. Interpreting David Janiak more as a symbol, there is a final reference to his death (221) after a nondescript career staging his falls.

His posture mirrors that of the Hanged Man, who is suspended upside down and crosses his legs in a similar fashion. As modern allusions go, T. S. Eliot's famous use of the Hanged Man as a representation of the Fisher King in the poem *The Waste Land* is well known. In Eliot's poem the Hanged Man symbolized redemption by Christ, or in the pagan interpretation, renewal of the land. Redemption, if any, is found in how the symbolic import of his action live on in the mind of Lianne as reader; Janiak instead has mastered what Ernst calls in German *Gedankenubertrargung*, "the broadcasting of thoughts" (191). His artistic self-sacrifice is thus aligned with Eliot's Christianized image of the hanged man. But the deck itself is static and flat, like the decks of cards Keith plays poker with while the work of art is vital and dynamic. Rather, the symbolic art that David Janiak the Falling Man creates in images lives on through the broadcasting of thoughts. His successful "broadcasting" thus enables a symbolic bridging of the distance between artist and audience through the medium in creative opposition to the destructive motif of "organic shrapnel" seen in the symbolic act of the 9/11 terrorists. This portrayal, found in *Falling Man*, completes Don DeLillo's representation of the social dimensions of the artist's social responsibility in the early part of the 21st century.

If only real life in history could always work out in such beautiful and morally positive artful resolutions as does *The Body Artist* and *Falling Man*. Events in history transpiring between 2007 and the time of this writing do not provide significant hope for the Lauren Hartkes, David Janiaks, and Lianne Glenns of this world, forming the context for Don DeLillo and his readers. Attempts to live up to this ambitious vision of the artist's moral responsibility are fraught with social crises that show no sign of abating, such the Iraq war, written about by DeLillo in the final novel of the sequence terminating in 2011, *Point Omega*. The title refers to the writings of Jesuit scholar Teilhard de Chardin, which speak of the end of the world as phenomenal, an end point of maximum organized complexity, a state of ideal love and reason beyond that which can now be known (*Teilhard de Chardin's Evolutionary Philosophy* 1). The Iraq War could be seen as a kind of moral polar opposite; hence the title is actually a reversal. DeLillo's latest novel is not a metaphysical speculation on de Chardin, nor does it concern the war in direct representational form. The novel has been widely praised and also blamed for its lack of representational quality.

In light of the recent extreme divergence of reactions as to the quality and value of Don DeLillo's latest novel, *Point Omega*, here a defense of the novel is offered in terms of "liberal irony," an idea that finds its origin in the field of philosophy. Richard Rorty defines the liberal ironist in his book *Contingency, Irony and Solidarity* as the writer for whom a "sense of human solidarity is "a matter of imaginative identification with the details of others' lives" (Rorty 190). In terms of what we've called "the divided opinion" on DeLillo's *Point Omega*, the book has been criticized for disabling the reader's imaginative and compassionate identification with said details because it does not resolve its ambiguous plotlines and seems deliberately to avoid making concrete anti–Iraq war statements—for instance as Harriet Beecher Stowe's *Uncle Tom's Cabin* did against slavery in the mid-19th century through the use of traditional realist modes of plot and character that condemned the cruelty of slavery through clear portrayals of the same. But it is precisely the ironic strategy of *Point Omega* to subvert traditional identification with the novel's details via omission. This strategy forces readers to look for imaginative identification between the sparse details he or she is afforded and significant conditions of the war itself. What we are given is the tragic and forever unexplainable disappearance of Jessie Elster, daughter of Bush-era Iraq mastermind Richard Elster, whose visit to her father provides a temporary respite from his visit with James "Jim" Finley, a documentary filmmaker who wishes to make an *Americana*-style soliloquy film of Elster as "a flawed character in a chamber drama, justifying his war and condemning the men who made it" (99). The narrative is abruptly truncated when the two return to find nothing left of the gentle Jessica. The inexplicability of her disappearance is complicated by the fact (among other causes) that the local sheriff is reluctant to suspect the house caretaker, the only other man to hold a key to Elster's home where Jessie and the men were staying because he has known this caretaker for 30 years (82). Accountability and criminal investigation are obstructed, finally impassibly. As the novel ends with Jessie's disappearance, the truth of her situation remains an unsolved mystery.

Therefore, it would seem that DeLillo has failed us in the traditional realist sense by refusing to provide an allegorical resolution to illustrate more fully the evil of the Iraq conflict. Yet this insolvability is the perfect motif with which to represent the phenomenon of embedded journalism. On April 8, 2003, a U.S. tank attacked the Palestine hotel in Baghdad, a well-known haven for international journalists who were not embedded with the American military and therefore not committed to give a pro-American bias to their reporting of the conflict. Just as this outrageous attack preempted true reporting of the many injustices involved in the war in Iraq, the truncated narrative of *Point Omega* preempts the true resolution of Jessie's disappearance. Ironically, Jessie's perspective on what might have happened is as lost as is the camera work of Ukrainian cameraman Taras Protysuk, an accomplished video journalist for Reuters killed in the attack ("Three Journalists Killed in Iraq"). Jim Finley's inane comment that "the story was here, not in Iraq or in Washington" (99) becomes ironic as well, because in both the fictional and historical cases the *real* story cannot be anywhere, as the readers' sole means of getting to the truth has been obstructed with DeLillo's termination of the story artistically representing the effect of the Palestine hotel attack. In contrast to the age of Stowe, the contemporary American fiction writer presents social evil with a stunned silence, like the silence of the antinuclear protester Matt Costanza Shay tries to engage in *Underworld* (412). Inquiring readers interested in the real story in Baghdad must be inspired to find the truth on their own. If they do, then they'll find Rorty's ironic "imaginative identification with details of others' lives," or as DeLillo puts it more eloquently, "The omega point has narrowed, here and now, . . . funneled down to local grief, one body, out there somewhere, or not" (99).

How does this irony fit into the vision of the artist's moral responsibility as outlined through my close readings of *The Body Artist* and *Falling Man* presented above? Perhaps it seems not to, and that lack of fit is precisely the point. As established in 16 novels, the author has fulfilled the demands of a leadership role by engaging personal and social ethics so frequently. Are we, his audience of readers, really listening? If the answer was yes, why has nothing changed as the world did change through American readers heeding the call of earlier socially engaged writers like Stowe and Twain? I don't mean to say that *Point Omega* is a frozen act of bitterness in its silences—maybe it would be more accurate to suggest that prolonged analysis of the Iraq war or critique of artistic treatments of the same as a surrogate for protest action to stop it would simply be a prolongation of witness to murderous violence, perfectly metaphorized in the presentation of *24-Hour Psycho* that is described in the opening of the novel, which is the centerpiece of DeLillo's frame. Irony is a perfectly appropriate response on behalf of an author who has done much to bring his world closer to the ideal presented in de Chardin and the moral vision I have attempted to outline for readers here.

Indeed, what else has DeLillo done? It is fair to bring in the well-publicized life of the writer not simply because of the indeterminacy we must face in *Point Omega*. It is fair because it is inescapable and DeLillo knows this, largely living a life of strategically limited public engagement. Unlike his characters, the writer knows how to preserve the integral self and yet answer to the moral call to be the "man for others," as the Jesuits would put it. Some notable examples can be found in his recent activities: Don DeLillo's participation in the 2009 PEN New Year's Eve rally for the release of Chinese writer and crusader for freedom Liu Xiaobo and his participation in the public reading of the testimonies of victims of U.S. torture also sponsored by PEN on October 13, 2009. That reading also featured philosopher and critic Amrit Singh, novelist Paul Auster, and the graphic novelist Art Spiegelman, whose Holocaust novel *Maus* criticizes state tyranny in a manner similar to many of Don's works. Whether by indicating the proper boundaries of personal self-integration in *The Body Artist*, elaborating a profound new vision of contemporary terrorism and a new perspective on the artist's socially ethical response in response to the same in *Falling Man*, or simply undercutting the act of representation with deep irony in *Point Omega*, DeLillo completes the redefinition of the moral accountability of the artist/writer for our age. Therefore, in the life of the author we see lived out the social vision of the personal moral accountability of the artist presented in three of his latest novels. It is time to appreciate DeLillo's moral vision in the only way left to us readers: by taking heed and living it out.

Bibliography

Algren, Nelson. *The Neon Wilderness*. New York: Seven Stories Press, 1986.

"An Appeal for Reflection." *Statement of Jesuit Priests of Columbia*. Fr. Francisco De Roux Rengifo, S. J. Barrancabermeja. 15 April 2008.

Boston College Website. *Address of the Very Reverend Peter-Hans Kolvenbach*. Originally appeared in Assembly 89, Jesuit Ministry of Higher Education. 6 March 2009. 1 November 2010. <http://www.bc.edu/content/dam/files/offices/mission/pdf1/ju1.pdf>.

"Catonsville 9 40th Anniversary." *Jonah House/Community-Nonviolence-Resistance*. 17 May 2008. 2 July 2008. <http://www.jonahhouse.org>.

Chaplin, Charles, dir. *The Great Dictator* (2 Disc Special Edition). 1940. Warner Home Video, 2003.

Consorzio del Prosciutto di Parma (Italian Association of Parma Ham producers). *Di Parma. The Basics: History and Traditions*. 2003. 11 July 2008. <http://www.parmaham.com>.

Conte, Joseph. "Writing Amid the Ruins: 9/11 and *Cosmopolis*." *Cambridge Companion to Don DeLillo*. Ed. John Duvall. Cambridge, UK: Cambridge University Press, 2008. 179–192.

Cowert, David. "DeLillo and the Power of Language." *Cambridge Companion to Don DeLillo*. Ed. John Duvall. Cambridge, UK: Cambridge University Press, 2008. 151–165.

DeLillo, Don:

Americana (1971). New York: Penguin Books, 1989.

End Zone (1972). New York: Penguin Books, 1986.

Great Jones Street (1973). New York: Penguin Books, 1994.

"Hitler, Manson and the Millennium." *White Noise: Text and Criticism*. Ed. Mark Osteen. New York: Viking Press. 498–516.

"In the Ruins of the Future." *Harper's* December 2001: 33–40.

Schuster, Marc. *Don DeLillo, Jean Baudrillard, and the Consumer Conundrum.* Youngstown NY: Cambria Press, 2008.

Soccio, Douglas F. *Archetypes of Wisdom: An Introduction to Philosophy.* Beverly, MA: Thompson and Wadsworth, 2007. 167–192, 227–252, 291.

Tagliabue, John. "A Nation Challenged: The Investigation; Retracing a Trail to the September 11 Plot." *New York Times.* 19 September 2001.

Teilhard de Chardin's Evolutionary Philosophy. Kheper Home Page. 21 June 1998 1–4. 11 Feb. 2011. <www.kheper.net/topics/Teilhard/Teilhard-evolution.htm>.

"Three Journalists Killed In Baghdad." *Online Newshour Update.* PBS. 8 April 2003. 15 April 2010. <www.pbs.org>.

Tolstoy, Leo. "Death of Ivan Ilyich." *A Treasury of Short Stories: Favorites of the Past Hundred Years.* Ed. Bernardine Kielty. New York: Simon and Schuster, 1947.

Union Carbide Corporate Media Relations Website. "The Incident, Response and Settlement." *Bhopal Information Center.* 2011. <http://www.bhopal.com/union-carbide-statements>.

University of St. Andrews, Scotland. School of Mathematics. "Biographies: Srinivasa Aiyangar Ramanujan." *MacTutor History of Mathematics.* University of St. Andrews, Scotland, 1998. 11 Feb. 2011. <http://www.mcs.st-andrews.ac.uk/>.

"Zbigniew Herbert (1924–1998)." Poetry Foundation. <http://www.poetryfoundation.org>.

Index

Ratner's Star, 37–45; analysis of plot and characters in, 37–41; critique of militarism and technology in, 41–42; Evariste Galois discussed in, 42; morality and the "value-dark dimension," 41; simulated disaster as a shared theme with *White Noise,* 42; theoretical science and empiricism as themes, 42

Rorty, Richard, 177

Running Dog, 52–57; analysis of plot and characters in, 52–53; *Apocalypse Now* and, 55; Hitler and the Reich chancellery in, 52; Pentagon Papers and left-wing media in, 54; portrayal of North Vietnamese in, 53; Watergate scandal and, 54

Russo, John Paul: on Catholicism, 139; *The Future Without a Past,* 122; on Nick Costanzo-Shay as narrator of *Underworld,* 120–121

Salinger, J. D., 100–101

Saltzman, Arthur, 84

Schuster, Mark, 12–13

"Scucciamente," 131

Terrorism as major theme: al-Qaeda, 169; East German terrorism, 171; nuclear war as terrorism 58–64; post-9/11 approaches to, 162; as replacement of art, 102; sexual immorality and, 50; terrorism and ancient history, 73; terrorism as pervasive force, 75

Tolstoy, Leo, "Ivan Ilyich," 91

Trickster, Jungian figure of, 125, 131

Underworld: analysis of plot and characters, 127–138; artist and modernism in, 15; artist and society in, 12, 17; Eisenstein film in, 137; and Italian American culture, 114–155, 127–138; moral contradictions and Catholicism in, 138–159; moral good portrayed in, 155–157; moral responsibility and, 21; unspeakable evil in, 114, 117–118

Unification Church of Sun-Myung Moon, 100–101

Unspeakable evil as theme, 35, 65, 91, 93–115; response to, 117–160

Velleity in St. Thomas Aquinas, 146

Volterra, city of, 125

Wall Street, 2008 collapse of, 104

Warhol, Andy, "Dead White Andy," 103

White Noise, 79–92; analysis of plot and characters, 71–84; Bhopal India and, 86; language as theme, 89; moral transcendence in, 91; natural environment as theme, 86; power of television as theme, 87–88; religion in vs. religion in *The Names,* 91

Writers and social/moral accountability, 161–179

Xenophobia as American response to 9/11 crisis, 167–168

Yost, Glen, in *Americana,* 123

Zapruder film, 96, 100, 103

About the Author

PAUL GIAIMO has presented papers and published several articles on topics in American literature, including Don DeLillo, Italian American culture, and literature and religion, in such journals as *M.E.L.U.S.* (the journal of the Multi-ethnic Literature Society of the United States), *VIA (Voices in Italian Americana)*, and others. He also has published entries in *The Greenwood Encyclopedia of Multiethnic American Literature*. He currently teaches English and Philosophy at Highland Community College in Freeport, Illinois.